Geographies of Sexual

Focusing on locations as diverse as the rural southern United States, Brazil, Istanbul, and South Korea, this book advances our understandings about how lesbian, bisexual, and queer women navigate identity, community, and politics. It brings together international scholars whose work addresses how meanings about sexuality and place intertwine.

The chapters in this edited volume challenge the assumption that certain places are inhospitable to LGBTQ lives by examining the varied ways that expressions of same-sex sexualities manifest across contexts. They explore questions about how and why the spaces for lesbian, bisexual, and queer-identified women are shifting. They take us to spaces as varied as women-only exotic dance venues, dyke bar commemoration events, and queer-friendly college campuses. By doing so, the scholars in this volume provide cutting-edge, rigorous, and interdisciplinary insights about what queer spaces might look like in the future.

This book will be valuable to students and scholars interested in Sociology, Gender Studies, Geography, and LGBTQ Studies. The chapters in this book were originally published as a special issue of the *Journal of Lesbian Studies*.

Emily Kazyak is Associate Professor of Sociology and Women's and Gender Studies at the University of Nebraska-Lincoln, USA. Her areas of specialization include sexuality, geography, law, and family.

Geographies of Sexualities

Edited by
Emily Kazyak

Routledge
Taylor & Francis Group

LONDON AND NEW YORK

First published 2023
by Routledge
4 Park Square, Milton Park, Abingdon, Oxon, OX14 4RN

and by Routledge
605 Third Avenue, New York, NY 10158

Routledge is an imprint of the Taylor & Francis Group, an informa business

Introduction, Chapters 1–10 © 2023 Taylor & Francis

British Library Cataloguing-in-Publication Data
A catalogue record for this book is available from the British Library

ISBN13: 978-1-032-43920-4 (hbk)
ISBN13: 978-1-032-43921-1 (pbk)
ISBN13: 978-1-003-36942-4 (ebk)

DOI: 10.4324/9781003369424

Typeset in Minion Pro
by codeMantra

Publisher's Note
The publisher accepts responsibility for any inconsistencies that may have arisen during the conversion of this book from journal articles to book chapters, namely the inclusion of journal terminology.

Disclaimer
Every effort has been made to contact copyright holders for their permission to reprint material in this book. The publishers would be grateful to hear from any copyright holder who is not here acknowledged and will undertake to rectify any errors or omissions in future editions of this book.

Contents

Citation Information

The chapters in this book were originally published in the *Journal of Lesbian Studies*, volume 24, issue 3 (2020). When citing this material, please use the original page numbering for each article, as follows:

Introduction

Introduction to special issue "Geographies of Sexualities"
Emily Kazyak
Journal of Lesbian Studies, volume 24, issue 3 (2020) pp. 173–185

Chapter 1

Not in our community: Queer women challenge religious homophobia in rural Kentucky
Bernadette Barton and Ashley Currier
Journal of Lesbian Studies, volume 24, issue 3 (2020) pp. 186–198

Chapter 2

"Not in my name": The anti-racist praxis of Mab Segrest & Minnie Bruce Pratt
Amanda Mixon
Journal of Lesbian Studies, volume 24, issue 3 (2020) pp. 199–213

Chapter 3

Racialized sexualization & agency in exotic dance among women
Cristina Khan
Journal of Lesbian Studies, volume 24, issue 3 (2020) pp. 214–226

Chapter 4

Queer space and alternate queer geographies: LBQ women and the search for sexual partners at two LGBTQ-friendly U.S. universities
Janelle M. Pham
Journal of Lesbian Studies, volume 24, issue 3 (2020) pp. 227–239

Chapter 5

Queer Anthropophagy: Building women-centered LGBT+space in Northeastern Brazil
Sarah Nicholus
Journal of Lesbian Studies, volume 24, issue 3 (2020) pp. 240–254

For any permission-related enquiries please visit:
http://www.tandfonline.com/page/help/permissions

Notes on Contributors

Ozlem Atalay is PhD Student in Urban and Regional Planning at Florida State University, Tallahassee, USA. In her study of LGBTQ spaces in Istanbul, she plans to analyze several inclusive queer spaces and neighborhoods to understand the effects of national and local government politics, especially the urban planning decisions that lead to rapid gentrification and displacement of individuals from their settlements.

Bernadette Barton is Professor of Sociology and Director of Gender Studies at Morehead State University, USA. She is the author of *Stripped: More Stories from Exotic Dancers* (2017), *Pray the Gay Away: The Extraordinary Lives of Bible Belt Gays* (2014), and *Raunch Culture*.

Japonica Brown-Saracino is Professor of Sociology and WGS at Boston University, USA. She is the author, most recently, of *How Places Make Us: Novel LBQ Identities in Four Small Cities* (2018).

Ashley Currier is Professor and Head of Women's, Gender, and Sexuality Studies at the University of Cincinnati, USA. She is the author of *Politicizing Sex in Contemporary Africa: Homophobia in Malawi* (2018) and *Out in Africa: LGBT Organizing in Namibia and South Africa* (2012).

Petra L. Doan is Professor of Urban and Regional Planning at Florida State University, Tallahassee, USA. She conducts research on transgender experiences of the city and explores the relationship between urban planning and the wider LGBTQ community. Most notably, she has edited two books: *Queerying Planning: Challenging Heteronormative Assumptions and Reframing Planning Practice* published in 2011 and *Planning and LGBTQ Communities: the Need for Inclusive Queer Space* published in 2015.

Chelle Jones is Doctoral Candidate in Sociology researching the migration of LGBTQ skilled laborers.

Emily Kazyak is Associate Professor of Sociology and Women's and Gender Studies at the University of Nebraska-Lincoln, USA. Her areas of specialization include sexuality, geography, law, and family.

Cristina Khan is Lecturer in the Department of Women's, Gender, & Sexuality Studies at Stony Brook University, USA. She received her PhD from the Department of Sociology at the University of Connecticut, USA, in 2019. Her specializations include race and ethnicity, embodiment, sexualities, and qualitative research methods. She is the co-author of *Race and Sexuality* (Vidal-Ortiz et al., 2018). Her work has appeared in *Gender & Society*.

Liz Millward is the author of *Making a Scene: Lesbians and Community across Canada, 1964-84* and is the co-author with Janice G. Dodd and Irene Fubara-Manuel of *Killing Off the Lesbians: A Symbolic Annihilation on Film and Television*.

Amanda Mixon is PhD Candidate in the Department of Comparative Literature at the University of California, Irvine, USA, and American Association of University Women Dissertation Fellow. Her dissertation theorizes the anti-racist activism and political thought of a group of twentieth-century white lesbian writers from the U.S. south. Duke University, the University of Virginia, and UCI Humanities Commons have supported the project.

Sarah Nicholus is Postdoctoral Scholar in the Center for Women's and Gender Studies at the University of Texas at Austin, USA, where she earned her PhD in the Department of Spanish and Portuguese. An interdisciplinary, media, and cultural studies scholar, Sarah's research examines articulations of queerness within traditional forms of culture as they migrate into urban and technologically mediated spaces and engages queer epistemologies of the Global South.

Janelle M. Pham is Assistant Professor of Sociology at Oglethorpe University, Atlanta, USA. Her research focuses on the development of sexual cultures within institutional settings.

Amy L. Stone is Professor of Sociology and Anthropology at Trinity University, San Antonio, USA, and the author of *Gay Rights at the Ballot Box* and *Cornyation: San Antonio's Outrageous Fiesta Tradition*. They study lesbian, gay, bisexual, and transgender (LGBT) politics, urban life, and health.

Introduction: "Geographies of Sexualities"

Emily Kazyak

ABSTRACT

In this foreword to the special issue "Geographies of Sexualities," I provide a review of the scholarly discussions about place and sexuality that have occurred in the past 20 years. I highlight five major themes in my synthesis of this scholarship: (1) how narratives about geography and sexuality are co-constitutive; (2) a critical interrogation of these narratives to demonstrate how more nuances exist than these narratives suggest; (3) assessments of the spatial distribution of women in same-sex relationships, comparisons to the spatial distribution of men in same-sex relationships, and analyses of the experiences of women in areas with high concentrations of women in same-sex relationships and urban lesbian, gay, bisexual, transgender, and queer (LGBTQ) neighborhoods; (4) comparisons across spaces to address the effect of place on outcomes such as well-being and how mobilities and movements across geographies matter; and (5) discussions as to whether, how, and why the geographies and spaces of lesbian, bisexual, and queer-identified women are shifting. My goal is to highlight these themes in order to contextualize how the articles in this special issue continue discussions and introduce new questions for the field.

In my introduction to this special issue, I synthesize scholarship published in the past 20 years that focuses on geography and sexuality. I discuss five key themes that emerge from this scholarship. My synthesis is crafted with the intent to contextualize the special issue articles within the broader interdisciplinary dialogues out of which and to which they contribute. In my introduction, I use the terminology lesbian, bisexual, and queer women, same-sex sexualities, and LGBTQ in reference to identities and lives, communities, and spaces. My use of these terms reflects how they are used in the literature, with the recognition of the imprecise and imperfect nature of any terminology to fully capture the range and variety of how individual women and communities may articulate non-heterosexual sexualities.

First, scholars have produced knowledge concerning how narratives about geography and sexuality are co-constitutive. Scholarship underscores how place is encoded with meanings about sexuality insofar as certain spaces are seen as LGBTQ-friendly and conducive to the creation of LGBTQ lives only through their juxtaposition to spaces that are seen as hostile and unfavorable to LGBTQ lives. The process of creating place-based distinctions that are intertwined with meanings about sexuality occur at a global level insofar as the West and the Global North are seen as more progressive and more conducive for the expression of same-sex sexualities and LGBTQ lives compared to the East and the Global South (Brown, Browne, Elmhirst, & Hutta, 2010; Puar, Rushbrook, & Schein, 2003; Puri, 2016; Swarr & Nagar, 2004; Wilson, 2006). Even within regions generally understood as less embracing of same-sex sexualities, distinctions are made such that certain cities or countries are understood in comparison to others as better spaces for LGBTQ people; for instance, Prague in the Czech Republic within Central and Eastern Europe (Nedbálková, 2016), Taipei in Taiwan within Asia (Brainer, 2019), Cape Town in South Africa (Oswin, 2005), and Beirut in Lebanon within the Middle East (Moussawi, 2018). Likewise, the distinctions made between urban and rural spaces continue to matter to narratives about sexuality insofar as rural areas are seen as inhospitable to LGBTQ lives in contrast to cities (Abraham, 2009; Halberstam, 2005; Myrdahel, 2016; Waitt & Gorman-Murray, 2011; Weston, 1995). Certain cities in the Global North in particular are seen as LGBTQ meccas, such as San Francisco, New York, Tel Aviv, Sydney, and Toronto (Fenster & Misgav, 2019; Gorman-Murray & Baganz, 2019; Stone, 2018). Importantly, these co-constituted narratives of place and sexuality manifest in multiple ways and are espoused not only by some LGBTQ people and those seeking to make spaces more supportive of LGBTQ lives, but also by anti-LGBTQ activists who seek to make claims about same-sex sexualities as being antithetical to certain spaces (Johnson, 2009; Valentine, 2001).

Further, scholars not only note, but also critically interrogate, the ways in which meanings about space and sexuality are intertwined. Two different avenues of inquiry reflect this critical interrogation and I address both avenues in the following: work that focuses on spaces assumed to be inhospitable to same-sex sexualities and LGBTQ lives (spaces that have historically received less attention within the literature, such as the Global South or rural areas) and work that focuses on LGBTQ urban meccas (spaces that historically have received more attention within the literature). Although different foci in terms of spaces, taken together this work ultimately challenges and provides more nuance to dominant narratives about geography and sexuality.

Scholarship focused on places assumed to be inhospitable to same-sex sexualities and LGBTQ lives challenges that assumption by documenting the varied ways that expressions of same-sex sexualities manifest in these spaces. Such work calls attention to how those expressions and identities may differ from ones in the Global North or LGBTQ urban meccas, but need not be read as less valid. For instance, in their analysis of poor women in same-sex relationships in South Africa and India, Amanda Lock Swarr and Richa Nagar (2004) illustrate how the women are able to assert same-sex intimacies in the context of experiencing extreme poverty and sociopolitical marginalization. Swarr and Nagar undermine the assumption that the women's location would make creating same-sex sexualities out of reach; rather, they argue that the women's assertion of same-sex sexualities is intertwined with their negotiations for daily survival. They note that the women's articulations and experiences of same-sex sexualities differ from Western ones (in terms of identity labels used or the absence of visible organized lesbian communities). As scholars work to create knowledge about same-sex sexualities in areas of the globe where there has been little attention thus far, scholars also acknowledge the barriers and challenges to doing such work (Blidon & Zaragocin, 2019; Pitoňák & Klingorová, 2019; Silva & Ornat, 2016). Further, scholarship focused on small towns and rural areas in the United States provides another challenge to dominant narratives that posit these spaces as wholly unfavorable for lesbian, bisexual, and queer-identified women's lives (Barton, 2012; Eaves, 2016; Forstie, 2018; Gray, 2009; Oswald & Culton, 2003; Oswald & Lazarevic, 2011; Woodell, Kazyak, & Compton, 2015). Such work highlights how some lesbian, bisexual, and queer-identified women experience small towns as spaces where they can be out, accepted, and visible, and that their interpretations rely on making distinctions between urban and rural LGBTQ identities (Kazyak, 2011, 2012; Thomsen, 2016). In a related vein, work in this area also calls attention to how manifestations of homophobia and anti-LGBTQ sentiments may differ across geographies (Abdi, 2014; Barton, 2012; Brainer, 2019). Thus, while work challenges the assumption that certain spaces are wholly unfavorable for LGBTQ lives, scholars also work to simultaneously call attention to how homophobia may still manifest in those spaces in ways that differ from manifestations in the Global North or LGBTQ urban meccas.

Another challenge to dominant narratives about geography and sexuality emerges from scholarship that critically analyzes LGBTQ urban meccas and the notion of a global queer identity, often via attending to processes of globalization and gentrification and histories of colonialization. For instance, work focused on tourism campaigns that market global LGBTQ urban meccas asserts that such efforts turn those spaces into commodities to be consumed; these scholars then question how global patterns of inequality shape who has the ability to consume the commodities

(Markwell, 2002; Puar, 2002; Rushbrook, 2002). Similarly, other work argues that the interpretation of certain cities as global LGBTQ meccas can obscure the struggles that LGBTQ people may experience within those cities (Markwell, 2002; Moussawi, 2018). Scholars have also addressed how attempts to create a shared global queer identity obscure the differences that exist across regions and between countries with regard to expressions, experiences, and articulations of same-sex sexualities (Hoad, 2007; Swarr, 2012). Further, scholarship also critically assesses LGBTQ urban meccas via analyzing how exclusions in these spaces occur based on factors like class, gender identity, and race. The topic of the effects of gentrification on urban LGBTQ neighborhoods has generated discussions about class and racial divisions with regard to which LGBTQ people are able to afford to be seen as legitimate in these spaces (Doan & Higgins, 2011; Hanhardt, 2013). Likewise, scholars draw attention to practices that marginalize and exclude transgender women within lesbian spaces (Browne, 2011). Finally, scholars have demonstrated how people of color experience marginalization and exclusion in LGTBQ communities and LGBTQ neighborhood in cities (Logie & Rwigema, 2014; Moore, 2010; Orne, 2017). These works underscore how the broader patterns of racial inequity and segregation that exist manifest in LGBTQ spaces.

In sum, all of this scholarship calls attention to how certain models of sexuality do not always translate across spaces (for instance, from Global North–Global South or from urban–rural), but that differences in expressions of same-sex sexualities or LGBTQ identities need not always be interpreted as a reflection of oppression. As a whole, this scholarship argues that holding up one space as a LGBTQ global mecca obscures the lived realities that LGBTQ people living in those cities may experience (which are not always as positive as assumed) and holding up one space as antithetical to LGBTQ life obscures the lived realities that LGBTQ people living in those areas may experience (which are not always as negative as assumed).

Additionally, another theme prominent in scholarship in the last two decades is a focus on assessing the spatial distribution of women in same-sex relationships, comparing it to the spatial distribution of men in same-sex relationships, and analyzing the experiences of women in areas with high concentrations of women in same-sex relationships and urban LGBTQ neighborhoods. Scholars have used census data (which allows for an assessment of same-sex couples) to document broad demographic patterns related to geography and sexuality in the United States and Australia (Baumle, Compton, & Poston, 2009; Gorman-Murray, Brennan-Horley, Kirsten Mclean, Waitt, & Gibson, 2010). Often, discussion of demographic trends centers on the fact that the areas with the highest concentration of female same-sex couples do not overlap with the areas with the concentrations of male same-sex couples (Brown-Saracino, 2018; Ghaziani, 2015). In particular, scholars note that female same-sex couples are less urban compared to male same-sex couples, a trend that occurs in both the United States and Australia (Gates & Ost, 2004; Gorman-Murray et al., 2010). Further, in addition to tracking these more general differences in geographies between female same-sex couples and male same-sex couples, scholars have focused specifically on urban LGBTQ neighborhoods. Such work highlights that the areas with high concentrations of women in same-sex couples are distinct from those with high concentrations of men in same-sex couples. For instance, in Chicago, Boystown is the visible area marked as that city's LGBTQ neighborhood, and yet the highest concentration of women in same-sex couples is in a different neighborhood, Andersonville (Ghaziani, 2014). Scholars focused on non-U.S. contexts, including Sydney, Toronto, and Montreal, have likewise documented the phenomenon that urban areas with high concentrations of lesbian, bisexual, and queer-identified women tend to be distinct from those areas with high concentrations of gay, bisexual, and queer-identified men (which are recognized more broadly as the LGBTQ district of that city) (Nash & Bain, 2007; Nash & Gorman-Murray, 2015; Podmore, 2006).

Along with documenting these demographic trends, scholars have also focused on analyzing the experiences of lesbian, bisexual, and queer-identified women who live in areas with high concentrations of women in same-sex relationships and lesbian, bisexual, and queer-identified women. This work includes attention to those living in intentional, often rural, lesbian communities to discuss how these communities function and why women seek to carve out spaces separate from mainstream society (Browne, 2009; Herring, 2007; Rabin & Slater, 2005; Stein, 2001). For instance, in their analysis of three lesbian land communities in Oregon, Arizona, and Arkansas, Rabin and Slater (2005) provide insight into the varied reasons women seek out intentional lesbian lands as part of their lesbian feminist perspective and how most communities self-govern through consensus. Analyses have also focused on the county town of Daylesford in Australia, which has a high number of LGBTQ people living there and a reputation for being LGBTQ friendly (Gorman-Murray, Waitt, & Gibson, 2008). Additionally, Japonica Brown-Saracino (2018) analyzes the identities and lives of lesbian, bisexual, and queer women in four small cities in the United States that have a high number of women in same-sex couples and are imagined as sites of acceptance for LGBTQ people: Ithaca, New York; San Luis Obispo, California; Portland, Maine; and Greenfield, Massachusetts. Her analysis illustrates how place shapes sexual identity insofar as the women in each city articulated very different narratives about sexuality; she argues that those sexuality narratives are in part influenced by the more general narratives about place and the city. For instance, she finds that in Portland, Maine, LBQ women stress that sexuality can change and adopt "hybrid" sexual identities and argues that, in part because Portland prides itself as an innovative and up-and-coming city, LBQ women likewise articulate their sexuality as something they can create and shape.

Additionally, along with analyzing the experiences of lesbian, bisexual, and queer-identified women in certain spaces, scholars have compared across spaces to study the effect of place on outcomes such as well-being and safety as well as to interrogate the importance of mobilities and movements across geographies. Work that addresses the effect of place tends to limit analytic comparisons either to urban vs. rural spaces or to regions with more supportive vs. less supportive laws related to LGBTQ rights. Research on whether differences in mental health exist between LGBTQ people living in rural areas vs. urban areas in the United States is mixed, with some work showing worse mental health outcomes for those living in rural areas, some work showing worse mental health outcomes for those living in urban areas, and some work showing no differences in mental health outcomes (Fisher, Irwin, & Coleman, 2014; Wienke & Hill, 2013; Woodell, 2018). Also, work has sought to assess differences in levels of victimization across urban and rural areas in the United States. Some research shows that LGBTQ people are less safe and experience more discrimination in rural areas compared to urban areas (Kosciw, Greytak, & Diaz, 2009; Swank, Fahs, & Frost, 2013; Swank, Frost, & Fahs, 2012). Other work suggests that cities with high concentrations of LGBTQ people can be correlated with higher levels of victimization (Green, Strolovitch, Wong, & Bailey, 2001; Spring, 2013, p. 692).

Further, scholars have analyzed the importance of mobility and movement across geographies. For instance, scholars attend to the ways in which migration is constitutive to LGBTQ identities insofar as part of what it means to be LGBTQ is to be displaced (Binnie, 2004; Fortier, 2001; Mai & King, 2009). The migration of people to regions and places like LGBTQ urban meccas speaks to the continued desire to find spaces to be able to freely express same-sex sexualities. For instance, Binnie and Klesse (2013), focus on some LGBTQ people's migration out of Poland and into other nations in the European Union reflects their perception and experience that Western Europe offers greater acceptance of LGBTQ identities compared to Central and Eastern Europe, particularly Poland. Likewise, scholarship highlights the continued appeal of LGBTQ urban meccas and the sentiment that these spaces offer a sense of safety and ability to explore sexual identities (Drabble, Veldhuis, Wootton, Riggle, & Hughes, 2019;

Ghaziani, 2014; Gorman-Murray, 2009). Yet work also points to nuances. For instance, focusing on migration patterns of LGBTQ people in France, Blidon (2016) finds that those migrating to Paris were actually more likely to already be from metropolitan areas (as opposed to the countryside), which she argues challenges the idea that rural LGBTQ seek out urban LGBTQ meccas. Other scholars address the fact that some LGBTQ people enjoy certain aspects of living in small towns or regions assumed to hostile and in fact migrate to those spaces from spaces assumed to be more accepting (Oswald & Lazarevic, 2011; Janovy, 2018; Kazyak, 2011; Waitt & Gorman-Murray, 2011). Scholars also argue for the importance of attending to how interpretations and experiences across geographies may differ by race, class, and gender identity (Abelson, 2014, 2018; Giesking, 2016; Hanhardt, 2013).

Finally, discussions as to whether, how, and why the geographies and spaces for lesbian, bisexual, and queer-identified women are shifting have occupied much of the literature in recent decades. Scholars have documented broad geographic demographic trends, and have provided more specific analyses of the changing nature of spaces in urban LGBTQ neighborhoods. This work attributes these changes to a variety of factors, but often highlights two factors in particular: an increased acceptance of LGBTQ people within the broader society and a shift in conceptualizations of sexuality that emphasize fluidity and queer identities. For instance, relying on demographic data, scholars note the fact that LGBTQ people in the United States live in more varied locales than reflected in academic literature, and document increasing numbers of female same-sex couples in rural areas and regions assumed to be inhospitable, such as the Midwest and South (Black, Gates, Sanders, & Taylor, 2000; Gates, 2006, 2007; Rosenfeld & Kim, 2005; Stone, 2018). Scholars point to these trends and speculate that they reflect an increasing acceptance within these areas. Work focused on non-U.S. contexts likewise situates analyses of geography and sexuality vis-à-vis discussions of changes in the broader culture (Nedbálková, 2016; Wimark, 2016). In his analysis of gays and lesbians in Izmir, Turkey, Wimark (2016) argues that increasingly cultural visibility gay and lesbian identities are one factor that makes it possible for younger generations to stay in that city (as opposed to migrating to a city or region more visibly marked as LGBTQ-friendly). Further, scholarship has also addressed more specifically the changing nature of spaces for lesbian, bisexual, and queer-identified women in urban areas. Most of this work focuses on how the number of community institutions visibly marked as lesbian, like bars and bookstores, have declined if not completely disappeared, which some scholars discuss vis-à-vis changes in communities' and individual's understandings of sexual identity (Forstie, 2019; Gieseking, 2016). For instance, in her work focused on lesbian spaces in Montreal, Podmore (2006) argues that those spaces became more fragmented alongside a shift away from a static-based notion of lesbian identity toward a more fluid notion of sexual identity. Nash and Gorman-Murray (2015) echo this in their assessment of changing lesbian spaces in Toronto and Sydney and argue that younger generations seek out a broader range of spaces outside of lesbian-marked venues that are not seen as restricted and identity-based. Other work focuses on how lesbian, bisexual, and queer-identified women experience conflicting reactions to these changes (Brown-Saracino, 2011).

In sum, a rich body of interdisciplinary scholarship underscores the importance that scholars interested in sexualities interrogate questions of geography, space, and location. The articles in this special issue continue these discussions and introduce new findings and questions for the field.

Acknowledgments

I would like to thank Esther Rothblum for inviting me to be a guest editor and for her guidance throughout the process. I would also like to Department of Sociology at the University of Nebraska-Lincoln for providing financial assistance to support my guest editorship in the form of a graduate student assistant. I am grateful to have had Trenton Haltom serve in this role. Finally, I want to thank the scholars who served as reviewers for the manuscripts submitted to this special issue and all of the authors who submitted their work.

References

Abdi, S. (2014). Staying I(ra)n: Narrating Queer Identity from Within the Persian Closet. *Liminalities: A Journal of Performance Studies, 10*(2), 1–20.

Abelson, M. (2014). Dangerous privilege: Trans men, masculinities, and changing perceptions of safety. *Sociological Forum, 29*(3), 549–570.

Abelson, M. (2018). *Men in place: Trans masculinity, race, and sexuality in America.* Minneapolis, MN: University of Minnesota Press.

Abraham, J. (2009). *Metropolitan loves: The homosexuality of cities.* Minneapolis, MN: University of Minnesota Press.

Barton, B. (2012). *Pray the gay away: The extraordinary lives of bible belt gays.* New York: New York University Press.

Baumle, A. K., Compton, D., & Poston, D. L. (2009). *Same-sex partners: The social demography of sexual orientation*. Albany, NY: SUNY Press.

Binnie, J. (2004). *The Globalization of sexuality*. London: Sage.

Binnie, J., & Klesse, C. (2013). Like a bomb in the gasoline station': East–West migration and transnational activism around lesbian, gay, bisexual, transgender and queer politics in Poland. *Journal of Ethnic and Migration Studies, 39*(7), 1107–1124.

Black, D., Gates, G., Sanders, S., & Taylor, L. (2000). Demographics of the gay and lesbian population in the United States: Evidence from available systematic data sources. *Demography, 37*(2), 139–154.

Blidon, M. (2016). Moving to Paris! Gays and Lesbians: Paths, experiences and projects. In G. Brown & K. Browne (Eds), *The Routledge research companion to geographies of sex and sexualities*, 201–212. New York, NY: Routledge.

Blidon, M., & Zaragocin, S. (2019). Mapping gender and feminist geographies in the global context. *Gender, Place & Culture, 26*, 915–925.

Brainer, A. (2019). *Queer kinship and family change in Taiwan*. New Brunswick, NJ: Rutgers University Press.

Brown, G., Browne, K., Elmhirst, R., & Hutta, S. (2010). Sexualities in/of the Global South. *Geography Compass, 4*(10), 1567–1579.

Browne, K. (2009). Womyn's separatist spaces: Rethinking spaces of difference and exclusion. *Transactions of the Institute of British Geographers, 34*(4), 541–556.

Browne, K. (2011). Beyond rural idylls: Imperfect lesbian utopias at Michigan Womyn's music festival. *Journal of Rural Studies, 27*(1), 13–23.

Brown-Saracino, J. (2011). From the lesbian ghetto to ambient community: The perceived costs and benefits of integration for social ties. *Social Problems, 58*(3), 361–388.

Brown-Saracino, J. (2018). *How place makes us: Novel LGB identities in four small cities*. Chicago: University of Chicago Press.

Doan, P. L., & Higgins, H. (2011). The demise of queer space? Resurgent gentrification and the assimilation of LGBT neighborhoods. *Journal of Planning Education and Research, 31*(1), 6–25.

Drabble, L. A., Veldhuis, C. B., Wootton, A., Riggle, E. D. B., & Hughes, T. L. (2019). Mapping the landscape of support and safety among sexual minority women and gender non- conforming individuals: Perceptions after the 2016 US Presidential election. *Sexuality Research & Social Policy, 16*, 488–500.

Eaves, L. E. (2016). Outside forces: Black southern sexuality. In M. L. Gray, C. R. Johnson, & B. J. Gilley (Eds). *Queering the countryside* (pp. 146–158). New York, NY: New York University Press.

Fenster, T., & Misgav, C. (2019). Israeli feminist geography: women, gender and queer geographies. *Gender, Place & Culture, 26*, 1119–1127.

Fisher, C. M., Irwin, J. A., & Coleman, J. D. (2014). LGBT health in the midlands: A rural/urban comparison of basic health indicators. *Journal of Homosexuality, 61*(8), 1062–1090.

Forstie, C. (2018). Ambivalently post-lesbian: LBQ friendships in the rural Midwest. *Journal of Lesbian Studies, 22*(1), 54–66. doi:10.1080/10894160.2017.1309901

Forstie, C. (2019). Disappearing dykes? Post-lesbian discourse and shifting identities and communities. *Journal of Homosexuality, 1*. doi:10.1080/00918369.2019.1613857

Fortier, A. M. (2001). Coming home: queer migration and multiple evocations of home. *European Journal of Cultural Studies, 4*(4), 405–424.

Gates, G. J. (2006). *Same-sex couples and the gay, lesbian, bisexual population: New estimates from the American community survey*. Los Angeles, CA: The Williams Institute. http://www.law.ucla.edu/williamsinstitute/publications/Policy-Census-index.html

Gates, G. J. (2007). *Geographic trends among same-sex couples in the U.S. census and the American Community Survey*. Los Angeles, CA: The Williams Institute. http://www.law.ucla.edu/williamsinstitute/publications/Policy-Census-index.html

Gates, G. J., & Ost, J. (2004). *The gay & lesbian atlas*. Washington, D.C.: Urban Institute Press.

Ghaziani, A. (2014). *There goes the gayborhood?* Princeton, NJ: Princeton University Press.

Ghaziani, A. (2015). Lesbian geographies. *Contexts*, *14*(1), 62–64. doi:10.1177/1536504214567848

Gieseking, J. J. (2016). Crossing over into territories of the body: Urban territories, borders, and lesbian-queer bodies in New York City. *Area*, *48*(3), 262–270. doi:10.1111/area.12147

Gieseking, J. J. (2016). Dyked New York: The space between geographical imagination and materialization of lesbian-queer bars and neighbourhoods. In G. Brown & K. Browne (Eds.), *The Routledge research companion to geographies of sex and sexualities* (pp. 29–36). New York, NY: Routledge.

Gorman-Murray, A. (2009). Intimate mobilities: Emotional embodiment and queer migration. *Social & Cultural Geography*, *10*, 441–460. doi:10.1080/14649360902853262

Gorman-Murray, A., & Baganz, E. (2019). Geographies of gender and sexuality in Australia, from 1994 to 2018. *Gender, Place & Culture*, *26*, 945–955. doi:10.1080/0966369X.2018.1555150

Gorman-Murray, A., Brennan-Horley, C., Kirsten Mclean, K., Waitt, G., & Gibson, C. (2010). Mapping same-sex couple family households in Australia. *Journal of Maps*, *6*(1), 382–392. doi:10.4113/jom.2010.1094

Gorman-Murray, A., Waitt, G., & Gibson, C. (2008). A queer country? A case study of the politics of gay/lesbian belonging in an Australian country town. *Australian Geographer*, *39*(2), 171–191. doi:10.1080/00049180802056849

Gray, M. L. (2009). *Out in the country: Youth, media, and queer Visibility in rural America*. New York, NY: New York University Press.

Green, D. P., Strolovitch, D. Z., Wong, J. S., & Bailey, R. W. (2001). Measuring gay populations and antigay hate crime. *Social Science Quarterly*, *82*(2), 281–296. doi:10.1111/0038-4941.00023

Halberstam, J. (2005). *In a queer time and place: Transgender bodies, subcultural lives*. New York, NY: New York University Press.

Hanhardt, C. B. (2013). *Safe space: Gay neighborhood history and the politics of violence*. Durham, NC: Duke University Press.

Herring, S. (2007). Out of the closets, into the woods: RFD, Country women, and the post-stonewall emergence of queer anti-urbanism. *American Quarterly*, *59*(2), 341–372. doi:10.1353/aq.2007.0043

Hoad, N. (2007). *African intimacies: Race, homosexuality, and globalization*. Minneapolis, MN: University of Minnesota Press.

Janovy, C. J. (2018). *No place like home: Lessons in activism from LGBT Kansas*. Lawrence, KS: University of Kansas Press.

Johnson, C. (2009). *Just queer folks: Gender and sexuality in rural America*. Philadelphia, PA: Temple University Press.

Kazyak, E. (2011). Disrupting cultural selves: Constructing gay and lesbian identities in rural locales. *Qualitative Sociology*, *34*(4), 561–581. doi:10.1007/s11133-011-9205-1

Kazyak, E. (2012). Midwest or lesbian? Gender, rurality, and sexuality. *Gender & Society*, *26*, 825–848. doi:10.1177/0891243212458361

Kosciw, J. G., Greytak, E. A., & Diaz, E. M. (2009). Who, what, where, when, and why: Demographic and ecological factors contributing to hostile school climate for lesbian, gay, bisexual, and transgender youth. *Journal of Youth and Adolescence, 38*(7), 976–988. doi:10.1007/s10964-009-9412-1

Logie, C. H., & Rwigema, M. (2014). The normative idea of queer is a white person: Understanding perceptions of white privilege among lesbian, bisexual, and queer women of color in Toronto, Canada. *Journal of Lesbian Studies, 18*(2), 174–191. doi:10.1080/10894160.2014.849165

Mai, N., & King, R. (2009). Love, sexuality and migration: Mapping the issue(s). *Mobilities, 4*(3), 295–307. doi:10.1080/17450100903195318

Markwell, K. (2002). Mardi Gras tourism and the construction of Sydney as an international gay and lesbian city. *GLQ: A Journal of Lesbian and Gay Studies, 8*(1-2), 81–99. doi:10.1215/10642684-8-1-2-81

Moore, M. R. (2010). Black and gay in L.A.: The relationships black lesbians and gay men have with their racial and religious communities. In D. Hunt & A. Ramon (Eds.), *Black Los Angeles: American dreams and racial realities* (pp. 188–214). New York, NY: New York University Press.

Moussawi, G. (2018). Queer exceptionalism and exclusion: Cosmopolitanism and inequalities in 'gay-friendly' Beirut. *The Sociological Review, 66*(1), 174–190. doi:10.1177/0038026117725469

Myrdahel, T. T. (2016). Visibility on their own terms? LGBTQ lives in small Canadian cities. In G. Brown & K. Browne (Eds.), *The Routledge research companion to geographies of sex and sexualities* (pp. 37–44). New York, NY: Routledge.

Nash, C., & Bain, A. (2007). Reclaiming raunch'? Spatializing queer identities at Toronto women's bathhouse events. *Social & Cultural Geography, 8*, 47–67. doi:10.1080/14649360701251809

Nash, C., & Gorman-Murray, A. (2015). Lesbian spaces in transition: Insights from Toronto and Sydney. In P. Doan (Ed.), *Planning and LGBTQ Communities: The need for inclusive queer spaces* (pp. 181–198). New York, NY: Routledge.

Nedbálková, K., (2016). Idle ally: LGBT community in the Czech Republic. In I. Jusova and J. Siklova (Eds.), *Czech Feminisms: Perspectives on Gender in East Central Europe* (pp. 205–221). Bloomington, IN: Indiana University Press.

Orne, J. (2017). *Boystown: Sex and community in Chicago*. Chicago, IL: University of Chicago Press.

Oswald, R. F., & Culton, L. S. (2003). Under the rainbow: Rural gay life and its relevance for family providers. *Family Relations, 52*(1), 72–81.

Oswald, R. F., & Lazarevic, V. (2011). You live where?!" Lesbian mothers' attachment to nonmetropolitan communities. *Family Relations, 60*(4), 373–386. doi:10.1111/j.1741-3729.2011.00663.x

Oswin, N. (2005). Researching 'gay Cape Town' finding value-added queerness. *Social & Cultural Geography, 4*, 567–586. doi:10.1080/14649360500200304

Pitonˇák, M., &., & Klingorová, K., (2019). Development of Czech feminist and queer geographies: identifying barriers, seeking progress. *Gender, Place & Culture, 26*, 1001–1012. doi:10.1080/0966369X.2018.1563528

Podmore, J. (2006). Gone 'underground'? Lesbian visibility and the consolidation of queer space fin Montreal. *Social & Cultural Geography, 7*(4), 595–625. doi:10.1080/14649360600825737

Puar, J. K. (2002). Circuits of queer mobility: Tourism, travel, and globalization. *GLQ: A Journal of Lesbian and Gay Studies, 8*(1-2), 101–137. doi:10.1215/10642684-8-1-2-101

Puar, J. K., Rushbrook, D., & Schein, L. (2003). Guest editorial Sexuality and space: queering geographies of globalization. *Environment and Planning D: Society and Space, 21*(4), 383–387. doi:10.1068/d2104ed

Puri, J. (2016). *Sexual states: Governance and the struggle over the antisodomy law in India*. Durham, NC: Duke University Press.

Rabin, J. S., & Slater, B. R. (2005). Lesbian communities across the United States. *Journal of Lesbian Studies, 9*(1-2), 169–182. doi:10.1300/J155v09n01_16

Rosenfeld, M. J., & Kim, B. (2005). The independence of young adults and the rise of inter-racial and same-sex unions. *American Sociological Review, 70*(4), 541–562. doi:10.1177/000312240507000401

Rushbrook, D. (2002). Cities, queer space, and the cosmopolitan tourist. *GLQ: A Journal of Lesbian and Gay Studies, 8*(1-2), 183–206. doi:10.1215/10642684-8-1-2-183

Silva, J. M., & Ornat, M. J. (2016). Wake up Alice, This is not wonderland!' Power, diversity, and knowledge in geographies of sexualities. In G. Brown & K. Browne (Eds.), *The Routledge research companion to geographies of sex and sexualities* (pp. 185–194). New York, NY: Routledge.

Spring, A. (2013). Declining segregation of same-sex partners: Evidence from Census 2000 and 2010. *Population Research and Policy Review, 32*(5), 687–716. doi:10.1007/s11113-013-9280-y

Stein, A. (2001). *The stranger next door: The story of a small community's battle over sex, faith, and civil rights*. Boston, MA: Beacon Press.

Stone, A. (2018). The geography of research on LGBTQ Life: Why sociologists should study the South, rural queers, and ordinary cities. *Sociology Compass, 12*(11), e12638–15. doi:10.1111/soc4.12638

Swank, E., Fahs, B., & Frost, D. M. (2013). Region, social identities, and disclosure practices as predictors of heterosexist discrimination against sexual minorities in the United States. *Sociological Inquiry, 83*(2), 238–258. doi:10.1111/soin.12004

Swank, E., Frost, D. M., & Fahs, B. (2012). Rural location and exposure to minority stress among sexual minorities. *Psychology and Sexuality, 3*, 226–243. doi:10.1080/19419899.2012.700026

Swarr, A. L. (2012). *Sex in transition: Remaking gender and race in South Africa*. Albany, NY: SUNY Press.

Swarr, A. L., & Nagar, R. (2004). Dismantling assumptions: Interrogating 'lesbian' struggles for identity and survival in India and South Africa. *SIGNS: Journal of Women in Culture and Society, 29*(2), 491–516. doi:10.1086/378573

Thomsen, C. (2016). In plain(s) sight: Rural LGBTQ women and the politics of visibility. In M. L. Gray, C. R. Johnson, & B. J. Gilley (Eds). *Queering the Countryside* (pp. 244–265). New York, NY: New York University Press.

Valentine, G. (2001). *Social geographies: Space and society*. London: Pearson.

Waitt, G., & Gorman-Murray, A. (2011). Journeys and returns: Home, life narratives and remapping sexuality in a regional city. *International Journal of Urban and Regional Research, 35*(6), 1239–1255. doi:10.1111/j.1468-2427.2010.01006.x

Weston, K. (1995). Get thee to a big city: Sexual imaginary and the great gay migration. *GLQ: A Journal of Lesbian and Gay Studies, 2*, 253–277. doi:10.1215/10642684-2-3-253

Wienke, C., & Hill, G. (2013). Does place of residence matter? Rural-urban differences and the well-being of gay men and lesbians. *Journal of Homosexuality, 60*(9), 1256–1279. doi:10.1080/00918369.2013.806166

Wilson, A. (2006). Queering Asia. Intersections: Gender, history and culture in the Asian Context, 14. Retrieved on 7 November 2019 from: http://www.intersections.anu.edu.au/issue14/wilson.html.

Wimark, T. (2016). The impact of family ties on the mobility decisions of gay men and lesbians. Gender. *Place & Culture, 23*, 659–676.

Woodell, B. (2018). Understanding sexual minority health disparities in rural areas. *Sociology Compass, 12*(2), e12553–17. doi:10.1111/soc4.12553

Woodell, B., Kazyak, E., & Compton, D. R. (2015). Reconciling LGB and Christian identities in the rural South. *Social Sciences, 4*(3), 859–878. doi:10.3390/socsci4030859

Not in our community: Queer women challenge religious homophobia in rural Kentucky

Bernadette Barton and Ashley Currier

ABSTRACT

"Not in my backyard" (NIMBY) movements emerge when a social or political event spurs opposition from local residents. Much research on NIMBY movements concentrates on local residents' efforts to defend their community from unwanted "outsiders" or elements, such as a waste incinerator or sex offenders. Little is written on how NIMBY activism can redefine a place to be more inclusive of sexual minorities and supportive of progressive social initiatives. After the Supreme Court's 2015 ruling in favor of marriage equality in *Obergefell v. Hodges*, Rowan County Clerk Kim Davis refused to issue marriage licenses to same-sex couples citing her religious beliefs. Davis' actions galvanized marriage-equality and religious-freedom activists in the region. Pro-marriage-equality activists included lesbian, bisexual, pansexual, and queer women who viewed Davis' action as an attack on their legitimacy in the community. Drawing on 11 interviews with queer women in Kentucky, we explore how their activist work in Rowan County challenged small-town intolerance and religious homophobia and helped to re-form the region as more a progressive space for sexual minorities.

Introduction

The June 2015 Supreme Court ruling *Obergefell v. Hodges* found state marriage bans on same-sex marriages unconstitutional. Directly following this decision, Kentucky made national news when Rowan County Clerk Kim Davis refused to issue marriage licenses to same-sex couples, citing a conflict of faith. Like their counterparts in urban areas (Bernstein & Taylor, 2013), rural lesbian, gay, bisexual, transgender, and queer (LGBTQ) (LGBTQ) residents and supportive heterosexual allies immediately began picketing outside Davis's office. They swiftly established the Rowan County Rights Coalition (RCRC), a face-to face and online activist organization. RCRC members included residents from Rowan and neighboring counties and Morehead State University (MSU) faculty, staff, and students. Rowan County also houses many Davis supporters who considered her actions a testament to her Christian faith. Led by pastors and members of local churches, a loose coalition of religious-freedom activists quickly rallied, motivated both by Davis' action and the religious homophobia institutionalized in many conservative Christian churches (Apostolic, Church of Christ, Baptist, and non-denominational among others) throughout the region (Barton, 2012). The two groups protested outside the Rowan County courthouse for weeks.

Among socially conservative Kentucky towns, Morehead, the Rowan County seat, is a progressive enclave and a destination spot for many LGBTQ people from Appalachia. Home to a rural community of artists, farmers, and university employees, few residents expected Morehead to host a battle in the "culture wars." In this article, we explore how Davis's actions and the subsequent protests transformed Rowan County for LGBTQ people. Citing their disagreement with Davis' stance, lesbian, bisexual, pansexual, and queer women participants viewed activism as a way to combat homophobia in their community. We treat their activism as a form of "not in my backyard" (NIMBY) mobilization. In doing so, we challenge the scholarly tendency to ignore queer lives in rural spaces (Stone, 2018) by illustrating how NIMBY organizing can be a viable strategy to create progressive social change for rural queer people.

Methods comprise eleven interviews with white lesbian, bisexual, queer, and pansexual women who participated in the courthouse protests.[1] Our data include face-to-face, digitally recorded audio interviews with seven women and four transcribed interviews collected by researchers involved with MSU's Rowan County Marriage Equality and Religious Liberty Project (MERL). We conducted interviews with anti- and pro-marriage-equality protesters in 2017–2018, and MERL interviews were collected in 2016–2017. We assigned interviewed women pseudonyms to ensure their confidentiality. Interview questions explored participants' thoughts about and experiences of the courthouse protests, the role of RCRC, and the effects of the 2015 events in Rowan County.

Making space for sexuality in analyses of NIMBY organizing

What is the relationship between LGBTQ activism and NIMBY organizing? Most studies on NIMBY organizing explore how residents object to a group, event, or institution menacing their communities (Stein, 2001). Describing how political contexts affect social movements, McAdam and Tarrow (2018, p. 32) write that "reactive, NIMBY-style, collective action against all manner of perceived threats, remains perhaps the single most common type of protest world-wide." Much research on NIMBY movements concentrates on residents' reactive efforts to defend communities from unwanted "outsiders," such as registered sex offenders (Williams, 2018) or environmentally harmful projects (Hager & Haddad, 2015). When scholars research sexuality in NIMBY organizing, they often focus on conservative mobilization in urban spaces. For example, in the US, some evangelical Christians have initiated vigilante-style "backyard abolitionism" to find victims of human-trafficking and eliminate commercial prostitution from their communities (Shih, 2016).

LGBTQ-led NIMBY organizing in urban queer spaces can also be motivated by intolerance, such as when privileged lesbians and gay men wage class-based battles over access to and the reputations of LGBTQ spaces (Jerolmack & Walker, 2018). For example, in some LGBTQ urban neighborhoods, white, wealthy lesbian and gay residents eject poor, working-class queers and queer residents of color by organizing to criminalize public behavior like loitering or solicitation for sex (Ross, 2010). In other affluent, gay urban enclaves, privileged community members have blocked shelters for homeless queer youth (Cruz, 2011). Manalansan (2005, p. 142) explains that well-off white gay and lesbian residents' NIMBY organizing ushers in "homonormativity" by "anesthetiz[ing] queer communities into passively accepting alternative forms of inequality in return for domestic privacy and the freedom to consume." In other words, "gating" their communities allows privileged, white lesbian and gay elites to ignore racial and class inequalities that make life difficult for LGBTQ residents of color.

Rural queer studies offer ways to understand NIMBY organizing in rural LGBTQ communities. First, these approaches examine how queer residents feel connected to their "close-knit" communities (Kazyak, 2011, p. 573; Luis, 2018), for instance, through friendships among lesbians (Forstie, 2018). Brown-Saracino (2018, p. 198) characterization of how small cities influence lesbian, bisexual, and queer women's sexualities contests "metronormative" narratives that dominate queer studies. Halberstam (2005, p. 36) defines "metronormative" perspectives as casting "[r]ural and small-town queer life-…as sad and lonely." The willingness of lesbian, bisexual, pansexual, and queer women to stay in and fight for acceptance in their communities challenges metronormative narratives. Second, rural queer studies approaches allow scholars to consider rural lesbian and queer women's NIMBY organizing as a key process in both generating a "close-knit" community and remaking their town to better include lesbian and queer difference.

Findings

Participants expressed that the events of 2015 had a lasting impact on Rowan County and noted ways that the protests changed the community. Primarily, many LGBTQ people shed the "toxic closet" (Barton, 2012), became more visible in their home county, found one another, and participated in a public conversation about LGBTQ rights. Staunch heterosexual allies also fought alongside LGBTQ people for marriage equality, bolstering lesbian, bisexual, pansexual, and queer women participants' sense of belonging and community. The months-long protests at the courthouse also offered progressive residents opportunities to meet and connect, laying a foundation for future grassroots organizing.

Interview participants acknowledged class inequalities, rejected regional prejudices about rural Appalachian communities, and actively challenged stereotypes of Kentucky as culturally "backward" (Donesky, 1999, p. 295). Like other queer people committed to their rural homes (Gray, 2009; Staley, 2012), the women featured in this article wanted to *transform* not *leave* their community. Lesbian, bisexual, pansexual, and queer women activists' experiences illustrate both how "places make us" (Brown-Saracino, 2018, p. 198) and how activism makes places. All observed that pro- and anti-LGBTQ protestors maintained a respectful civility until *outsiders* entered Rowan County at which point tensions between protest groups escalated. We analyze the NIMBY tactics lesbian, bisexual, pansexual, and queer women used to confront religious homophobia in their community.

Dissolving the "toxic closet"

Participating in pro-LGBTQ demonstrations at the courthouse helped lesbian, bisexual, pansexual, and queer women dismantle the "toxic closet," a homophobic socialization "to hold back, to not express ourselves, to accept that we do not deserve the taken-for-granted social courtesies, legal rights, respect, care, and support that heterosexuals enjoy without thought" (Barton, 2012, p. 88). They also brought people together in ways that furthered LGBTQ rights and facilitated a richer public conversation about sexual and gender minorities. For example, Caroline, a lesbian said, "We're less invisible and it's more comfortable to talk about" LGBTQ experiences. Sydney, a lesbian, admitted,

> It was a conversation we needed to have in Morehead. So, Kim Davis, I'll pat her on the back for allowing that to happen. Because if you were in Morehead, you pretty much had to be closeted. I think that [the protests] opened that up a little bit. It also brought the conversation out and made it more explicit. So we're now dealing with it. ... So, I'm really proud of what happened.

Like Sydney, Kristen, a lesbian, believed the events increased local LGBTQ visibility and forced community members to reckon with LGBTQ issues. She said, "It made people more aware of our rights, that we're here and we're not going away."

The fact that the early days of the demonstrations were mostly positive, empowering, and civil encouraged participants to protest as "out" lesbian, bisexual, pansexual, and queer women. Terry, a lesbian, and Christine, who is pansexual, each described the environment. Terry narrated:

> Well, the first day [early July 2015], it was fun. Friends, people I hadn't seen in a long time, are showing up and there's flowers and signs. Lots of rainbows. I've had people show up in support. So it was, "What do we do here? We stand, okay. Oh, let's chant. Yeah, good. I don't want to chant. Let's all hold hands." It was interesting. Fun. Hot.

Christine rushed to her first protest without saying "bye to my significant other. I just went on down there, and it was pretty active already." She recalled seeing a number of marriage-equality supporters at the courthouse and that Kim Davis's "people had started to congregate as well." She said, "By mid-day, she had people there representing her and her theology and her 'right to do as she saw fit in accordance with her beliefs.'" Although Christine observed a "lot of energy on both sides," she emphasized the "passion" marriage-equality activists displayed, and was determined to show up and support "our friends trying to pursue their right to get married [and] protect themselves."

Most participants expressed that it was important to demonstrate for those who couldn't—those who were closeted, scared, young, and struggling. Caroline shared that she was "stunned" and then filled with "joy" when she first learned about the Supreme Court decision legalizing same-sex marriage, knowing she would be able to marry in her hometown. She said, "People getting married [in Kentucky] the same day that it became legal was astounding." Outrage complicated Caroline's joy when she learned that Kim Davis was refusing marriage licenses to same-sex couples in Rowan County. Caroline explained she was inspired to join the "movement" because, she said, "This is a place that matters. Being from the area, it was something I knew I had to do." She understood her involvement as a "responsibility" to the "young people in the area that are LGBTQ that I'm related to and that I love, who aren't able to easily make a stand because of who their family is or what their relationships are." For Caroline, allowing the religious homophobia of Davis and her supporters to go unopposed further marginalized LGBTQ youth.

Alice, a lesbian, also explained that "there are kids in our community who have said, 'I can't go home because I came out as gay or lesbian and my family has shunned me,' or 'if I came out, my family would never speak to me again.'" A middle-aged woman with a stable job, Alice felt securely enough positioned to "stand up for those who can't." Similarly, Terry expressed her commitment to join the groups standing up against bigotry for "little dudes in Eastern Kentucky:"

I protested because I wanted people in the community to know that it wasn't just one person that was interested in this. I was there because the [college LGBTQ student group], affirmative action statements, LGBT offices, Pride events, protesting, to me, those are beacons. Beacons of light for curly-haired girls that live in [a town south of Morehead] that think that not only is the world against them, but their entire religious system is against them. Or for little dudes that live in far eastern Kentucky that haven't had the opportunity to tell their parents, "Hey, I'm gay," and for them to be like, "That is so awesome! I love you! Your boyfriend is amazing!" I will stand out there so you know that people like me exist.

Terry hoped that the work of a diverse group of LGBTQ rights and marriage-equality supporters might make the future a little brighter for sexual and gender minorities in the region.

Lesbian, bisexual, pansexual, and queer women recognized and appreciated the hard work and fierce support of many heterosexual allies in RCRC. "Allies are movement adherents who are not direct beneficiaries of the movements they support and do not have expectations of such benefits" (Myers, 2008, p. 168). For example, informants explained that heterosexuals helped found RCRC and stood side by side with LGBTQ people outside the courthouse day after day in the summer heat. Caroline described the heterosexual allies as:

the group of people who showed up to protest and who kept showing up and who organized and helped walk people in as they went to the courthouse. They were there to support us. They called and said, "We've got your back and don't worry about this." [They were] group of local citizens, again, most of them not gay, not a part of the queer community but just really unhappy with the fact that this injustice was happening in our community and were willing to come out and bodily put themselves between us and harm. That's really the truth of it. To make sure that justice was done and to say this is not the kind of community we want.

Participants found this solidarity with supportive heterosexuals very meaningful and some, like Caroline, experienced a new level of community support. Caroline and her partner Savannah obtained a marriage license at the Rowan County courthouse while Davis was in jail. She said, "There was a moment that was really surreal and felt full circle for me. I could look down the street and see where my grandmother lived most of my life. It's probably the most accepted or the most belonging I had ever felt."

Natalie, an RCRC leader, and daily regular at the demonstrations, observed LGBTQ people in the region actually *discover* themselves and one another in front of the Rowan County courthouse. She explained, "People felt like [the protests] gave them a voice that they didn't have: 'I thought I was the only one in Morehead, but I'm not. Look at all these people who came out.' Especially transgender individuals. We ended up finding a whole pocket who identified as transgender and they found each other because of this." The demonstrations for marriage equality created a space where sexual and gender minorities came, met one another, and formed support networks.

How NIMBY activism transformed this rural Kentucky town

From early July through mid-August 2015, relations between the pro-equality and religious-freedom protestors were cordial as small-town norms of civility governed their interactions. Natalie explained:

You have generations of families here, and this divided us even within families. So you would protest each other during the day, but then you have to go church with them on Sunday. Or you're going to Kroger [grocery store], and they're there. You can't escape them. It's not a big city where you can disappear. These were people that you saw every day.

Protestors on both sides of the sidewalk recognized the importance of being neighborly. According to the 2010 census data, Rowan County has 24,517 residents. It is stressful to share a town with, and regularly encounter, those with whom one has unresolved tension. Both marriage-equality and religious-freedom demonstrators knew that, when the dust settled, they still had to work and live together.

Yet, when several same-sex couples and one opposite-sex couple who were denied marriage licenses sued Davis and outsiders arrived, local norms of courtesy were upended. The case made its way to an appeals court in Ashland, Kentucky, where a federal judge ordered Davis to issue marriage licenses to all couples, including same-sex couples (Associated Press, 2015; Southall, 2015). Davis refused and the judge ordered her to jail. When Davis was incarcerated, churches from outside Rowan County began bussing in religious-freedom protestors to Morehead. At this point the tone of the courthouse protests changed, and "things got scary" for participants like Terry. She explained, "We had reports of this armed militia on its way in." Emulating a hypothetical, armed religious-freedom supporter, Terry grabbed an imaginary belt recalling that they "'were going to show the police chief what they were going to do.'"

During this time, Alice and her then-partner (and now wife) Kristen went to get their licenses. The courthouse was, as Alice described, "a media circus":

There were tents with different media outlets. There was MSNBC, CNN, MBC, CBS. There were Lexington outlets. There were helicopters flying over top because they had heard that at noon, we were coming to get our licenses that day. The AP [Associated Press] person had called me and said, "When are you coming? We thought you would be at eight this morning. When are you coming?" And I said, "It'll be around noon. I'm working." And so Kristen and I went down there and helicopters flying over—I mean that's just shocking that there were news helicopters in Morehead, Kentucky. And I was the subject of those helicopters. And there were protesters. There were protesters for both sides. There were people who were passing out flowers. There were ministers willing to marry us right there and invited us to church in Lexington. There were people yelling, "You're going to hell," "It's against the rules in the Bible," and "You're going to burn," and sodomy—it always something about sodomy.

With media vans and busloads of strangers appearing, protests grew more raucous and contentious. Terry recalled seeing "people playing drums and trumpets, stomping around, and retirees in camping chairs with Bible verses. They were saying things that are very hurtful to people who've already been ostracized and bringing guns into this." Deborah, a lesbian, explained that she felt very unsafe the day that men brought guns strapped to their backs to the courthouse. She also described a disturbing encounter with a Davis supporter: "One man got in my face and said, 'The reason you're a lesbian is because you were raped as an infant.'" Several informants described two vans painted with Bible verses, featuring lurid antiabortion images and proclaiming AIDS as God's punishment for "homosexuals," parked in visible areas around town. Terry was particularly bothered by a plane with a banner advertising an anti-LGBTQ movie promoting conversion therapy flying across Rowan County at all times of the day. Overall, informants noted a decline in respectful protest norms when *outsiders* entered Rowan County. Davis supporters bussed in from North Carolina and Tennessee churches had no investment in the place, no expectation of a continued relationship with the people on the other side, and thus no social pressure to be respectful.

Lesbian, bisexual, pansexual, and queer women participants overwhelmingly perceived Davis supporters as more aggressive and insulting than marriage-equality proponents. However, they did note that LGBTQ activists from outside Morehead were sometimes more confrontational than RCRC preferred. Anticipating possibly belligerent counterprotestors, some of whom would likely espouse homophobic ideas, RCRC leaders developed a set of protest "guidelines" in early July. Natalie and other RCRC representatives shared the "rules" with new people rotating in and out of the demonstrations. For example, one guideline forbade "vulgarity." She said, "We're going to be representing our community. We need to be able to be respectful and responsible." Natalie explained that RCRC members wrote the rules "on the back of our posters so if people showed up, we could give them a poster, and they had the guidelines on the back so they can see where we were coming from."

Not only did these rules help protestors cultivate a "collective identity" rooted in defending LGBTQ rights and marriage equality in Kentucky (Taylor & Whittier, 1992), but they also projected an image of marriage-equality supporters as "respectful and responsible" community members. However, like the

religious-freedom protestors arriving from other states, some progressive outsiders also showed little interest in abiding by the RCRC rules of civility.
Natalie illustrated, "I remember there was this one woman in particular, and
I gave her a sign and I said, 'The media is watching us so it's really important
that we stay focused and here are some guidelines that we came up with so this
can be helpful.' And she was not having it. She wanted to fight and was ready
and willing to engage with anybody."

As protests and media scrutiny became somewhat routine, Rowan
County residents had new conversations about LGBTQ rights with one
another. Respondents like Christine used the events to initiate dialogs with
those opposed to or ignorant about LGBTQ rights. She recalled that "a lot
of friendships ended up being broken off because of people trying to
defend what [Davis] was doing, asking questions like, 'Why can't [couples]
go to another courthouse? Why does it have to be here [where Davis] signs
the license?'" Yet, over time, Christine observed some people change from
being supportive to critical of Davis as they mulled over the implications of
her actions. Christine described one interaction: "'You know, you're right.
It isn't right that she did that.' These are people … 50-, 60-year-old men
and women. … All you needed to say was: 'These are our rights. These
are the things that we get from this—like what if the spouse dies?"
Christine was even able to "have that conversation with" her "own grand-
parents … and have them see what [Davis was] doing isn't right."
Although it was taxing for Rowan County residents to be ground zero in
the battle over marriage equality, those featured in this manuscript
observed many positive developments explicitly manifest because the
NIMBY protests happened in a *rural* place.

Fueling and dismantling stereotypes about Appalachia

Over the summer and fall of 2015, international news outlets ridiculed the
appearances of Kim Davis and her husband, Joe Davis, and dozens of satir-
ical memes of Davis circulated on social media. Clerk Davis, with her
uncut hair, lack of makeup, long skirts, four marriages, and bigoted ideas
about gay people was easy to mock. Bethany, a bisexual woman, noted how

> the media fixated on her [Davis], like a trend, a flash. She physically embodied and
> religiously embodied a stereotype that drew a lot of media attention. She practices an
> Apostolic religion that's charismatic in which women don't cut their hair and always
> wear skirts. So, I think all of that was easy for the media to fixate on as freakish.

Although Bethany did not agree with Davis' actions, she deplored how
the media and US public vilified her: "I didn't appreciate any of the snarky
memes floating around, making fun of the way she looked at all. But I
think that exotic visual look was very arresting to media folks from New

York and California." Coupled with her "extreme" "religious ideology ... in that she was basically choosing to discriminate against a group of people in the name of religion," Davis' physical appearance "drew their attention," Bethany believed. "So, I think that whole package together was really attractive to the media. It's easy for the media also to put down Kentucky as a place of backward hillbillies."

Many news articles also featured images of anti-LGBTQ activists waving flags, Bibles, and guns outside the Rowan County courthouse. Kentuckians have much experience facing and combating stereotypes of rural Appalachians as poor, unsophisticated, and out of touch with popular culture. Unsurprisingly, several participants lamented that Davis's actions reinforced negative stereotypes about the region. Some, like Christine, viewed it as their moral obligation to protest and resist harmful stereotypes of Appalachia that galvanized local homophobia. Christine elaborated:

> When we tell people, "I'm from Morehead," two out of three times, people say, "Oh, that place where that Kim Davis lady is from," and that stinks. It doesn't make us look great, but there's also a lot of people that after that say, "Oh, were you there with those people who were out there protesting?" And so that gives us an opportunity to say, "Yeah, there are a lot of good people in our community. They realize when bad things happen, and they know they need to take action." I do think a lot of people think, "They must be stereotypical Kentuckians: backwoods, they're ignorant." But, on the flipside, a lot of people say, "That same day, a bunch of those kids went out there with their signs and their flags, and they protested for what is right."

Several pro-LGBTQ activists stressed that one reason they protested was to remind observers that there are left-leaning progressives in rural Kentucky and to challenge outdated stereotypes of Appalachia. Natalie shared, "We were already being made fun of for being in the Kentucky county that was standing up against [Davis] so there was this negative image of Morehead and Rowan County. It was really important to me that we were representing a better part of Rowan County. I wanted them to see us as passionate, vibrant activists; people that were not stereotypical, but peaceful and respectful." Lesbian, bisexual, pansexual, and queer women activists felt that it was important to challenge the stereotypes of others and model what a progressive community looks like for locals. By participating in daily protests, local LGBTQ residents experienced a greater sense of belonging in the region while challenging negative stereotypes about what makes up a "Kentuckian."

Conclusion

In Rowan County, Kentucky, pro-equality advocates challenged small-town intolerance and religious homophobia to create a more a progressive space for sexual and gender minorities. Whereas much scholarship on NIMBY organizing explores the motivations of sociopolitical conservatives, here we highlight progressive queer women's resistance to religious homophobia in a rural Kentucky community. In doing so, we make a substantive contribution to rural queer (Gray, Johnson, & Gilley, 2016) and NIMBY studies. As noted, most research on US LGBTQ organizing focuses on major metropolitan areas (Armstrong, 2002; Ghaziani, 2008), excluding rural queer people from national conversations about gender and sexual diversity politics. Our research shifts the center of movement organizing around LGBTQ rights away from the urban by interrupting "metronormative" assumptions guiding queer and social movement studies. Simply stated, our findings counterassumptions that no LGBTQ organizing exists in rural areas. Rather, we find that norms of rural life can sometimes *accelerate* social change. In 2015, the spectacularly public events in Rowan County, coupled with the tight-knit structure of small town life, facilitated relationship-building that weakened the toxic closet and made possible future progressive grassroots organizing. The continued persistence of pro-LGBTQ organizing, among other social justice initiatives in Morehead, suggests that the rural US south is a new frontier for LGBTQ activism.

Note

1. According to 2018 US Census estimates, approximately 94 percent of Rowan County, Kentucky, residents identified as non-Hispanic whites. Therefore, it is unsurprising that all of our respondents identified as white.

Acknowledgments

The authors thank Anna Blanton, Kathleen M. Blee, Toni Hobbs, Nashia Fife, and all the interview participants for their support of the project. The authors gratefully acknowledge the data collected by, and the support of, MSU's Rowan County Marriage Equality and Religious Liberty Project (MERL). We also acknowledge Research and Sponsored Programs and the Department of Sociology, Social Work and Criminology at Morehead State University and the University of Cincinnati's University Research Council and Charles Phelps Taft Research Center for generously supporting this study. Finally, we thank Emily Kazyak and three anonymous reviewers at the *Journal of Lesbian Studies* for their thoughtful feedback.

References

Armstrong, E. A. (2002). *Forging gay identities: Organizing sexuality in San Francisco, 1950-1994*. Chicago, IL: University of Chicago Press.

Associated Press. (2015). Kentucky: Clerk ordered to issue wedding licenses to same-sex couples. *New York Times.* August 13, A10.

Barton, B. (2012). *Pray the gay away: The extraordinary lives of Bible belt gays.* New York: New York University Press.

Bernstein, M. & Taylor, V. (Eds). (2013). *The marrying kind? Debating same-sex marriage within the lesbian and gay movement.* Minneapolis, MN: University of Minnesota Press.

Brown-Saracino, J. (2018). *How places make us: Novel LBQ identities in four small cities.* Chicago: University of Chicago Press.

Cruz, C. (2011). LGBTQ street youth talk back: A meditation on resistance and witnessing. *International Journal of Qualitative Studies in Education, 24*(5), 547–558.

Donesky, F. (1999). America needs hillbillies: The case of the Kentucky cycle. In D. B. Billings, G. Norman, & K. Ledford (Eds.) *Back talk from Appalachia: Confronting stereotypes* (pp. 283–299). Lexington, KY: University Press of Kentucky.

Forstie, C. (2018). Ambivalently post-lesbian: LBQ friendships in the rural midwest. *Journal of Lesbian Studies, 22*(1), 54–66.

Ghaziani, A. (2008). *The dividends of dissent: How conflict and culture work in lesbian and gay marches on Washington.* Chicago, IL: University of Chicago Press.

Gray, M. L. (2009). *Out in the country: Youth, media, and queer visibility in rural America.* New York, NY: New York University Press.

Gray, M. L., Johnson, C. R., & Gilley, B. J. (Eds.). (2016). *Queering the countryside: New frontiers in rural queer studies.* New York, NY: New York University Press.

Hager, C. & Haddad, M. A. (Eds.). (2015). *NIMBY is beautiful: Cases of local activism and environmental innovation around the world.* New York, NY: Berghahn.

Halberstam, J. (2005). *In a queer time and place: Transgender bodies, subcultural lives.* New York, NY: New York University Press.

Jerolmack, C., & Walker, E. T. (2018). Please in my backyard: Quiet mobilization in support of fracking in an Appalachian community. *American Journal of Sociology, 124*(2), 479–516.

Kazyak, E. (2011). Disrupting cultural selves: Constructing gay and lesbian identities in rural locales. *Qualitative Sociology, 34*(4), 561–581.

Luis, K. N. (2018). *Herlands: Exploring the women's land movement in the United States.* Minneapolis, MN: University of Minnesota Press.

Manalansan, M. F. IV. (2005). Race, violence, and neoliberal spatial politics in the global city. *Social Text, 84-85*, 141–155.

McAdam, D., & Tarrow, S. (2018). The political context of social movements. In D. A. Snow, S. A. Soule, H. Kriesi, & H. J. McCammon (Eds.) *The Wiley Blackwell companion to social movements* (2nd ed., pp. 19–42). Hoboken, NJ: John Wiley & Sons.

Myers, D. J. (2008). Ally identity: The politically gay. In J. Refer, D. J. Myers, & R. L. Einwohner (Eds.) *Identity work in social movements* (pp. 167–187). Minneapolis, MN: University of Minnesota Press.

Ross, B. L. (2010). Sex and (evacuation from) the city: The moral and legal regulation of sex workers in Vancouver's West End, 1975-1985. *Sexualities, 13*(2), 197–218.

Shih, E. (2016). Not in my 'backyard abolitionism': Vigilante rescue against American sex trafficking. *Sociological Perspectives*, 59(1), 66–90.

Southall, A. (2015). Court rules clerk must issue licenses for same-sex marriages. *New York Times*, August 27, A15.

Staley, K. (2012). Gay liberation comes to Appalachian State University (1969-1979). *Appalachian Journal*, 39(1/2), 72–91.

Stein, A. (2001). *The stranger next door: The story of a small community's battle over sex, faith, and civil rights*. Boston, MA: Beacon.

Stone, A. L. (2018). The geography of research on LGBTQ life: Why sociologists should study the south, rural queers, and ordinary cities. *Sociology Compass*, 12(11), e12638.

Taylor, V., & Whittier, N. E. (1992). Collective identity in social movement communities: Lesbian feminist mobilization. In A. D. Morris & C. M. Mueller (Eds.) *Frontiers in social movement theory* (pp. 104–129). New Haven, CT: Yale University Press.

Williams, M. (2018). *The sex offender housing dilemma: Community activism, safety, and social justice*. New York, NY: New York University Press.

"Not in my name": the anti-racist praxis of Mab Segrest & Minnie Bruce Pratt

Amanda Mixon

ABSTRACT

Minnie Bruce Pratt (1946-) and Mab Segrest (1949-) are white middle-class lesbians that both came of age during the classical phase of the Civil Rights Movement in rural Alabama. Today, they are considered influential figures in feminist and lesbian, gay, bisexual, transgender, and queer (LGBTQ) literary movements and recognized as important activists in late twentieth-century feminist, LGBTQ, and anti-racist political struggles. Examining Pratt's *Rebellion: Essays, 1980-1991* (1991) and Segrest's *Memoir of a Race Traitor* (1994), I argue that both texts deconstruct the sociopolitical dynamics and ideologies that inform the inculcation of white middle-class southern womanhood specifically and hegemonic white southern culture generally through performing a form of anti-racist praxis that I call *geospatial critique*. This term addresses how Pratt and Segrest mine spaces that they occupy for histories of struggle, paying specific attention to how white settler-colonialism and chattel slavery produced particular epistemologies of race, class, gender, and sexuality that continue to influence social identities and practices in the present. Initially developed during Pratt and Segrest's collaboration on *Feminary*, a lesbian-feminist journal located in Durham, North Carolina, between 1978 and 1982, *geospatial critique*, I suggest, is a direct response to or a way of undoing the racial training that was part of the production of whiteness in the south from the turn to the first half of the twentieth century.

Introduction

In the acknowledgements to *My Mama's Dead Squirrel: Lesbian Essays on Southern Culture*, Mab Segrest (1985) writes, "to the women of *Feminary* for the time together, and for leaving when they needed to; and especially to Minnie Bruce Pratt for those years we drove all over the South in her VW bug, and I was not sure when she was stealing my ideas or I was stealing hers" (p. 7). Today, Pratt and Segrest have made names for themselves as important LGBTQ writers and activists. The former is best known for her poetry, primarily her collection *Crime Against Nature* (1990), and commitment, with her late partner, Leslie Feinberg, to Marxist organizations like Workers World Party, while the latter is better known for her nonfiction, especially *Memoir of a Race Traitor* (1994), and involvement with multiracial, multiissue southern grassroots organizations, such as NCARRV (North Carolinians Against Racist and Religious Violence) and SONG (Southerners on New Ground).[1] But what is less acknowledged, except by a handful of academics that have written about *Feminary*—the lesbian-feminist journal with which Pratt and Segrest were involved between 1978 and 1982—is the relationship and history that these two women share.

For anyone reading Pratt and Segrest together, the personal memory that Segrest describes above—the overlap of ideas between her and Pratt—is often a textually reproduced experience. Their critiques of whiteness, classism, anti-Blackness, misogyny, homophobia, and other vectors of power and oppression usually bolster each other's claims rather than challenge them. While, as Segrest implies, this mirroring is partly a consequence of them having come into consciousness together in the Research Triangle of North Carolina during the seventies and early eighties, it is also a consequence of them having grown up white and middle class during the classical phase of the Civil Rights Movement within a one hundred-mile radius of each other in rural Alabama.[2] As sociologists and anthropologists have noted, local, regional, and national discourses influence perceptions and understandings of race, but place *itself* and the specific power relations therein play an equally important role.[3]

This essay reads Pratt's *Rebellion: Essays, 1980–1991* (1991) and Segrest's *Memoir of a Race Traitor* (1994) alongside of materials from *Feminary* in order to: 1) examine how their autobiographical accounts of developing anti-racist consciousness offer insight into the white cultural training that was endemic to their shared spatio-temporal locations; and 2) identify the anti-racist praxis that they employed to understand and deconstruct this cultural training. Beginning with a brief sociohistorical contextualization of Pratt's and Segrest's backgrounds and their work on *Feminary*, I argue that they initially developed a form of anti-racist praxis that I call *geospatial critique* during their collaboration on *Feminary*. This term addresses how Pratt and Segrest mine spaces that they occupy for histories of struggle, paying specific attention to how white settler-colonialism and chattel slavery produced epistemologies of race, class, gender, and sexuality that continue to influence social identities and practices in the present. I then turn to *Rebellion* and *Memoir* to trace their textual incorporations of geospatial critique and reveal how this anti-racist praxis is a direct undoing of the racial training involved in the production of whiteness in the south from the turn to the first half of the twentieth century. More specifically, geospatial critique challenges white possessive logics of history and space, which Pratt and Segrest show are primarily instilled through gendered knowledges within the heteronormative nuclear family.

Of the small niche of scholarship about Pratt and Segrest that currently exists, the majority of studies concern *Feminary* and their contributions to the journal. These pieces historicize the publication within local, regional, and national spheres of the second wave feminist movement, while analyzing its content and how it politically dialogs with feminist and lesbian-feminist discourses of the time (Cantrell, 2015; Cherry, 2000; Enszer, 2015; Gilbert, 1993; Harker, 2018; Powell, 2000). Comparatively, Pratt has received more critical attention than Segrest, who is the subject of just one published article (Hill, 1997) that analyzes *Memoir* alongside of Noel Ignatiev and John Garvey's *Race Traitor* to trace epistemological issues in whiteness studies. While a few articles and book chapters survey Pratt's poetics, perhaps the most influential vein is feminist scholarship of the late eighties and early nineties that took up Pratt's essay "Identity: Skin Blood Heart" as a means to elaborate emerging theorizations of feminist geographies and mapping (Aldrich & Gilmore, 1992; Martin & Mohanty, 1986). This essay not only pushes back against the latter scholarship's deracination of Pratt's theory and praxis from local and regional forms of knowledge production, but initiates an outline of Pratt and Segrest's political thought that accounts for the influence of *Feminary* and their friendship. Together, they offer insight into how racializing and regionalizing feminist and queer critiques of the heteronormative nuclear family is essential to understanding the production of white supremacy and anti-Blackness in the 20th-century U.S.

Shared history & space

Brought together by the organizing currents of the Women's Liberation and Women in Print Movements (WLM & WIPM) that began sweeping across the U.S. in the mid-sixties, Pratt and Segrest met at a solstice ritual hosted by the Atlanta Lesbian Feminist Alliance (ALFA) in 1975.[4] Both were literature Ph.D. students in the Research Triangle at the time: Pratt had enrolled at UNC-Chapel Hill in 1969 and Segrest at Duke in 1971, as the area was rapidly becoming one of the most important southern nodes of the nationwide WLM network.[5] Hearing that Segrest was headed from Atlanta to her hometown of Tuskegee, Alabama, which was within proximity to Pratt's hometown of Centreville, Pratt offered her a ride, and a friendship developed that would lead to collaboration on a number of feminist projects, including WomanWrites, a yearly writing conference for southern lesbians that is still in existence today, and *Feminary*.

But *Feminary* had a long history in the Triangle area prior to Segrest joining the collective in 1976 and Pratt joining in 1978. First published as the *Research Triangle Women's Liberation Newsletter* on August 11, 1969, the newsletter was re-branded and published as a magazine called *A Feminary* on October 6th, 1974 and later renamed *Feminary* in 1976. In the summer of '78, Pratt and Segrest published the first issue of a new iteration titled *Feminary: A Feminist Journal for the South Emphasizing the Lesbian Vision.*[6] Featuring artwork and photography, short stories, nonfiction, poetry, interviews, book reviews, and feminist scholarship and criticism, *Feminary* resembled other popular feminist journals of the period, such as *Sinister Wisdom*, *Quest*, and *Conditions*, and was eventually recognized as the premier feminist journal of the south. From the journal's initial publication, the collective was direct about its goals and motivations, desiring to showcase an array of voices in an intersectional conversation about lesbian experience in the south, as seen in the collective's full statement in Figure 1. The collective lived up to these guidelines over its five years of existence by publishing women across races, socioeconomic statuses, urban

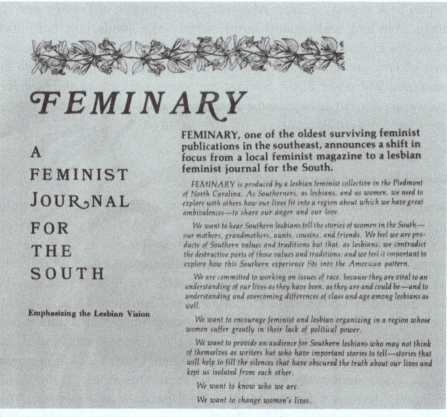

Figure 1. Feminary collective statement, Minnie Bruce Pratt papers, David M. Rubenstein rare book & manuscript library, Duke University.

and rural spaces, and southern states while including the voices of less well-known or regional writers, as well as those making a mark nationally, such as Barbara Smith and Ann Allen Shockley.[7]

However, as much as *Feminary* is a documentation of the WLM and WIPM in the south, it is also a repository of the shifting political thought of Pratt, Segrest, and other collective members. This is especially the case concerning the 1979 Greensboro massacre, in which KKK and American Nazi Party members murdered local members and associates of the Communist Workers' Party at a "Death to the Klan" march just fifty-five miles west of Durham. In *Rebellion* and *Memoir*, Pratt and Segrest narrativize this event as prompting a critical shift in their anti-racist consciousness. Because KKK and ANP members justified their actions in the name of protecting white women, an identity that included Pratt and Segrest, the two felt compelled to understand the history of this defense. They thus began intensively reading histories of struggle in North Carolina and the south more broadly, discovering how indigenous peoples, Black people, and some white people had resisted and critiqued forces of white supremacist dominance. Well trained in the consciousness raising techniques of the WLM, which championed using personal experience as a means of understanding political thought and action, Pratt and Segrest began situating themselves and their families within these historical narratives, noticing how they challenged what that they had been taught by their families, secondary and postsecondary institutions, and white hegemonic southern culture generally.

We see evidence of this process in the first issue of *Feminary* post Greensboro, titled "Being Disobedient" (Volume 11, No. 1 & 2). In the collective comments in *Feminary* Volume 11, number 3—the second issue after Greensboro—Segrest explains that "Being Disobedient" was severely delayed because of technical difficulties, the physical and mental exhaustion of the group as whole, and members trying to process how to respond to national political events, like the presidential election of Ronald Reagan, and local ones, like the acquittal of white supremacists involved at Greensboro.[8] That contemplation is apparent not just in the issue's title, which implies disobedience to oppressive social structures, but also in its opening selection, "Rebellion." This was Pratt's first essay that explicitly deconstructed the white cultural training of her youth, and it would later open her collection of essays, *Rebellion*, that I discuss here. Finished in 1980, "Rebellion" contextualizes Pratt as a historical subject implicated in the production of whiteness. Structurally, the essay intersperses quotes from older white southern women who critiqued anti-Blackness between accounts of how Pratt's childhood and education in rural Alabama trained her to propagate white supremacist ideologies. This structuring allows Pratt to suggest that there is an alternative history and legacy of southern rebellion that she is a part of that has been purposely written out.

WomanWrites materials created shortly after the 1981 publication of "Being Disobedient" also exhibit Segrest referencing histories of struggle, land, and space as a technique for understanding and positioning one's self. To the 1982 WomanWrites participants, Segrest describes Indian Springs State Park in Georgia as follows:

> It's one of the oldest state parks in the United States, with important historical associations for us as lesbians. Its sulphur springs restored health to the Creek Indians, and this resource for healing drew thousands of vacationing and health-seeking nineteenth century Georgians during its heyday as a popular resort. But with this healing, there has also been more destructive energy: the State of Georgia took the land from the Creeks, with the help of a slave trader; and Klansmen met near the camp in the 1960s in response to the Freedom Rides. This is the land we come to for our fourth year, for community as lesbians, for power as writers, and for healing. (Mab Segrest Papers)

Segrest's connection between the importance of knowing histories of land and the struggles over it to lesbian identity is similarly reflected in the final publication of *Feminary* in 1982. Titled "The South as Home: Staying or Leaving," the issue, in addition to its typical staples of poetry, book reviews, and short nonfiction, maintains a host of graphic art, specifically six maps of the south listed as "Maps" in the table of contents. These maps, as seen in Figure 2, give meaning to lesbian experience in the south across racial and economic lines. Figure 2, in particular, invokes white lesbian experience in the type-written narrative on the bottom-half—"how my Anglo-Scot-Irish family made a place for me on stolen ground"—while the words on the top-half are evocative of general feelings of oppression that racial, sexual, and gender minorities might experience in the south (Mab Segrest Papers). Other maps also invoke specific racialized experience, as the one on pages 110-111, which includes information about Jews in the south, describing both their subjection to anti-Semitism and their participation in anti-Black oppression (Mab Segrest Papers). This map, as well as the one about Black experience on pages 24-25, always connect southern experience with happenings in the north and on the international scale to suggest that the south is not a closed space or region, but one intimately interconnected with and influenced by the rest of the world (Mab Segrest Papers). Other maps offer critiques of the exploitative labor systems in the south, focusing on migrant agricultural workers in the seventies and eighties but critically connecting their experiences to those in systems of the past by, for example, incorporating analogies: "LABOR CAMP: SLAVE CABIN: GHETTO: DETENTION CENTER" (Mab Segrest Papers).

I would flag these examples as early manifestations of *geospatial critique* in Pratt's and Segrest's work. I use geospatial critique to name how Pratt

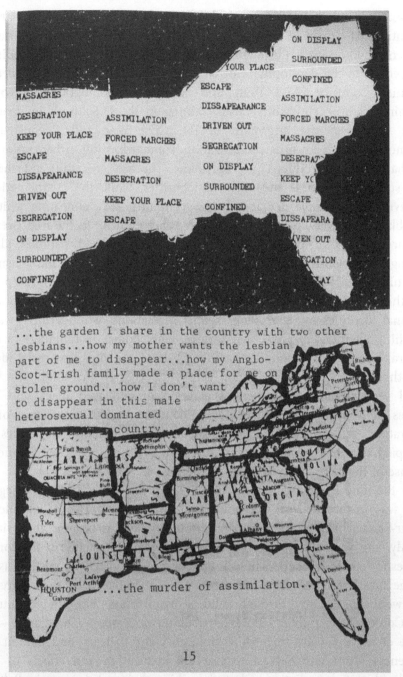

Figure 2. Map in Feminary volume 12, issue 1, Mab Segrest papers, David M. Rubenstein rare book & manuscript library, Duke University. Eleanor Holland and Helen Langa, as the graphics/design team of Feminary, created the map.

and Segrest cite geography and space as sources of anti-racist knowledge that provide insight into how epistemologies of race, gender, sexuality, and class are tied to violence beginning with and proceeding from white settler colonialism and chattel slavery. I identify and elaborate this particular form of anti-racist praxis in relation to Pratt and Segrest because historians of whiteness, like Grace Elizabeth Hale, have shown that spatial mediations are central to the development of U.S. white identity in the first half of the twentieth century. And Pratt and Segrest's autobiographical writings explain this aspect of white racial training in the U.S. south in detail. As Hale writes, in the aftermath of the Civil War and Reconstruction, "economic trends towards centralization, standardization, urbanization, and mechanization" produced an epistemic rupture in white northerners and southerners' local and regional identities, while the emancipation of enslaved Black people demanded new techniques for delineating whiteness and blackness (1999, p. 6). From the late nineteenth up to the mid-twentieth century, whites in the U.S. created a white racialized national identity through imperialist wars, consumer culture, media, and scientific racism—all of which trafficked in racist imagery and ideas about non-whites (p. 5-8). But they also tried to make sense of the remaining vestiges of their local and regional identities by developing "spatial mediations of modernity—ways of attaching identities to physical moorings, from bodies to buildings to larger geographies like region and nation" (p. 6). Hale contends that racial identity was the primary spatial mediation across the U.S. In the south, Jim Crow racial segregation, or the literal separation of perceived Black and white bodies in public spaces and the embodied and psychic experience of that separation, as well as narratives created by whites about the spaces they occupied and their people's history there, colluded to give white southerners a sense of their regionally specific, racialized self.

By the time Pratt and Segrest were born in the 1940s, Jim Crow segregation was instantiated to the point that for the majority of middle and upper-class white southern children, domestic spaces became the primary, if only, site where they engaged with Black people, usually in the form of domestic female workers. These interactions with Black domestics, as well as the racial instruction and lessons of history offered by their parents— that were substantiated through cultural organizations like the Daughters of the Confederacy, public school curriculum, and often Christianity—were some of the key ways that white children came to learn and inhabit their whiteness. Pratt and Segrest expose the inculcation and effects of these racialized spatial mediations when describing their upbringings in *Rebellion* and *Memoir*. There, they focus on domestic spaces and primarily their parents to show how male relatives passed down knowledges of land and ideas of ownership, while female relatives passed down knowledges of family and ideas of kinship. For example, Pratt frequently shares reveries from her childhood, in which her father teaches her about their family's land, which was given to them for fighting Muscogee Indians in the Creek War led by Andrew Jackson. Similarly, *Memoir* opens with Segrest traveling through the southern countryside as a child with her father, learning about white settler-colonial history as they search for the birthplace of Osceola, a Muscogee Indian freedom fighter (her family had also been given land for their participation in the Creek War). These interactions with their fathers constitute what Aileen Moreton-Robinson calls *white possessive logics*, which "are operationalized within discourses to circulate sets of meanings about ownership of the nation, as part of commonsense knowledge, decision making, and socially produced conventions" (2018, p. 212). In other words, their fathers were instilling in Pratt and Segrest an unconscious means, which they will be able to later diagnose, of knowing themselves, as racialized subjects, through their people's history of manipulating and controlling space and their own ability to do the same.

Complementing their fathers' information about land and space were stories of family history shared by female relatives that were embedded in white settler-colonial practices and the establishment of white supremacy. As Segrest notes, her mother offered genealogical work that she could use to join the United Daughters of the Confederacy, the Daughters of the American Revolution, and the Colonial Dames: "the genealogies were designed to help me 'know who I am'"; they were "part of her mother's legacy" (p. 55). Likewise, Pratt reminisces on how all the women in her family "could and can talk" (p. 20). Her grandmother would tell "about her childhood during the Reconstruction" and about how her mother, MaMa Carr, "could make the most elegant dessert out of nothing but day-old biscuits, milk, sugar, and cinnamon" (a story that all the women in Pratt's family knew) (p. 11). But Pratt and Segrest both write that these stories were the extent of information that they could glean from their mothers and other female relatives. That is, female relatives did not reveal deeply personal thoughts, desires, or opinions about the south's sociopolitical structure. As Pratt explains, women would not delve into "the hidden depths of their lives, and the lives of the people"—poor whites and Blacks—"who live[d] down in the Quarters or in Four Points by the sawmill" (p. 20). And Segrest only gained these insights upon her mother's passing, when she had access to her personal journal.

Contrastingly, Pratt and Segrest describe their fathers as brooding figures who often subjected their families to racist and misogynistic political tirades that family members were expected to agree with. Pratt's mother never publically challenged her husband's political beliefs, and Segrest recounts her mother often saying she "agreed with [her], but at the dinner table [she] was on [her] own" (p. 24). Pratt and Segrest read this denial and silencing of the self among women of their mother's generation and class as necessary for white supremacy to function and maintain itself as a system. Taught to be and idealized as the cultivators of civilization, women, in deferring to and letting men dictate and take up space with their ideas and beliefs, were, in the words of Segrest's mother, practicing "courtesy" or "the mortar of civilization" (1985, p. 64). To act otherwise or to exhibit "anger" would "destroy both" (p. 64). Or as Pratt notes in reference to her mother's behavior, in a social system where identity was policed by spectacles of psychological and physical violence, many folks adopted a fatalistic belief that "there was nothing to be done but keep your manners, lower your voice, and go through life to your death with intense grace" (p. 23). As Pratt and Segrest make clear, the heteronormative family structures in which they were raised, and the forms of gendered socialization, behavior, and knowledges that were communicated therein, helped ensure that lessons of whiteness were learned and transmitted from one generation to the next.

Geospatial critique

Spatial metaphors and imagery of nature and land tend to dominate Pratt's poetry and prose generally, but within the context of *Rebellion*, the essays compel the reader to consider how geospatial critique can be a practice for daily personal accountability in relationality to others, whether that's to a stranger on the street, a neighbor, a colleague, or a lover. Due to article limitations, I'll take as my sole example the second essay in *Rebellion*, "Identity: Skin Blood Heart." I choose this essay because of its coverage in feminist scholarship, as mentioned in my introduction, and because it was written and published shortly after Pratt's time with *Feminary*, over the course of 1983–1984, and she explicitly thanks and acknowledges the collective's influence on it. With its focus on relationality, "Identity" repeatedly situates Pratt, in terms of geography and space, at both panoramic and intimate levels. For example, the essay opens with Pratt mining the history of the production of space in her neighborhood and how specific gendered, racialized, sexualized, and/or classed bodies move through that space in relation to each other:

> I live in a part of Washington, D.C., that white suburbanites called 'the jungle' during the uprising of the sixties—perhaps still do, for all I know. When I walk the two-and-a-half blocks to H Street, N.E., to stop in at the bank, to leave my boots off at the shoe-repair-and-lock shop, I am most usually the only white person in sight. I've seen two other whites, women, in the year I've lived here. (This does not count white folks in cars, passing through. In official language, H. Street, N.E. is known as the "H Street Corridor," as in something to be passed through quickly, going from your place on the way to elsewhere). (p. 27)

Pratt's observations here reflect Katherine McKittrick and Clyde Woods's thoughts about "how black human geographies are implicated in the production of space" (p. 4). When Pratt describes her neighborhood as a place that the general white population and ruling elite of Washington, D.C.,

view as just a place to "pass through quickly," (p. 27) her comment resonates with McKittrick and Woods's argument that Black geographies, or
neighborhoods with large Black demographics, are typically "geographies of
exclusion," places that are rendered as "invisible/forgettable" so that the
struggles and concerns of the subjects and communities within that space
can be erased or forgotten (p. 4).

Soon after this panoramic view of bodies moving through space, the text
hones in on an intimate encounter between specific bodies, those of Pratt
and Mr. Boone, that offers an alternative experience to white people just
passing through:

> The pain, of course, is on the other side of this speaking, and the sorrow, when I have
> only to turn two corners to go back in the basement door of my building, to meet Mr.
> Boone, the janitor who doesn't raise his eyes to mine, or his head, when we speak. He
> is a dark red-brown man from the Yemassee in South Carolina—that swampy land of
> Indian resistance and armed communities of fugitive slaves, that marshy land at the
> headwaters of the Combahee, once site of enormous rice plantations and location of
> Harriet Tubman's successful military action that freed many slaves. When we meet in
> the hall or on the elevator, even though I may have just heard him speaking in his
> own voice to another man, he "yes-ma'ams" me in a sing-song; I hear my voice
> replying in the horrid cheerful accents of a white lady. And I hate my white
> womanhood that drags between us the long bitter history of our region. (p. 28)

Crucial here is Pratt's configuring of bodies and their relationality to
each other. Pratt always contextualizes herself and others as specific historical subjects, temporally and spatially, in order to account for the ways in
which bodies register contemporaneous epistemologies of race, class, gender, sexuality, region, and nation. But she also makes it a point to trace
how those present epistemologies have evolved from and are influenced by
those of the past. Amidst this contextualization, she acknowledges the
affective experience and charge that occurs for a person and between
people as a consequence of their individual identity positions. Pratt
thus consistently pushes the reader-activist to consider how white settler-
colonialism and chattel slavery—key practices upon which the U.S. was
founded—produced forms of categorical distinction, in terms of race, gender, class, sexuality, and region, that continue to enact quotidian forms of
psychological and physical violence in the contemporary moment. For
example, in terms of whiteness in the quotes above, notice how she exposes
the psychological violence of her body being racialized and gendered as a
white woman, without erasing the responsibility she has as a white person
to know the history of white supremacy, how she is implicated, and how
she might undo it. Segregating herself from Black people to avoid their
experiences and perspectives or simply feeling white guilt are not sufficient
coping mechanisms to practically heal the wounds of white supremacy and
anti-blackness in the U.S.

While Pratt's use of geospatial critique is colored by her profession as a poet, Segrest's use in *Memoir* is marked by her work as a grassroots political organizer. There, geospatial critique is a practical organizing strategy that not only has potential concrete ramifications for local communities but taps into longstanding psychological trauma with the hope of working towards collective healing. For instance, in chapters about different locales in which she was battling white supremacist organizations, like "Robeson, Bloody Robeson" and "The Bookstore Murders," Segrest uncovers histories of indigenous peoples, Blacks, and poor whites in the area through an approach very similar to that of the 1982 WomanWrites Participant Letter. She then demonstrates how this information explains the coalition that develops between these demographics as they organized against police corruption and a slew of white supremacist hate crimes towards racial, gender, and sexual minorities in the county. In short, the takeaway for the reader-activist is that knowing histories of local struggles and past coalitions and political divides can help one build better organizing strategies against white supremacy in the present.

Alongside of this incorporation of geospatial critique, is also the repeated invocation of Osceola's head. Osceola was eventually captured by Andrew Jackson's troops and died in Charleston, South Carolina, where the doctor attending him, Frederick Weedon, supposedly severed his head post-mortem and placed it in a preserving jar that sat in the window of Weedon's drugstore. Chapter 1 of *Memoir*, titled "Osceola's Head," begins with a historical contextualization of Osceola, explaining that Weedon family stories tell of Frederick removing Osceola's head from the jar and tying it to his sons' bedposts at night whenever they misbehaved. Segrest's invocation of Osceola and his head some five to six times across the autobiography creates a haunting effect. This strategy could be mistakenly read as Segrest representing land through deceased and disappeared indigenous populations—a trope that is problematic because in mythologizing and relegating indigenous people to the past, their contemporary social lives and political struggles are obscured. However, as Segrest notes in the first chapter, Osceola and his head function as a metaphor for how "fetishized racism ... within white families" is part of the psychological training ground that teaches individuals how to enact white supremacy and pass down behaviors and ideas of whiteness generationally (p. 4). At times in Segrest's narrative when incidents seem to be repeating themselves spatially and historically—as in similar sociopolitical dynamics and struggles in different counties or similar demonizing metaphors of bad blood in relation to a person's race and a person's human-immunodeficiencyvirus (HIV)/AIDS status—Segrest brings up Osceola's head to symbolize the violence of the past influencing the present and repeating itself in new forms. In effect, the violence that produced Osceola's severed head is representative of how the land and people of the region have been traumatized by the intertwined material and discursive practices of white supremacy, which, Segrest suggests, require a serious psychical accounting for if real political change is ever expected to occur.

Conclusion

It is fair to say that Pratt and Segrest are both understudied as writer-activists. This might seem somewhat remarkable given their political and literary contributions, but considering that queer theory has dominated the study of LGBTQ populations and cultural productions since the early nineties, their elision should come as no surprise. That is, although scholars have engaged queer theory and race to address racialized genders and sexualities of people of color,[9] little attention—as documented by Black and Black queer scholars—has been paid to engaging queer theory and whiteness studies to ask questions about white racialized genders and sexualities.[10] And almost anything written by Pratt and Segrest is going to function at that critical intersection. In this essay, I wanted to describe just one example of anti-racist praxis that Pratt and Segrest use: both because I believe it is a skill that anyone, but especially white people, can incorporate to explore histories of racialized violence and disenfranchisement that are often denied us by U.S. educational institutions and culture generally, and because contextualizing its significance for Pratt and Segrest reveals a nuanced glimpse into how whiteness was partly produced in the south across the twentieth century. But more importantly, I wanted to encourage a curiosity about what it might mean to racialize and regionalize, specifically through whiteness, critiques of the heteronormative nuclear family. Geospatial critique may manifest itself differently in Pratt and Segrest's respective texts, but there seems to be an overarching political consensus: whiteness is pathological, and working towards an anti-racist world, in part, requires understanding that pathology, from its initial transmission through family systems on to how it is worked out through social and political institutions.

Notes

1. Segrest co-founded both of these organizations. NCARRV existed from 1984 until the mid-nineties. Founded in 1993, SONG remains active and is expanding its chapters throughout the south.
2. The Research Triangle, or The Triangle, refers to an area in the North Carolina Piedmont between these cities and their respective universities: Raleigh (North Carolina State University), Chapel Hill (The University of North Carolina), and Durham (Duke University).

3. An extensive list of sources could be included here, but Hartigan (2005) and Frankenberg (1993) especially inform my work.
4. The Women in Print Movement was an important arm of the Women's Liberation Movement. Between the late sixties and mid-eighties, there was a proliferation of feminist and lesbian-feminist print cultures across the U.S. The journals, newspapers, newsletters, novels, poetry chapbooks, etc. that were produced by women-run collectives and presses, as well as their byways—or circulation methods via word of mouth, conferences, meetings, feminist bookstores, and the mail, for example—make up what recent scholarship has termed the Women in Print Movement. For more detailed histories of the WIPM, see, for instance, Harker (2018), Hogan (2016), and Enszer (2013).
5. For a detailed history of the area at this time, see Enszer (2015).
6. The journal's title was revised from "vision" to "visions" by its penultimate issue.
7. For more historical contextualization and analysis of the journal, consult sources in endnote 4.
8. "Being Disobedient" was published in March 1981 rather than October 1980.
9. A long list of sources could be catalogued here, but consider, for example, scholarship by Roderick Ferguson (2003) and José Esteban Muñoz (1999)
10. This critique begins with Evelynn Hammonds (1994) and extends itself in *Black Queer Studies: A Critical Anthology* (2005), edited by Mae G. Henderson and E. Patrick Johnson, as well as Sharon Holland's *The Erotic Life of Racism* (2012).

Disclosure statement

I have no potential conflicts of interest.

Funding

Archival research for this article was supported by the Sallie Bingham Center for Women's History and Culture and the Program in Gender, Sexuality, and Feminist Studies at Duke University under a 2018–2019 Mary Lily Research Grant. The article was written with support from a 2019–2020 American Association of University Women Dissertation Fellowship.

References

Aldrich, M., & Gilmore, L. (1992). Writing home: 'Home' and lesbian representation in Minnie Bruce Pratt. *Genre: Forms of Discourse and Culture, 25*(1), 25–46.

Cantrell, J. (2015). Subscribe to feminary! Producing community, region, and archive. In A. L. Stone & J. Cantrell (Eds.), *Out of the closet, into the archives: Researching sexual histories* (pp. 311–336). Albany, NY: SUNY Press.

Cherry, W. (2000). Hearing me into speech: Lesbian feminist publishing in North Carolina. *North Carolina Literary Review, 9*, 82–90.

Enszer, J. R. (2013). *The whole naked truth of our lives: Lesbian-feminist print culture from 1969 through 1989* (Doctoral dissertation). Retrieved from Proquest Dissertations & Theses Global (3590787), Ann Arbor, MI.

Enszer, J. R. (2015). Night heron press and lesbian print culture in North Carolina. *Southern Cultures, 22*(2), 43–56.

Ferguson, R. (2003). *Aberrations in black: Towards a queer of color critique.* Minneapolis, MN: University of Minnesota Press.

Frankenberg, R. (1993). *White women, race matters: The social construction of whiteness.* Minneapolis, MN: University of Minnesota Press.

Gilbert, J. (1993). *"Feminary" of durham-chapel hill: Building community through feminist press* (Unpublished masters thesis). Duke University, Durham, NC.

Hale, G. E. (1999). *Making whiteness: The culture of segregation in the south, 1890–1940.* New York, NY: Vintage.

Hammonds, E. (1994). Black (w)holes and the geometry of black female sexuality. *Differences: A Journal of Feminist Cultural Studies, 6*(2–3), 126–145.

Harker, J. (2018). *The lesbian south: Southern feminists, the women in print movement, and the queer literary canon.* Chapel Hill: University of North Carolina Press.

Hartigan, J. (2005). *Odd tribes: Towards a cultural analysis of white people.* Durham, NC: Duke University Press.

Henderson, M. G., & Johnson, E. P. (Eds.). (2005). Black queer studies: A critical anthology. Durham, NC: Duke University Press.

Hill, M. (1997). What was (the white) race? Memory, categories, change. *Postmodern Culture, 7*(2), n.p.

Hogan, K. (2016). *The feminist bookstore movement: Lesbian antiracism and feminist accountability.* Durham, NC: Duke University Press.

Holland, S. (2012). The erotic life of racism. Durham, NC: Duke University Press.

Mab Segrest Papers, David M. Rubenstein Rare Book & Manuscript Library, Duke University, Durham, NC.

Martin, B., & Mohanty, C. T. (1986). Feminist politics: What's home got to do with it?. In T. de Lauretis (Ed.), *Feminist studies/critical studies* (pp. 191–212). Bloomington, IN: Indiana University Press.

McKittrick, K., & Woods, C. (2007). *Black geographies and the politics of place.* Toronto: Between the Lines.

Minnie Bruce Pratt Papers, David M. Rubenstein Rare Book & Manuscript Library, Duke University, Durham, NC.

Moreton-Robinson, A. (2018). White possession and indigenous sovereignty matters. In T. Das Gupta, C. E. James, C. Andersen, G. E. Galabuzi, & R. C. A. Maaka (Eds.), *Race and racialization: Essential readings* (pp. 211–218). Toronto: Canadian Scholars.

Muñoz, J. E. (1999). *Disidentifications: Queers of color and the performance of politics.* Minneapolis, MN: University of Minnesota Press.

Powell, T. M. (2000). Look what happened here: North Carolina's feminary collective. *North Carolina Literary Review, 9*, 91–102.

Pratt, M. B. (1990). *Crime against nature.* Ithaca, NY: Firebrand Books.

Pratt, M. B. (1991). *Rebellion: Essays, 1980–1991.* Ithaca, NY: Firebrand Books.

Segrest, M. (1985). *My mama's dead squirrel: Lesbian essays on southern culture.* Ithaca, NY: Firebrand Books.

Segrest, M. (1994). *Memoir of a race traitor.* Boston, MA: South End Press.

Racialized sexualization & agency in exotic dance among women

Cristina Khan

ABSTRACT

Through the analysis of two years of ethnographic observations and 40 in-depth interviews with a collective of Black and Puerto Rican exotic dancers (referred to herein as "Divine Dancers") who perform exotic dance for other women, this article explores how spatial expressions of sexuality within the context of a woman-only exotic dance venue enables both the resistance and reinforcement of circulating discourses of race, gender, and sexuality that construct sexual desirability under the male gaze. In contrast to literatures on exotic dance that center the heteromasculinist arrangement of the U.S. gentleman's club, this article centers the construction of a woman-only exotic dance space that is absent of men and white women. I situate this analysis within critiques put forward by the feminist sex wars to argue that space and place, in tandem with racialized sexualization, shapes women's potential to enact agency in the domain of exotic dance. In this article, I focus on the contestation of whiteness as a normative standard of beauty by Divine Dancers, and the ways in which norms regarding touch and intimacy are regulated within this exotic dance setting, which I argue allows for new interactions between dancers and audience members. This article disrupts binary understandings of exotic dance as either exploitative or demeaning, focusing instead on dancers' interpretations of agency as expressed through the body in space. I find that the extent to which Divine Dancers find this spatial context sexually empowering is shaped through gendered sexuality and their experiences with racialized sexualization.

Within the heteromasculinist setting of the U.S. gentleman's club, white eroticized embodiment rooted in hegemonic beauty standards are generally rewarded in women (Hunter, 2002; Thompson, 2009). The hierarchical readings attributed to white women in such settings tend to attach privilege to not only light skin, but other racialized representations of whiteness, including thinness, tallness, and long, flowing hair, all of which are constructed as sexually desirable. Michelle Newton-Francis and Young (2015) refer to this embodiment as the FFW or "fuckable fantasy woman" who embodies a "girl next door" appearance reminiscent of the stereotypical "Hooters girl." This construction of beauty and sexual desirability is not exclusive to the domain of exotic dance; it exists more broadly in the U.S. context and conditions women's potential to become employed by a number of erotic labor industries (Brooks, 2012; Gimlin, 2002; Kwan & Trautner, 2009; Mears, 2014). Yet it is also true that there are spaces that seemingly would challenge the idealizations circulating in white heteromasculinist exotic dance clubs, including the space that is the center of this analysis: the Divine Dancers. In this article, I explore how white eroticized conceptualizations of beauty are reinforced and challenged within the context of a woman of color-only (both in terms of clients and dancers) exotic dance space (referred to by the pseudonym "Divine Dancers"). I situate this analysis within critiques put forward by the feminist sex wars (Duggan & Hunter, 2006) to argue that space and place (Hammers, 2009), in tandem with racialized sexualization (Vidal-Ortiz, Robinson, & Khan, 2018), shapes women's potential to enact agency (Ferguson, 2012) in the domain of exotic dance. I find that the extent to which Divine Dancers find this spatial context sexually empowering, and by extension, one in which whiteness as normative is challenged, is shaped through gendered sexuality and their experiences with racialized sexualization. This article disrupts binary understandings of exotic dance as either exploitative or demeaning (Barton, 2002), focusing instead on dancers' interpretations of agency as expressed through the body in space.

In the section that follows, I briefly survey the feminist sex wars of the 1970s and 80s, illustrating how the composition of Divine Dancers as a woman of color-only collective offers significant new insight to previous discourses on erotic labor, which posited that heteropatriarchal power structures present in erotic labor industries limited women's potential to enact agency over the conditions of their participation. Specifically, I ask to what extent the male gaze (Mulvey, 1975) and conceptualizations of beauty born from it shape how erotic capital, which references an individual's level of sexual attractiveness and is understood by Brooks (2012) as an inherently racialized interchangeable currency, is understood and deployed within a woman of color-only setting. I then explore racialized sexualities as a framework for theorizing the lived experiences of Divine Dancers, linking the contestation of hegemonic beauty standards and the enactment of norms regarding touch and intimacy to space and place.

The feminist sex wars

During the 1970s and 80s, feminist thinkers debated a range of issues relative to sexuality and sexual practices, including the place of erotic labor within feminist organizing (Ferguson, 2012; Freedman & Thorne, 1984;

Hollibaugh & Moraga, 2003; Duggan & Hunter, 2006; Rubin, 1998; Vance & Snitow, 1984). Second wave feminist activism around issues of sexual representation were the subject of critique by women of color feminist academics and activists, who suggested that the racialized underpinnings of women's lived experiences and grappling with inequality were not being sufficiently attended to. The Combahee River Collective Statement (1979) as well as Cherríe Moraga & Gloria Anzaldúa's 1983 publication of *This Bridge Called My Back: Writings by Radical Women of Color*, among other works, introduced intersectional theorizing to feminist discourses, which linked gender, race, sex, and class as a lens to analyze the lived experiences of women of color, linking the interpersonal to the structural.

The experiences of women of color within erotic labor settings were not central throughout the feminist sex wars, which instead explored gender, sexuality, and class as relevant axes of women's participation in the erotic. Anti-violence campaigns led by feminist activists and thinkers centralized pornography as an erotic labor site from which to analyze whether agency could be claimed by participating women (Barry, 1980). Although later problematized by Chapkis (1997), such debates were often thought of as existing on a polarized spectrum. On one end, "radical feminists" posited that as a heteropatriarchal institution, pornography, and other forms of sexual labor, were inherently exploitative and demeaning enterprises that victimized women. In contrast, "sex radical" feminists saw erotic labor as a potential site of erotic expression and financial independence for women. The monolithic reduction of the feminist sex wars into these two arenas erased "the multilayered nature of human experience" (Barton, 2002, p. 586), and masked the variation of experience within sexual labor (Weitzer, 2000) by making essentialist claims of empowerment vs. oppression.

Significantly, the settings in which women's experiences were analyzed throughout the feminist sex wars were ones in which women performed for men. The potentiality of a woman-only space for subverting these traditional power structures have seldom been explored in literatures on erotic labor (see Brooks, 2012; Hammers, 2008; Pilcher, 2012). The question of race and racialization (Omi & Winant, 2014) as mediators of women's experiences in the erotic has recently been undertaken by trailblazing Black feminist scholars, including Brooks (2012), Miller-Young (2014), Nash (2014), and Jones (2015; forthcoming). These texts speak to Black women's experiences with structural inequality within erotic labor industries, including pornography, camming, and exotic dance. The racialized experiences of Latinas within exotic dance demonstrate how the embodiment of structural expectations around Latinidad is rewarded (Khan, 2019). In this article, I draw upon these works to locate race and sexuality as co-constitutive formations that shape Divine Dancers' experiences.

Racialized sexualities and erotic capital

Racialized sexualities was developed as a product of both feminist and critical race scholarship to highlight the co-constitutive nature of race and sexuality (Brown, 2012). Historically, race and sexuality have operated as mutually exclusive fields of study, leaving the interarticulated nature of the two largely disregarded (Vidal-Ortiz et al., 2018). The co-constitutive nature of race and sexuality is attentive to the construction of erotic deviance, which McClintock (1992) asserts "was constituted in Europe to serve a specifically modern form of social dominance ... the analogy between erotic deviance and racial deviance emerged as a necessary element in the formation of the modern European imagination (p. 71)." Miller-Young (2014) notes that this legacy imbues Black women's bodies with a simultaneous fascination and "othering." This, in effect, positions whiteness as innocent and the penultimate symbol of piety, and racialized "others" as hypersexual deviants. This racialized hierarchy in reference to sexual desirability and erotic capital forces women of color who participate in erotic labor to rely on "racialized sexual stereotypes in order to make a profit" (Vidal-Ortiz et al., 2018, p. 105). Attention to race and sexuality reveals the racist structural discrimination that women of color face in erotic labor industries, which position them as less sexually desirable than their white counterparts (see Jones, 2015; forthcoming).

A body seen as in possession of erotic capital in one space may not exist as such in the next. Although whiteness is a hegemonic standard of beauty across the U.S. context, what constitutes a sexually desirable body varies across time and space (Craig, 2006). Gentles-Peart (2018) notes an embodied emphasis on thickness in Black Caribbean contexts, where largeness in the hips, buttocks, and thighs is prized. Similarly, Newton-Francis and Vidal-Ortiz (2013) find that within Hooters establishments in Colombia, it is large buttocks, rather than large breasts (that are constructed as a prized embodiment for women in the U.S.), which are imbued with erotic capital. Space and place co-determine what kinds of bodies become inscribed with erotic capital.

Methods

This multimethodological study draws from two years of participant observation and 40 in-depth interviews with members of Divine Dancers. I became employed by the collective as a cocktail waitress and worked in that capacity, and as a coat-check attendee, making change for audience members, and collecting tips on dancers' behalf, over the course of my fieldwork. On average, 10 to 12 Divine Dancer shows take place annually. In total, I conducted participant observation at 19 Divine Dancer shows, each of which lasted between 8 to 9 h, including preparation time and clean-up. All participants were aware of my status as a researcher, and I obtained IRB approval from the University of Connecticut.

During Divine Dancer shows, I paid close attention to the body, including attire, body adornment, the performance of dance, and interactions between customers and dancers, including lap dances. I recorded observations in a written notebook following each event. Interviews took place on the phone, either through FaceTime or only through voice, depending on the preference of the participant. Each participant was compensated $25 for participating in an interview. I transcribed each interview and saved them onto a password-protected USB drive. All identifying information was removed from these interviews and each participant was issued a pseudonym.

Divine Dancers host shows at several venues throughout the Northeast Corridor Region, including a rented banquet hall, a private home, and a Latin dance club that is rented from a private owner. I refer to the most frequently used venue of Divine Dancer shows as El Aguila. Despite the lack of a permanent venue for the show, a 120+ person audience has been consistent at shows since its onset. Attendees purchase tickets, learn of the location of the show, and communicate with Divine Dancers through a publicly accessible Instagram and Facebook account. Typically, 10-15 dancers participate in each show although many more attend to perform duties such as hosting, bartending, set-up and clean-up. In addition to performing with Divine Dancers, many members also perform at gentleman's clubs,[1] male revue shows.[2] Dancers also perform on an individually-contracted basis for private events such as birthday parties or bachelor/bachelorette celebrations.

Spatial expressions and understandings of sexuality

Agency is a highly contested, slippery concept that has been taken up at length in both the social sciences and humanities (Mahmood, 2001). While I do not propose a static definition for agency, I understand it as it is appears within interview data; when participants report that their participation in Divine Dancers makes them feel good, gives them heightened confidence in their body and self-presentation, and resulted in financial capital that enabled them to lead a richer and fuller life, I coded these instances as enactments of agency. In this section, I highlight these instances to demonstrate how some participants understand Divine Dancers as a space that affords them a level of agency within their labor.

Negating white hegemonic beauty standards

Disco is a Black masculine-presenting dancer who describes herself as a BBW, or big beautiful woman. She refers to herself as a performer, emcee, and host. When she is not dancing with Divine Dancers, she performs free-lance work hosting at nightclubs in the D.C., Maryland, and Virginia areas. When asked during an interview how Divine Dancers is different from the other work she does, she recounted:

> I'm gonna say this because it's the way it is. But when you're a BBW, you don't get a lot of work in the industry. And I'm not just a big girl, I'm Black, and whether or not people like to acknowledge it, there's a lot working against me. So when I emcee, when I host, I have to be on point with the jokes. Jokes and personality. I gotta sell it. But at Divine Dancers, I get to be sexy. I show my body, I move, I dance. And I'm not a spectacle cause people are laughing.

Disco views the "industry" as one in which she must use her personality to earn the right to emcee or host. In contrast, Divine Dancers affords her the opportunity to "be sexy" without existing as a spectacle, which she suggests she has experienced by way of others' laughter at her body. Divine Dancers enables Disco to contest the idea that her body is undesirable and assert herself as a sexually desirable subject. Disco expressed that because she is both Black and a BBW, she has "a lot working against [her]." The racialized and sexualized meanings attributed to her body, specifically the expectation that she is desirable if she is funny and expresses personality rather than sensuality and sex appeal, points to an inherent desexualization in spaces where she emcees or hosts, which sometimes includes hetero-nightclub settings. In her exploration of the racialized underpinnings of fat stigma, Strings (2019) posits that the imaginary of the "'fat Black woman' was created by racial and religious ideologies that have been used to both degrade Black women and discipline white women" (p. 6). Utilizing an intersectional lens to uncover the proliferation of fat phobia, Strings finds that this imaginary positions "slenderness as the proper form of embodiment for white women" (p. 212), and simultaneously "others" Black women and inscribes them with a racialized excess.

When asked to reflect on the relationships she's built with Divine Dancers audience members, Disco affirmed that "one of the best things to hear is other women talking about how they never thought they could get up on stage and dance like I do … sometimes they tell me I inspire them, and that's always good to hear." Here, Disco refers to a level of empowerment shared between herself and audience members, which affirms that her presence and performance as an exotic dancer is meaningful to those who see themselves reflected in her embodied presentation. Similarly, Jones (2019) finds that erotic webcam performers who self-identify as BBWs challenge normative standards of beauty, and experience what Jones refers to as "pleasures of fetishization," through which they experience heightened levels of empowerment and experience pleasure within their labor. The spatial setting of Divine Dancers affords Disco the opportunity to experience pleasure, and ultimately find agency and empowerment as a BBW exotic dancer.

The regulation of the body within the gentleman's club setting extends beyond weight, and includes dress, adornment, and make-up. Elisa, a feminine-presenting Puerto Rican dancer who works at a gentleman's club in addition to her work with Divine Dancers, expressed the ways in which the bodily regulation women experience in the gentleman's club setting becomes internalized and shapes how they understand themselves as possessing erotic capital, or not.

> There's things they expect you to do at the [Chain Strip] club, like you always have to be perfectly waxed, make-up has to look a certain way. I know it sounds dumb but it's the little things with Divine Dancers. I got a new lipstick from Mac, it's this really pretty deep brown color. And I loved how it looked on me, like a real dramatic dark lip. And when I wore it to The Chain Strip Club, my manager told me to take it off and put on something lighter. I didn't fight it but it made me really question like did I look ugly with it on? And I like, LOVED it before that so... but nobody is ever gonna tell me that at Divine Dancers. If anything, they're gonna say hey, Elisa, I see you, or some shit. Or maybe nothing at all. But I never was one to question myself there.

The questioning of the self that Elisa points to is symbolic of her need to negotiate with dominant gazes within the gentleman's club setting. Rather than focus on an embodied presentation that provides her with heightened confidence, she manages the presentation of her body to avoid being told by club management that she needs to alter her presentation in some way, be it the color of her lipstick or being perfectly waxed. Elisa experiences Divine Dancers as a setting in which she is free from such stringent regulating, and experiences encouragement to experiment with her self-presentation. Significantly, dark lips are associated with a "sexual-esthetic excess" (Hernandez, 2009, p. 63) that is marked as a simultaneously racialized and sexualized representation of Latinas.

Divine Dancers enables both Disco and Elisa opportunities to express an embodied presentation that resonates as sexy, desirable, and most importantly, is constructed outside of whiteness. Having discussed how participants understand Divine Dancers as a comparatively transgressive space in terms of how erotic capital becomes attributed to bodies, I turn to touch and intimacy at Divine Dancers to elucidate how this space, compared to conventional hetero dance clubs, allows for new interactions between dancers and audience members.

Touch and negotiated intimacies at divine dancers

In typical gentleman's clubs, there are rules regarding touch between customers and dancers. The rules regulating how bodies perform extend to the attire that dancers wear; although it varies by state, in many cases gentle-man's clubs in which women dance fully nude do not permit the sale of alcohol. These same rules do not exist within Divine Dancer events; the security team that works Divine Dancer shows includes dancers who have retired from the collective, and, sometimes, security personnel who are employed by El Aguila. This means that dancers are given full autonomy over their attire, and touch between those in the audience and those per-forming is the norm.

Flame, a Black, self-identified dom (or masculine presenting) dancer, expressed feeling that the lack of regulation regarding touch within the Divine Dancer space dictated the parameters of how she could- and felt required- to perform.

> Everyone, especially the femmes (feminine presenting dancers), thinks that Divine Dancers is an easy show because everyone's gay but it's not like that. Everyone's competing about who is the strongest, the most aggressive dom out there and they expect it. Women there expect you to grab on them and do all this kind of stuff to them because you call yourself a dom. I've had a woman literally bend over in front of me when I was performing, I didn't ask her to for the show or anything and in my head I was like I guess I gotta do this, everyone's crowding me watching, ain't anywhere for me to go and if I don't they're gona tell me that I dissed a fan.

Flame indicates that she experiences pressure to engage in physical inter-actions with audience members, who she refers to as "fans," that she would otherwise prefer not to. She posits that the assumption that Divine Dancers is an "easy" show by femme dancers is false, suggesting that femme dancers feel Divine Dancers is "easier" work than that they perform at the gentle-man's club specifically because it is a woman-only space. By and large, femme dancers did indeed find Divine Dancers space to be more conducive to their agency and autonomy compared to the gentleman's club setting. For Flame, the false assertion that Divine Dancers is "easier" work erases the existence of abuse in this woman-only space, as it naturalizes women as inherently safer or less aggressive than men. There is also the assumption that because Flame is masculine presenting, that she is expected to express strength and sexual aggression in ways that feminine presenting dancers are not expected to, which makes her job more difficult than theirs, accord-ing to her. Dom identity is the most prized embodiment in the context of Divine Dancers, and is defined through muscularity, strength, and sex-ual dominance.

Flame recounts feeling pressure to not reject a "fan." Flame's reflection on this interaction reveals that she views herself as having supporters who are devoted to her success, and sees them as possessing a heightened level of enthu-siasm about her as a dancer. Rather than seeing herself as a dancer who has customers (or "regulars"), she conceptualizes her labor as one that garners the appreciation, and following of women, reminiscent of that of a celebrity. She rationalizes succumbing to the demands of the audience member in question as a means of preserving this fan base, so as to not threaten her clout and following. For her, this interaction is part and parcel of what it means to have fans, and to preserve her fan base, she feels she must use her body in ways that cross a boundary she would have preferred to keep. For Flame, this prompting represents a violation and interruption to her as she dances, regardless of the potential for this exchange to be financially lucrative. Flame's negotiations with the unwanted advances of the audience member in question as well as her positioning of her audience as fans are exemplary of Teela Sanders' findings, which posit that erotic laborers develop "a character constructed only for the workplace" not only as an emotion-management strategy, but to "create a marketable character that will appeal, and implicitly conform, to the demands and expectations of the client" (2005, p. 337).

Significantly, femme performers see Divine Dancers as a space in which the unwanted advances of audience members typical of the gentleman's club are less frequent, which they report makes Divine Dancers feel to them like a "safer" setting in which to perform exotic dance. The lack of physical distance between herself and audience members is viewed by Flame as not only an impediment to her performance, but as enabling audience members to force her into sexual exchanges she does not find sexually empowering. The lack of distance placed between dancers and performers is deliberate on behalf of Divine Dancers, who see the lack of physical separation between both parties as part of its mission to differentiate itself from the typical gentleman's club.

Before dancers begin their performances, they prepare for the evening in an area near the restrooms that is partitioned by long folding tables, which is unlike gentleman's clubs, which typically provide dancers with dressing rooms that customers are not allowed in. It is common practice for audience members to approach dancers as they get ready for the evening for pictures or casual conversation. Flame expressed feeling that this results in ambiguity between performer/companion, causing confusion for both herself and audience members:

> I like it, don't get me wrong. But there was a time I was talking to this girl at the bar, and we were having a good time and all that and we're dancing. And I'm enjoying myself, like I'm feeling her, and she whispers in my ear: "should I be tipping you?" and then she starts laughing. And that moment was weird for me because I'm there to make money, and if I don't go home with a certain amount I'm gona be set back, so that's gotta be priority. But what do you do when you find someone you like but you're working? Saying yes woulda' made it awkward, especially if we were going to see each other outside of the show.

Flame's comments reflect her grappling with what it means to work, or perform a certain labor for pay, and simultaneously finding pleasure in it.

Her comments show that she relies on the income she accumulates at Divine Dancers for her financial livelihood, and that this sense of closeness, intimacy, and pleasure between herself and the audience member in question resulted in her feeling as though she must make a choice between finding pleasure in her work and garnering income. The notion that it would be awkward to ask for a tip if she were to see this customer again, outside of her workplace, signals that Flame worries that her connection to her would be seen as inauthentic or premised entirely on the exchange of money, when for Flame, that is not true.

Divine Dancers' emphasis on reducing power differentials between audience members and performers, evidenced by the lack of distance placed between both parties (specifically, the proximity of the preparation space used by dancers and the space in which audience members congregate before performances), produces a feeling of intimacy for event-goers that Flame reports grappling with. For her, this enables what feels like authentic exchanges while she works, which she prefers to not compromise by agreeing to be tipped. While Flame sees this as a positive effect of the Divine Dancers setting, it also forces her to choose between expressing what feels like authentic for customers and earning tips, both of which she sees as diametrically opposed. Bernstein (2007) theorizes the exchange of authentic emotional connection as "bounded authenticity" (p. 6), locating erotic labor as a site of possibility for producing intimate and genuine connections between erotic laborers and customers, though limited in terms of their temporality.

Conclusion

In this paper, I explore to what extent the heteropatriarchal power structure embedded within erotic labor domains can become contested and destabilized in a woman-only space that is also absent of whiteness. Divine Dancers provides Black and Puerto Rican participants a temporal space in which white hegemonic beauty standards are negated, enabling participants to contest the ways in which beauty is constructed under the male gaze. While some participants reported taking pleasure in their ability to express embodied subjectivities in ways otherwise inaccessible to them across different industries and erotic labor settings, Divine Dancers does institute alternative regulatory mechanisms that compromise the extent to which participants find this space sexually empowering.

Whereas Divine Dancers is lauded as a transgressive space in which to perform exotic dance by feminine presenting participants (many of whom also perform at gentleman's clubs), masculine presenting participants experienced this spatial setting as one that forced them to contend with unwanted sexual advances on behalf of audience members. Masculine presenting participants also grappled with issues of intimacy and ambiguity relative to tipping practices, specifically, managing the need to garner tips while experiencing authentic sexual and romantic connections with customers. While feminine presenting dancers reported heightened feelings of autonomy over their labor, masculine presenting dancers who do not perform in the gentleman's club setting found Divine Dancers to be a less autonomous exotic dance site. Their grappling with intimacy, ambiguity, and unwanted advances on behalf of customers mirror the issues that feminine presenting participants contend with in the gentleman's club setting. Participants' potential to enact agency within Divine Dancers is defined in contrast to the other settings in which they work, and shaped through the gendered sexuality of participants.

This study opens a line of inquiry for studies at the intersection of race, sexuality, and the erotic to examine how space and place condition erotic laborers' capacity for expressing autonomy. Specifically, the question of how erotic labor spaces that are constituted differently in terms of ethno-racial composition, classed status, and geographic setting, shape how dancers experience the conditions of their labor.

Notes

1. Gentleman's clubs are hetero-masculinist exotic dance clubs in which women perform for men.
2. Male revue shows are exotic dance shows in which men perform for women. Sometimes, masculine presenting women who perform with Divine Dancers perform alongside men at these shows.

Acknowledgments

I am indebted to Nancy Naples for her thoughtful guidance and feedback throughout the development of this manuscript. I am grateful to the three anonymous reviewers and guest editor for their thoughtful feedback.

Funding

This research received generous support from El Instituto: Latina/o, Caribbean, & Latin American Studies at the University of Connecticut.

References

Barry, K. (1980). Beyond pornography: From defensive politics to creating a vision. In L. Lederer (Ed.) *Take Back the Night* (pp. 307–312). New York, NY: William Morrow & Co, Inc.

Barton, B. (2002). Dancing on the Mobius strip: Challenging the sex war paradigm. *Gender & Society, 16*, 585–602.

Bernstein, E. (2007). *Temporarily yours: Intimacy, authenticity, and the commerce of sex.* Chicago, IL: University of Chicago Press.

Brooks, S. (2012). *Unequal desires: Race and erotic capital in the stripping industry.* Albany, NY: State University of New York.

Brown, M. (2012). Gender and sexuality I: Intersectional anxieties. *Progress in Human Geography, 36*(4), 541–550.

Chapkis, W. (1997). *Live sex acts: Women performing erotic labor.* New York, NY: Routledge.

Craig, M. L. (2006). Race, beauty, and the tangled knot of a guilty pleasure. *Feminist Theory, 7*(2), 159–177.

Duggan, L., & Hunter, N. D. (2006). *Sex wars: Sexual dissent and political culture.* 10th anniversary edition. New York, NY: Routledge.

Ferguson, R. (2012). Of sensual matters: On Audre Lorde's 'Poetry is Not a Luxury' and 'Uses of the Erotic, WSQ: Women's Studies Quarterly, 40*(3–4), 295–300.

Freedman, E. B., & Thorne, B. (1984). Introduction to 'the feminist sexuality debates'. *Signs: Journal of Women in Culture and Society, 10*(1), 102–105.

Gentles-Peart, K. (2018). Controlling beauty ideals: Caribbean women, thick bodies, and white supremacist discourse. *WSQ: Women's Studies Quarterly, 46*(1–2), 199–214.

Gimlin, D. L. (2002). *Body Work: Beauty and self-image in American culture.* Berkeley, CA: University of California Press.

Hammers, C. (2008). Making space for an agentic sexuality? The examination of a lesbian/queer bathhouse. *Sexualities, 11*(5), 547–572.

Hammers, C. (2009). An examination of lesbian/queer bathhouse culture and the social organization of (im)personal sex. *Journal of Contemporary Ethnography, 38*(3), 308–335.

Hernandez, J. (2009). "Miss, you look like a Bratz doll": On Chonga girls and sexual-aesthetic excess. *NWSA Journal, 21*(3), 63–90.

Hollibaugh, A., & Moraga, C. (2003). What we're rollin' around in bed with. In J. Escoffier (Ed.) *Sexual Revolution* (pp. 538–552). New York, NY: Thunder's Mouth Press.

Hunter, M. (2002). If You're Light You're Alright. *Gender & Society, 16*(2), 175–193.

Jones, A. (2015). For Black models scroll down: Webcam modeling and the racialization of erotic labor. *Sexuality & Culture, 19*(4), 776–799.

Jones, A. (2019). The pleasures of fetishization: BBW erotic webcam performers, empowerment, and pleasure. *Fat Studies, 8*(3), 279–298.

Jones, A. (forthcoming). *Camming: Money, power, and pleasure in the sex work industry.* New York, NY: NYU Press.

Khan, C. (2019). Constructing eroticized latinidad: Negotiating profitability in the stripping industry. *Gender & Society, 33*(5), 702–721.

Kwan, S., & Trautner, M. N. (2009). Beauty work: Individual and institutional rewards, the reproduction of gender, and questions of agency. *Sociology Compass*, 3(1), 49–71.

Mahmood, S. (2001). Feminist theory, embodiment, and the docile agent: some reflections on the Egyptian Islamic revival. *Cultural Anthropology*, 16(2), 202–236.

McClintock, A. (1992). Screwing the system: Sex work, race, and the law. In *Boundary 2* (Vol. 19, No. 2, pp. 70–95). Durham, NC: Duke University Press.

Mears, A. (2014). Aesthetic labor for the sociologies of work, gender, and beauty. *Sociology Compass*, 8(12), 1330–1343.

Miller-Young, M. (2014). *A taste for brown sugar: Black women in pornography*. Durham, NC; London: Duke University Press.

Moraga, C., & Anzaldúa, G. (1983). *This bridge called my back: Writings by radical women of color*. 2nd ed. New York, NY: Kitchen Table/Women of Color Press.

Mulvey, L. (1975). Visual pleasure and narrative cinema. In *The feminism and visual culture reader* (pp. 44–53). New York, NY: Psychological Press.

Nash, C. J. (2014). *The Black body in ecstasy: reading race, reading pornography*. Durham, NC; London: Duke University Press.

Newton-Francis, M., & Young, G. (2015). Not winging it at hooters: Conventions for producing a cultural object of sexual fantasy. *Poetics*, 52, 1–17.

Newton-Francis, M., & Vidal-Ortiz, S. (2013). ¡Más que un bocado! (More than a mouthful) comparing hooters in the United States and Colombia. In A. Jafar & E. Masi de Casanova (Eds.) *Global beauty, local bodies*. New York, NY: Palgrave Macmillan.

Omi, M., & Winant, H. (2014). *Racial formation in the United States*. New York, NY: Routledge.

Pilcher, K. (2012). Dancing for women: Subverting heteronormativity in a lesbian erotic dance space? *Sexualities*, 15(5–6), 521–537.

Rubin, G. S. (1998). Thinking sex: Notes for a radical theory of the politics of sexuality. In P. M. Nardi and B. E. Schneider (Eds.) *Social perspectives in lesbian and gay studies* (pp. 100–133). New York, NY: Routledge.

Sanders, T. (2005). It's just acting': Sex workers' strategies for capitalizing on sexuality. *Gender, Work and Organization*, 12, 319–342.

Strings, S. (2019). *Fearing the black body: The racial origins of fat phobia*. New York, NY: NYU Press.

The Combahee River Collective. (1979). A black feminist statement. *WSQ: Women's Studies Quarterly*, 42(3–4), 271–280.

Thompson, C. (2009). Black women, beauty, and hair as a matter of being. *Women's Studies*, 38(8), 831–856.

Vance, C. S., & Snitow, A. B. (1984). Toward a conversation about sex in feminism: A modest proposal. *Signs*, 10(1), 126–135.

Vidal-Ortiz, S., Robinson, B., & Khan, C. (2018). *Race and sexuality*. Cambridge: Polity Press.

Weitzer, R. (2000). *Sex for sale: Prostitution, pornography, and the sex industry*. New York, NY: Psychology Press.

Queer space and alternate queer geographies: LBQ women and the search for sexual partners at two LGBTQ-friendly U.S. universities

Janelle M. Pham

ABSTRACT

The postgay era – marked by decreased stigmatization of non-heterosexual identities and increasing assimilation of gays and lesbians into the heterosexual mainstream – may be indicative of a broader pluralization of queer geographies expanding the social and sexual opportunities of lesbian, gay, bisexual, transgender, and queer (LGBTQ)-identified individuals beyond queer spaces. Less is known, however, about how LBQ women experience these pluralized geographies in a postgay era in their search for sexual partners, and how the perceived accessibility of queer and heterosexual spaces informs the search process. Drawing upon twenty-six in-depth qualitative interviews, this study examines queer-identified undergraduate women's searches for same-sex sexual partners at two LGBTQ-friendly universities in the United States. The women in this study described experiences with dating, sex and relationships within three distinct campus "sexual geographies" – queer spaces, virtual communities and heteronormative campus parties – with entry to each of these sites negotiated in relationship to place-based gender and sexual dynamics. While women at both schools viewed their LGBTQ communities as viable spaces to both build community and meet potential sexual partners, this was paired with the understanding that one needed sufficient "queer capital" to stake a claim there. Counter to the notion that a postgay era has rendered queer space obsolete, or just one of many options, this study suggests that perceptions of queer community spaces as exclusionary or inaccessible may partially contribute to the production of alternative queer geographies beyond marked LGBTQ campus spaces.

Introduction

Increased public and political support of LGBTQ persons in the United States over the past several decades, and their subsequent assimilation into the mainstream, have prompted the declaration that we have entered a "postgay" era (Seidman, 2002). Scholars of sexuality and geography have since debated what these cultural changes mean for LGBTQ communities, with some asserting a postgay era has contributed to the gentrification of urban gayborhoods and the subsequent decline of marked queer spaces (Simon Rosser, West, & Weinmeyer, 2008; Usher & Morrison, 2010). Others argue that postgay life has positively aided in the "queer pluralization of sexuality," (Brown, 2014:1), expanding the social and sexual options of LGBTQ persons beyond gayborhoods (Ghaziani, 2015; Lea, de Wit, & Reynolds, 2015; Nash, 2013; Nash & Gorman-Murray, 2014).

Sexual identity in a postgay era is said to matter less for determining where one lives or whom one interacts with (Ghaziani, 2011), though recent literature finds LBQ women experience queer and heterosexual spaces in different ways. Consistent with both the "queer pluralization" and "postgay" narratives, studies of urban, suburban and rural towns find LBQ women are more apt to form friendships and communities around shared hobbies, interests and activities than sexual identities (Brown-Saracino, 2011; Forstie, 2018; Rothblum, 2010). Studies of queer spaces such as bars (Taylor, 2008), bathhouses (Hammers, 2009) and pride celebrations (Ward, 2003), however, find LBQ women feel palpable pressure to "prove" they belong, troubling the notion that postgay life has uniformly expanded the geographic and social boundaries for LBQ women. Even in a postgay moment, forms of queer capital such as dress, language or appearance continue to hold significant weight for determining affirmation from the LGBTQ community, predicated on collectively developed notions of what it means to be "authentically" queer (Valentine & Skelton, 2003). For LBQ women this may include asserting their bisexuality as a real identity (Fahs, 2009) or negotiating a "butch-femme divide" (Hutson, 2010) in queer spaces where feminine women may struggle for recognition. Collectively, these findings raise an additional question: how does their perceived accessibility to queer and heterosexual spaces inform where LBQ women search for sexual partners in a postgay era?

This study focuses on the experiences of LBQ-identified women in their search for sexual partners at two U.S. universities. Studies of LGBTQ college students' sexual lives detail the varied social networks and spaces, both material and virtual, within which students seek and find sexual partners (Kuperberg & Padgett, 2015; Lamont, Roach, & Kahn, 2018), to include use of heteronormative spaces such as large campus parties. While sexual encounters between women in these settings are often described as instances of "straight girls kissing" for the presumed benefit of heterosexual male onlookers (Esterline & Muehlenhard, 2017; Knox, Beaver, & Kriskute, 2011), these environments also serve as opportunistic sites for women to act on same-sex desire or affirm an LBQ identity (Rupp, Taylor, Regev-Messalem, Fogarty, & England, 2014).

Yet while these findings may suggest a pluralization of queer campus geographies consistent with a postgay narrative, LGBTQ students also describe exclusion or hostility in heteronormative spaces such as Greek life or athletics (Hamilton, 2007; Stone & Gorga, 2014; Tillapaugh, 2013), as well as within queer settings. In their study of a large metropolitan university in Australia, Waling and Roffee (2017) found LGBTIQ + students to harbor hostile or dismissive attitudes towards other LGBTIQ + students perceived to be "too queer" or "not queer enough," further evidence that LGBTIQ + individuals must continually affirm their right to community spaces via knowledge, actions and physical appearance in a postgay era.

In this article I examine how LBQ women perceive and negotiate varied campus geographies in their search for sexual partners using interviews with undergraduate women at two "LGBTQ-friendly" universities in the United States. Women on both campuses identified three distinct sexual geographies as viable places to meet other women – queer spaces, virtual communities and heteronormative campus parties – though sufficient "queer capital" to was deemed necessary to access queer space. I consider how, counter to the notion that a postgay era has rendered queer space obsolete, the perception of queer community spaces as exclusionary or inaccessible may actually contribute to the production of alternative queer geographies beyond the LGBTQ community.

Methods

Data for this study come from a larger study of the sexual cultures of two U.S. universities: the University of Pennsylvania (Penn), a mid-sized private university located in Philadelphia, and the University of California Santa Barbara (UCSB), a mid-sized public university located on the central coast of California. The data from this larger study consist of archival research and in-depth qualitative interviews with fifty-four undergraduate women, twenty-seven from each school. Participants were recruited by a combination of in-person advertising in sociology classrooms, flyers in on- and off-campus spaces, print ads in student newspapers and targeted social media advertising. The author purposefully oversampled for nonwhite and non-heterosexually-identified women to address the dearth of sexual research on these college populations – 42.6% of the overall sample identified as White, and half as heterosexual.

Coincidentally, both schools made Campus Pride's "Best of the Best Top 30 List of LGBTQ-friendly Colleges and Universities" in 2016, the same year data for this study were collected. Campus Pride is a nonprofit organization dedicated to creating safe and supportive college environments for LGBTQ students. Schools on its "Best of the Best" list scored highest on the Campus Pride Index, which measures a school's commitment to LGBTQ-friendly policies, programs and practices. Both institutions boast ample physical and social spaces for its LGBTQ community to meet and connect, to include campus resource centers with a full-time staff member (less than 5% of US universities offered such a resource in 2014 (Marine & Nicolazzo, 2014)). While UCSB offers student housing specifically for LGBTQ students, Penn is home to an unofficial "queer frat" known for its inclusive parties. Both schools also offer a number of student organizations, ranging from general (Queer Student Union) to specific (Queer People of Color, Trans Social Group), and each institution hosts an annual Pride Week.

Given the variability of sexual identities in a postgay era, I chose to focus on the twenty-six undergraduate women (twelve at UCSB, fourteen at Penn) who identified as something other than heterosexual. Participants identified as lesbian (2), bisexual (16), questioning, bi-curious or heteroflexible (4), queer (3) and pansexual (1), and ranged in age from 19 to 24. They self-identified as White (10), Asian (6), multiracial (3), Latina/Hispanic (3), African/African-American (3) and Caribbean American (1). All participants identified as cisgender, and thus this study cannot speak to how trans* or genderqueer students navigate the LGBTQ-friendly campus as a sexual space. Interviews ranged in length from 45 mins, to two hours, and were audio recorded with the participant's consent. All interviews were transcribed in full by the author and analyzed using inductive coding (Ragin, 1994), allowing prominent patterns and themes in the data to emerge organically.

The lesbian, gay, bisexual, and transgender (LGBT)-Friendly campus as post-gay space

Consistent with their status as students on "LGBTQ-friendly" campuses, the women in this study described their respective schools as safe spaces to be out – each of the women in this sample was out to at least their closest friends. They attributed their felt levels of comfort or support to institutional features catered to queer populations, such as student organizations and resource centers, though they described their campuses to be "tolerant" or "accepting" of LGBTQ students overall. "I feel pretty comfortable telling most anybody [about my identity] here," reflected Zoe, an Asian-American at UCSB who identified as pansexual.

> If you look around, there are rainbow flags everywhere... more so than other campuses. So even if people had an issue with it here what are you gonna do, speak out against it? Because you are going to have a lot of people on your ass about it.

These women's descriptions of their campus mirror the language of a postgay era, where perceived levels of acceptance made cloistering in queer spaces or social networks unnecessary or undesirable. Becca, a queer-identified White woman and a recent transfer from a private university on the East Coast, described her perception of UCSB's campus community.

> I feel in general UCSB's campus is a little more accepting of different genders and sexualities than [my previous school] was... if you were going to the queer events you would be a part of the 5% that was not dressing like everybody else, that was not studying the same things as everyone else. You could really tell. Whereas here I feel like there is so much more flexibility so there is less of a need to be in that space since it is less hostile.

Women at Penn shared similar sentiments, evoking a postgay language of assimilation and widespread acceptance. "The queer community at Penn is so ubiquitous," explained Shayla, a White bisexual. "I have never felt afraid to hold hands with my girlfriend on campus... girls kissing on a bench, that is normal. It is literally just as normal as straight people, and that makes me so happy." Alex, a bisexual Asian junior at Penn, added, "I have never met anyone who is discriminating. I pretty much just expect people to be okay with [my sexual identity]. Which I realize is a weird privilege."

Consistent with this postgay language of assimilation, friendships were formed through propinquity (living in the same dorm) or membership in a campus organization, as opposed to a shared sexual identity. To be sure, some women on campus prioritized involvement in their school's queer community; however, none of the women in the study stated their peer groups came solely from this population. Beyond matters of friendship, however, queer community and queer spaces took on a different meaning or value when it came to seeking sexual partnership.

Queer Capital and queer space

Women who considered themselves members of their campus' LGBTQ community described their involvement via social networks, participation in campus organizations and/or attendance at queer-identified parties. These forms of interaction with other queer-identified students provided varied opportunities to not only form friendships, but to meet potential hookups or long-term partners. Melanie, a lesbian attending Penn, had recently met a woman at a pizza party organized by a queer women's group, adding, "We are talking and flirting." She reflected further upon the benefits of attending events hosted by queer organizations. "It makes it a lot easier [to meet people]. It's like, 'oh I got your number, I already know that you are attracted to ladies, so let me flirt with you.' It helps a lot."

Other women in this study shared they had met current or previous partners within their campus' queer community. This included Shayla, who met her ex-girlfriend at Penn's LGBT Center, and Alex, who regularly attended queer parties and served on the board of a queer organization for Asian students. Alex found it "easy" to meet women on Penn's campus, whether through attending parties or becoming involved in queer organizations. She reflected on a recent hookup she met at a queer frat party.

> We were just talking and my friends were like, jokingly, 'You are already talking to the hottest person in the room, what are we going to do?' And then this person overheard it and said, 'Oh, you think I'm the hottest person in the room?' And then we danced and started kissing and went back to my room.

Not all of the women in this study expressed a desire for involvement in their campus queer community, with some of their reasons consistent with a postgay attitude that forming social ties around a shared sexual identity was not important. Though she had previously attended get-togethers of the queer women's group at Penn, Kiri, a White bisexual, explained, "I felt like other than being queer there wasn't a whole lot that we had in common ... I don't do much in the community ... I just don't get the idea of hanging out with people on the basis of this one character trait that I have." However, when it came to relationships or hooking up, the majority of the women in this study described the real or perceived value of queer campus space, regardless of their level of involvement within it. For those without social ties to these spaces, finding partners was thought to be more difficult. "If I was out there looking for a genuine same-sex partner I think I would [need to] be ... in the basic community," shared Zoe.

> If I headed over to [Queer Student Union] it would be like ok, here we go. Or the Rainbow House [the LGBTQ dormitory]. You have those places where you are there for a reason, to meet people like you. But if you are not involved in that ... just going out there trying to find a decent woman, I think that would be a little difficult.

Despite these feelings, some women admitted they avoided queer spaces completely, citing their lack of queer capital to stake a claim there. Jazmine, a multiracial senior at UCSB who described herself as questioning, expressed a desire to explore her identity and attractions to other women, but hesitated to do this in queer spaces.

> I wouldn't feel comfortable necessarily going into a queer-identified space ... I don't want them to be like, 'well, why are you here?' And it's one of those things where if I was going to venture and try to find a partner, that would probably be the first place that I would look and start hanging out in queer identified spaces, but I also want to be respectful of everyone's energy and everyone's time.

"It is almost like you have to have a certain resumé to qualify as queer," shared Cassie, a senior at Penn who identified as bisexual/queer. "I have found that difficult and isolating from the queer community in general." When prompted to describe what would need to be on one's resumé to qualify as queer, Cassie mentioned "friend groups, social activities, sexual experiences and relationships." Even women who described high levels of involvement in their school's queer community described feeling out of place or intimidated at times, such that the no one was exempt from the pressures to "perform queerness." Reflecting upon her attendance at meetings of UCSB's Queer Student Union, Teresa, a White pansexual, shared

> [QSU] is very much focused on social activism and the queer identity... so if [you] don't know a bunch of terminology and history it can be very intimidating... I already had a lot of the language and exposure to how they talked... even with that it still felt a little bit intimidating.

Women who identified as bisexual, and/or self-described as more feminine in their gender presentation, were especially likely to mention divisions within the queer community or feelings of "not measuring up." Recalling her experience attending an event for queer women at Penn her freshman year, Layla, a Black senior, shared, "I didn't really feel welcome because everyone I met identified as gay. It's weird, even though it's a community, the queer community, you still feel the lines... and not in a positive way."

Zoe, who shared earlier the importance of belonging to queer spaces when looking for a potential partner, described her prior attendance at a meeting of one of UCSB's queer organizations her freshman year.

> I was working out my own identity so it was like, 'I don't know if I belong here'... I identify as pansexual but... I had always been with men. I am very femme, I am with guys, I've never had sex with a woman, I've never kissed a woman, stuff like that... for me, I think I didn't feel queer enough to be a part of that.

Like Cassie, Zoe also equated sexual experiences with women as a form of queer capital, and a lack of these experiences as an impediment to fitting in within marked queer spaces. This presented a paradox for women who described themselves as "not queer enough," in that queer spaces were both plentiful and hyper visible, yet viewed as inaccessible.

Diffuse spaces: Dating applications

Women in this study looking to date or form hookups with other women also utilized various social media applications such as Tinder or Her, as well as online group pages on Facebook, to search for sexual partners. For some, these technologies were a means to bridge physical and virtual space by allowing women to confirm the sexual orientations of other women they had met on campus. Sharing that "I have the worst gaydar, which is so annoying," Vanessa, a queer junior at Penn, described a Facebook group for queer women at her school to be a valuable resource. "If I am attracted to a person who I don't know, I usually look them up in the Facebook group first to see if they are part of that." She recalled multiple sexual relationships with women while at Penn, meeting her partners through both social media and her attendance at queer frat parties, citing these parties to be "the one space I can typically count on, being with similar kinds of people and being myself."

For women who were not out or did not feel comfortable engaging in their campus' queer spaces, online communities were a primary means for searching for partners. This was true for Maisie, an Asian bisexual whose exclusive use of dating applications both helped to signal attraction and keep her sexual identity more private, sharing "I am not fully out at Penn. So it feels more comfortable to hide behind an app." While Maisie described efforts to become more immersed in Penn's queer community, to include attending a queer party where "I met someone that I was interested in," she also explained, "I don't quite fit into the queer community. Most of the females who are prominent in the queer community are more queer than I am." Consistent with a language of queer capital, Maisie's words suggest queerness is seemingly quantifiable, though she did not elaborate on what constitutes being "more queer" beyond perhaps not identifying as bisexual. In her identification of the queer community's most "prominent" members, Maisie asserts the power of visibility for conjuring up imagined notions of what queer looks like, and who is most apt to feel comfortable in queer spaces.

Finally, a few women described online communities as a way to build their "queer competence," another benefit of these spaces for women who were looking to become involved in the LGBTQ community but who felt they lacked the queer authenticity to participate. This was true for Elise, a bisexual and a member of one of UCSB's sororities. As a member of Greek life, Elise viewed social media as a means to both browse her options and learn how to "present" as bisexual.

> I am looking to explore women more right now. But I think that is difficult here. Just because I am in a sorority and I'm not going for anyone in my sorority… but I was looking through [an] app because I wanted to see girls here that were bisexual or lesbian because I don't know how to portray myself as one. Except going to a gay bar.

Elise mentions multiple geographies and subcultures to explain her use of dating applications, citing her membership in Greek life to be a non-opportunistic site for partnership. She mentions going to a gay bar as a way to "portray herself" as bisexual, presumably by occupying a space that is marked as queer in its orientation. For her, online applications became an alternative space to browse for potential partners and to see what bisexual or lesbian "looks like."

Spaces of contention: Frat parties

Finally, queer women described seeking out sexual opportunities with other women at heteronormative parties on campus, though opinions about this approach were contentious. Those who made strategic use of parties to meet women described varied levels of involvement in their campus' queer community. Roxy, a White bisexual junior at UCSB, was not involved in the campus' queer community. While most of Roxy's hookups were with men, she shared that "it's not for lack of trying," describing greater difficulty in meeting women. She recalled all of her sexual encounters with women to be "in a situation with alcohol."

> I've definitely made out with a lot of girls at frat parties who seem they might just be doing it because we're at a frat party. And I kind of feel like I'm almost taking advantage of people because they probably wouldn't be doing it normally... I actually haven't had sober hookups with women while I've been here.

Interestingly, Roxy views her engagements with women in fraternity party environments as potentially exploitative, rather than a limiting factor in her expressed desire for a more consistent hookup or relationship.

Another bisexual, Nicole, was a prominent figure in Penn's LGBTQ community, holding a leadership position in a queer student organization and regularly organizing queer parties for the campus. While Nicole felt that it was easy to find women if you are openly queer and "are in that kind of environment," she was not against hooking up with women in straight party settings. She did, however, recognize this type of behavior was problematic for some members of the queer community.

> I think in general if it is that kind of sexual experimentation, female specifically, [the queer female community is] generally really against it. I think it is the whole idea of possibly being used. It's a very general thing that a lot of straight people go into college saying 'oh I want to experiment with girls... this is on my bucket list' kind of thing. And so I think there are a lot of people that just don't want to be a bucket list kind of person.

Counter to Roxy's sentiments of using other women, Nicole considers how some members of the queer community fear the possibility of *being used* by women just looking to experiment. Making clear her position on the issue, Nicole added, "I'm totally fine with being somebody's drunken experiment!," sharing that she had hooked up with multiple women at "traditional" fraternity parties.

This was not the case for Vanessa, who preferred attending Penn's queer frat parties, where same-sex sexual interaction is less apt to be met with male ogling or propositions. Describing her interactions at traditional fraternity parties, Vanessa explained, "If I am making out with a girl in the corner, which I am totally cool with doing, a lot of the guys will say 'oh my God, that is so hot, let's have a threesome.'... then I become kind of a porn object... and that is really disappointing." Vanessa's recollection of being propositioned for a threesome by male party attendees is predicated on the assumption that women who kiss other women at parties are also attracted to men, and that their engagement in sexual activity is in an effort to garner male attention. Rather than being for her enjoyment, Vanessa suggests how her actions become a form of entertainment for male party-goers, marking her and her female partner as "porn objects." For some women, the attention that kissing between women draws at large parties was reason enough to avoid these spaces. Thus, queer women shared conflicting views of campus parties as both advantageous and exploitative spaces from which to meet other women.

Conclusions: Rethinking postgay sexual geographies

The experiences of queer-identified women at UC Santa Barbara and the University of Pennsylvania reveal how attendance at an LGBTQ-friendly campus in a postgay era informs experience of the university as a sexual space. Collectively, these women's narratives suggest the presence of three distinctive campus "sexual geographies" facilitative of same-sex encounters: queer spaces, virtual communities and heteronormative campus parties. Consistent with their attendance at LGBTQ-friendly institutions, women in this study described their schools as supportive and affirming places to be out, evoking a postgay language where segregating within queer networks or spaces was unnecessary. These descriptions of the LGBTQ-friendly university may appear to align with prior literature detailing the diffusion of queer geographies aided by postgay sensibilities (Ghaziani, 2015; Lea et al., 2015; Simon Rosser et al., 2008). However, these women's experiences across queer and non-queer spaces suggests the pluralization of queer geographies is also driven by the perceived inaccessibility of queer space.

While women's negotiation of campus space in their search for sexual partners was shaped by multiple factors, descriptions of queer spaces as intimidating or exclusionary presents the possibility of LGBTQ campus spaces, and the populations understood to circulate within them, as partially informing queer women's searches for sexual partners in alternative spaces. This significantly troubles the notion of a postgay campus where diverse identities, gender presentations and lived experiences are presumed equally celebrated or acknowledged (Ghaziani, 2011), and introduces the possibility that prominent LGBTQ campus communities may actually reify alternative queer geographies. That is, some queer students may find themselves negotiating alternative queer geographies in their search for sexual partners not because they have voluntarily "opted out" of queer spaces, but because they feel they are not welcome to "opt in."

Women at both schools detailed the "paradox of queer space" (Valentine & Skelton, 2003). While they described their LGBTQ communities as viable spaces to connect and meet potential sexual partners, this was paired with the understanding that one needed to meet certain criteria to feel comfortable in these spaces. Consistent with prior studies of student engagement within LGBTQ communities (Waling & Roffee, 2017), some women described avoiding queer spaces completely, feeling they lacked the proper "queer capital," such as language, identity, peer networks or a past sexual history with women. Women who were heavily involved in their campus' queer community described similar pressure to "prove their worth" within the queer community. This was especially pronounced for bisexual-identified women, who constituted the majority of the sample. While included under the LGBTQ umbrella, bisexual women suggest that their identity is considered less legitimate than if they had identified as lesbian, queer or even pansexual.

Virtual communities and heteronormative campus parties were also described as spaces to meet women. However, the existence of these alternative sexual geographies – and women's experiences navigating them – cannot be understood separate of their relationship to queer campus space. For some women virtual spaces were just one of many sexual geographies they felt were available to them. For those who described feeling unwelcome in queer spaces or difficulty "signaling" a queer identity in material spaces, however, online communities were the sole means to seek out sexual partners. Finally, the heteronormative campus party as an alternative sexual space for LBQ women is dependent on the role that heterosexual men play in its construction. The dynamics of this campus space divided the women in this study on whether or not these spaces were suitable places to meet women. The heteronormative campus party as a space of queer sexual potential is not a derivative of a postgay era, but an "opportunity structure" (Rupp et al., 2014) fortified by the (sometimes) unwanted attention from male onlookers.

These findings also provide broader insight about the perceived accessibility of LGBTQ-marked organizations and spaces for women of varying identities on university campuses. Despite attending an LGBTQ-friendly university, women in this study negotiated feelings of inadequacy and/or inauthenticity – feelings that might be *amplified* on campuses with a hypervisible queer community. Dedicated spaces on campus for the queer community are integral to providing the resources and support needed to this population, and more universities can and need to commit to these offerings. However, it is important that institutions are aware of how these spaces may also prove intimidating and/or exclusionary, and how to best support student accessibility to and affirmation within queer geographies. Finally, while a great deal of attention has been paid to postgay life across commercial, urban, suburban and rural settings, future research can begin to shift towards understanding if and how the postgay moment informs the sexual geographies of organizations. Beyond higher education, this could include a deeper understanding what effects a postgay culture has on the sexual geographies of work environments, and how organizational culture and membership shapes these geographies.

Acknowledgments

For their helpful comments and suggestions, the author would like to thank Beth Schneider, Verta Taylor, Leila Rupp, Sarah Thébaud, Maria Charles, Fatima Suarez and Anna Chatillon.

Disclosure statement

No potential conflict of interest was reported by the authors.

References

Brown, M. (2014). Gender and Sexuality II: There Goes the Gayborhood? *Progress in Human Geography*, *38*(3), 457–465.

Brown-Saracino, J. (2011). From the Lesbian Ghetto to ambient community: The perceived costs and benefits of integration for community. *Social Problems*, *58*(3), 361–388.

Esterline, K. M., & Muehlenhard, C. L. (2017). Wanting to be seen: Young people's experiences of performative making out. *Journal of Sex Research*, *54*(8), 1051–1063.

Fahs, B. (2009). Compulsory bisexuality?: The challenges of modern sexual fluidity. *Journal of Bisexuality*, *9*(3–4), 431–449.

Forstie, C. (2018). Ambivalently Post-lesbian: LBQ friendships in the rural midwest. *Journal of Lesbian Studies*, *22*(1), 54–66.

Ghaziani, A. (2015). *There goes the Gayborhood?* Princeton, NJ: Princeton University Press.

Ghaziani, A. (2011). Post-gay collective identity construction. *Social Problems*, *58*(1), 99–125.

Hamilton, L. (2007). Trading on heterosexuality: College women's gender strategies and homophobia. *Gender & Society*, *21*(2), 145–172.

Hammers, C. (2009). An examination of lesbian/queer bathhouse culture and the social organization of (im)personal sex. *Journal of Contemporary Ethnography*, *38*(3), 308–335.

Hutson, D. J. (2010). Standing OUT/Fitting IN: Identity, appearance, and authenticity in gay and lesbian communities. *Symbolic Interaction*, *33*(2), 213–233.

Knox, D., Beaver, T., & Kriskute, V. (2011). I Kissed a Girl": Heterosexual women who report same-sex kissing (and more). *Journal of GLBT Family Studies*, *7*(3), 217–225.

Kuperberg, A., & Padgett, J. E. (2015). Dating and hooking up in college: Meeting contexts, sex, and variation by gender, partner's gender, and class standing. *The Journal of Sex Research*, *52*(5), 517–531.

Lamont, E., Roach, T., & Kahn, S. (2018). Navigating campus hookup culture: LGBTQ students and college hookups. *Sociological Forum*, *33*(4), 1000–1022.

Lea, T., de Wit, J., & Reynolds, R. (2015). Post-Gay" Yet? The Relevance of the lesbian and gay scene to same-sex attracted young people in contemporary Australia. *Journal of Homosexuality, 62*(9), 1264–1285.

Marine, S. B., & Nicolazzo, Z. (2014). Names that matter: Exploring the tensions of campus LGBTQ centers and trans* inclusion. *Journal of Diversity in Higher Education, 7*(4), 265–281.

Nash, C. J. (2013). The age of the "Post-mo"? Toronto's gay village and a new generation. *Geoforum, 49*, 243–252.

Nash, C. J., & Gorman-Murray, A. (2014). LGBT neighbourhoods and 'New Mobilities': Towards understanding transformations in sexual and gendered urban landscapes. *International Journal of Urban and Regional Research, 38*(3), 756–772.

Ragin, C. (1994). *Constructing social research.* Thousand Oaks, CA: Pine Forge.

Rothblum, E. (2010). Where is the 'Women's Community?' Voices of lesbian, bisexual and queer women and heterosexual sisters. *Feminism & Psychology, 20*(4), 454–472.

Rupp, L. J., Taylor, V., Regev-Messalem, S., Fogarty, A., & England, P. (2014). Queer women in the hookup scene: Beyond the closet? *Gender & Society, 28*(2), 212–235.

Seidman, S. (2002). *Beyond the closet: The transformation of gay and lesbian life.* New York, NY: Routledge.

Simon Rosser, B. R., West, W., & Weinmeyer, R. (2008). Are gay communities dying or just in transition? Results from an International consultation examining possible structural change in gay communities. *AIDS Care, 20*(5), 588–595.

Stone, A. L., & Gorga, A. (2014). Containing pariah femininities: Lesbians in the sorority rush process. *Sexualities, 17*(3), 348–364.

Taylor, Y. (2008). That's not really my scene': Working-class lesbians in (and out of) place. *Sexualities, 11*(5), 523–546.

Tillapaugh, D. (2013). Breaking down the "Walls of a Façade": The influence of compartmentalization on gay college males' meaning-making. *Culture, Society and Masculinities, 5*(2), 127–146.

Usher, N., & Morrison, E. (2010). The demise of the gay enclave, communication infrastructure theory and the transformation of gay public space. In P. Pullen, & M. Cooper (Eds.), *LGBT identity and online new media* (pp. 271–287). New York, NY: Routledge.

Valentine, G., & Skelton, T. (2003). Finding oneself, losing oneself: The lesbian and gay 'scene' as paradoxical space. *International Journal of Urban and Regional Research, 27*(4), 849–866.

Waling, A., & Roffee, J. A. (2017). Knowing, performing and holding queerness: LGBTIQ+ student experiences in Australian Tertiary Education. *Sex Education, 17*(3), 302–318.

Ward, J. (2003). Producing 'Pride' in West Hollywood: A queer cultural capital for queers with cultural capital. *Sexualities, 6*(1), 65–94.

Queer Anthropophagy: Building women-centered LGBT + space in Northeastern Brazil

Sarah Nicholus

ABSTRACT

Through an ethnographic study of a party for lesbian, gay, bisexual, and transgender (LGBT)+ women, this article examines contemporary sociospatial practices LGBT+/queer women utilize to build community during the *festas juninas* in Natal, Rio Grande do Norte. While these popular festivals associated with the rural space of the Brazilian Northeast may seem to replicate colonial, religious, and traditional structures, they have also have become fertile ground for queer contestations of heteronormative structures in the Northeast. I argue that LGBT + women in Natal engage in a cultural and spatial anthropophagy: devouring, absorbing, and hybridizing different cultural influences and types of space to create new community formations. By consuming many of the symbols, images, and cultural productions of the *festas juninas* they actively construct a hybrid anthropophagic space for LGBT + women and challenge moralistic values associated with rural Northeastern culture.

Introduction

The month of June is a particularly important month in Brazil with regard to sex, marriage, and romance. Brazilians celebrate *Dia dos Namorados* (Brazilian Valentine's Day) on June 12th, the feast day of Saint Anthony, as part of the *festas juninas* – the popular June festivals associated with the rural space of the Brazilian Northeast. In an ethnographic study of a June party for LGBT + women (the *Arraiá do GAMI*), this article examines ephemeral sociospatial practices LGBT + women utilize to build community during the *festas*. An organization whose goal is to transform the lives of women and girls and to visibilize lesbian and bisexual women, The Affirmative Group of Independent Women (GAMI) promotes sexual diversity and gender equality in the city of Natal, Rio Grande do Norte. Through political activism, community programs, and annual events such as the *Arraiá*, GAMI engages a population of youth, women, LGBT, and black communities in a peripheral neighborhood of Natal.

As celebrations with religious, colonial, and heteropatriarchal origins, the *festas juninas* often replicate conservative structures associated with rural Northeastern culture. However, this article demonstrates some of the ways in which LGBT + women contest these heteronormative structures and reclaim the festivals as an important space for community formation. I utilize the Brazilian cultural concept of "anthropophagy" to theorize GAMI's interventions during the *festas juninas*. A term elaborated during the Brazilian Modernist movement of the 1920s, "anthropophagy" symbolically draws upon indigenous practices of consuming external influences, hybridizing them with internal influences, and producing original work. I argue that GAMI engages in a cultural and spatial anthropophagy: devouring, absorbing, and hybridizing different cultural influences and types of space to create new community formations. At its annual *arraiá* party the group merges modern, traditional, and queer cultural practices to configure new spaces with virtual, physical, ephemeral, visual, auditory, and performative dimensions. GAMI also consumes many of the symbols, images, and cultural productions of the *festas juninas* to actively construct a queer anthropophagic space for LGBT + women. These hybrid spaces offer networks that link individuals across space and time. They also produce alternate, resistant, and symbolic spaces that subvert traditional spatial organization and challenge moralistic values associated with rural Northeastern culture. Like others at the intersections of multiple marginalized identities, GAMI utilizes different dimensions of space to construct new community formations.

A cultural study in the Brazilian Northeast

This article is grounded in an interdisciplinary, cultural studies approach with explicit queer and intersectional feminist engagement. It contributes to women's, gender, and sexuality studies by exploring queer geographies and lesbian community formations of the Global South. Situated within the specific context of rural festivities in Northeastern Brazil, it contributes to a plural and multifarious understanding of identities and cultural practices beyond an already established Northern-metropolitan framework. It also challenges static understandings of space by investigating traditional rural culture as it has moved to the city with migration. Building off nine years of collaboration and interaction within Natal's LGBT + communities including two years living in Natal and three summers of immersed field research, this article also makes an impactful contribution in the field of Brazilian Studies where women-centered, queer, and Northeastern subjectivities remain understudied. Existing literature on Brazilian LGBT + culture focuses on the urban South from a male perspective (Green, 1999; Kulick, 1998; Parker, 1991), while scholarship on cultural productions of Northeastern Brazil highlights only their articulation of heteronormative values (Rowe & Schelling, 1991; Slater, 1982; Costa, 2015; Chianca, 2007a). The primary sources of my study have not been previously researched in academic literature, yet they represent important expressions of LGBT + culture and sociopolitical life. Rather than simply providing a study located in the Global South, this article seeks to better understand local models for understanding and theorizing lesbian and queer women's community configurations around gendered, sexed, raced, and classed LGBT + subjectivities in Northeastern Brazil.

The merged methods of cultural studies have been especially useful as they have allowed for flexibility in my choice of methods and materials. I utilize online ethnography and participant observation, applying techniques of close reading to various cultural phenomena including the geography of the city, virtual spaces such as Facebook, and the visual and auditory elements of the *Arraiá* event to locate queer anthropophagic practices within the festival, city, and culture. Rather than over-relying on the analysis of formal English language texts, I examine LGBT + culture as it is expressed in Portuguese, within folk traditions, and through ephemeral spatial practices in Northeastern Brazil. GAMI is an organization whose goal is to transform the lives of women and girls and to visibilize lesbian and bisexual women in Natal and beyond. This has been one of my central considerations as I conduct this research. For my online ethnography, I specifically chose a public Facebook site from which to draw material as it was deliberately placed in a public, online forum to be seen and recognized. My in-person ethnographic work was participant observation at an event in which I was both an insider and an outsider. For these reasons, I made sure to communicate with GAMI's organizers about my research and had permission to make my observations. I also spent a great deal of time in Natal's LGBT + community before beginning my work. I chose participant observation, rather than formal interviews, in order to focus on the cultural phenomena GAMI produces rather than the lived experiences of participants. Future research could explore the significance of the *festas juninas* and the *Arraiá do GAMI* to local women through formal interviews.

Finally, the merged methods of cultural studies are an important tool given my positionality as both an insider and outsider. Narrative and storytelling provide a space for critical feminist reflexivity and the articulation of lived experiences, especially those unrepresented in more conventional academic disciplines. As I introduce the *Arraiá do GAMI*, I also reflect on how my positionality affects my access to this LGBT + community. My sustained engagement in Natal's LGBT+ communities before I became a researcher has also resulted in a variety of relational dynamics including friendships and political allyships. I follow the work of feminist geographers who interrogate how a researcher's positionality directly affects their work and how this work is also a dialogical process structured by both researchers and participants (Brown, Browne, Elmhirst, & Hutta, 2010; England, 1994; Faria & Mollett, 2016; Kobayashi, 1994). These methods allow me to better interrogate the ways in which identities, positionalities, and power relations are historically, socioculturally, and geographically contingent rather than fixed, stable, or uniform.

LGBT(Q)+ identities and terminologies

The term "queer" is not commonly utilized in Brazil. In everyday language, Brazilians use more individualized terms such as *"lésbica," "gay," "bisexual," "travesti"* or *"não-binário* (lesbian, gay, bisexual, *travesti*, or non-binary)" for self-identification. In the Northeast, it is not uncommon for people to express anti-normative sexuality elliptically in expressions such as *"ela é entendida* (she is understood (to be gay))," *"ela faz parte do time* (she is part of the team)," or by conflating sexuality and gender identity, *"ela é um menino* (she is a boy)." In this article, I utilize the acronym LGBT+ (*lésbica, gay, bi, trans/travesti/transsexual*) to respect the umbrella term most widely used in public, activist discourse in Brazil. I also use the term "queer" to contribute to the elaboration of an intersectional feminist framework that bridges conversations in Latin America and the United States. I mobilize the term beyond conventional understandings of LGBT+ identities to refer to marginal, anti-normative, ambiguous, fluid, and intersectional subjectivities that also resist hegemonic hierarchies and systems of power (such as white supremacy, patriarchy, colonialism, etc.). My mobilization of the term follows the work of U.S. black feminist scholars (Cohen, 2005; Johnson & Henderson 2005), decolonial Latin American scholars (Costa, 2012; Lugones, 2007; Ruvalcaba, 2016; Quijano, 2000), and geographers of sexuality (Browne, 2006; Puar, 2002; Oswin, 2008) who contest binaries, encourage an intersectional understanding of queerness, and interrogate the sexed, raced, and gendered biopolitics of colonization. Finally, the term queer (or *cuir/kuir*) has recently appeared in Brazilian cultural productions, for example, in the internationally-screened films *Bixa Travesty* (2018) and *The Whisper of the Jaguar* (2018). These Brazilian films represent a queer diaspora which not only mobilizes queerness as anti-normative, ambiguous, intersectional, and subversive, but also applies queerness to (black, queer, trans, femme, rural, and indigenous) bodies that migrate beyond traditional borders[1].

Queer anthropophagy

While the term "queer" has not fully made its way into public discourse, many Brazilian scholars have approached queer theory through the notion of *cultural anthropophagy*: the cultural and metaphorical cannibalization of outside influences to produce original work and combat Eurocentrism (Colling & Pelúcio, 2015; Neto, 2015). While originally elaborated as an esthetic model during the Brazilian Modernist movement of the 1920s, *antropophagia* as a cultural movement has become one of the most important concepts in Brazil in the twentieth century. A movement that claimed a self-conscious stance of absorption (or critical devouring), *antropofagia* blended European avant-garde ideas with Brazilian traditions to negotiate transnational influences. While colonial frameworks position the metaphor of cannibalism as a paradigm of otherness, cultural anthropophagy re-purposes cannibalism as a trope of self-recognition in Brazil (Islam, 2012; Jáuregui, 2012). In his *Manifesto Antropófago* (1928), Oswald de Andrade elaborates key ideas of abjection and in-between-ness that complement subaltern and queer perspectives. The Manifesto presents an original strategy for resisting colonization by drawing from indigenous social practices and recognizing them as an important part of Brazilian culture. *Antropofagia* repositions Brazil's history of "cannibalizing" other cultures as its greatest strength, providing a queer decolonial methodology for Brazilians engaging with work from Europe and the United States[2]. GAMI's interventions within the *festas juninas* not only contest heteronormative narratives in the Northeast, but also highlight black and indigenous influences in the region. *Anthropophagia*, as a mode of intervention, relies on the strategies and social practices of people of color to resist colonization and free marginalized communities from white heteropatriarchal regimes.

Anthropophagy also provides important points of departure for dialog between Brazilian cultural theory and queer theory. Cultural studies scholar João Nemi Neto uses the term "anthropophagic queer" (2015) to propose both a queer analysis of the experimental, modernist spirit of *antropofagia* and an anthropophagic reading of queer theory. Neto asserts that anthropophagy is queer as it "revolutionizes the way the other is seen, the way the colony saw itself, the way abject bodies saw themselves, and the way local theory could be analysed" (p. 73). Emphasizing "devouring" as a critical lens through which one can question normative theories and practices, *antropofagia* also re-articulates that which is forbidden as a tool for intervention. Neto argues that the queerness in *anthropofagia* is the notion of emancipation and inclusion of indigenous people, people of color, and women, as well as the abject bodies that have been denied visibility (p. 44) He argues that "queer," as a theory invested with colonial power, "needs to be eaten by Brazilian queer bodies and devoured in ways that would fit their queer needs" (p. 45). He insists on its continued relevancy and importance to define local practices of reading and producing in Brazil. *Antropofagia's* cultural importance as well as its transgressive and subversive nature make it an essential lens through which to analyze local queer practices.

Anthropophagic spatialities

In this article, I utilize the term "queer anthropophagic space" to refer to hybrid, fluid, transgressive, intersectional, and radically inclusive spaces, such as that of the *Arraiá do GAMI*. I follow the work of previous scholars who differentiate "queer spatiality" from "gay and lesbian spatiality" (Browne, 2006; Nash & Bain, 2007). This definition is linked to how queer spatiality, unlike gay and lesbian spatiality, necessarily transgresses the normative and disrupts normalizing boundaries and binaries. Previous work has also noted how studies in gay and lesbian spatialities often reinscribe these binaries while isolating sexuality from its intersections with raced, classed, and gendered arrangements of space (Oswin, 2008; Puar 2002). I therefore look to queer geographies that position sexuality within "multifaceted constellations of power" (Oswin, 2008) including the raced, classed, and gendered ways in which sexuality and power are deployed in Natal, RN.

In the sections that follow, I first read Natal's queer anthropophagic spatialities as they intersect with raced and classed geographies of the city and region. I then introduce the *Arraiá do GAMI* alongside the ephemeral and network spaces in which the group operates. Highlighting the ways in which GAMI hybridizes space, I connect these ephemeral network spaces to the physical space in which the *Arraiá do GAMI* takes place. I conclude by describing various modes of GAMI's cultural anthropophagy during the event including visual and auditory interventions that effectively queer the *festas juninas*.

Raced and classed geographies of Natal, Rio Grande do Norte

Natal is a capital city located within a region that national imaginaries produce as conservative, rural, and traditional. To most people living in and around Natal, it is a modern, urban center that offers the opportunities and challenges of a big city. However, in relation to the large cosmopolitan centers of the South and Southeast, Natal is subject to regionalist stereotyping that casts the Northeast as an underdeveloped, highly religious, and closed region (Albuquerque, 2014; Valladares, 2000). The Northeast as a geopolitical construct relies on a broad cultural/ethnic category of "*nordestino.*" This category subsumes blackness and indigeneity to construct *sertanejo*[3] cultural affinities rather than racial ones (McCann, 2004; Nicholus, 2018; Packman, 2015). This emphasis of cultural affinities over racial ones is not unlike the framework of racial democracy first advanced by Gilberto Freyre in the 1930s that elided racial difference and reframed miscegenation as a unique and exceptional characteristic of the Brazilian nation. The heartland of *sertanejo* culture (including the traditions of the *festas juninas*) is located in the Northeastern hinterlands of Pernambuco, Paraíba, Rio Grande do Norte, and Ceará states. The ethnic category "*nordestino*" subsumes race and class into a geographical, regional category which marks (poor, black, indigenous) Northeasterners as "backwards" and underdeveloped like stereotypes of the region they inhabit.

A result of unequal patterns of development, Natal is characterized by a peripheral modernity - a form of modernity assumed in spaces of supposed historical backwardness and under-development (WREC 2010). These spaces have been conditioned by their positions on the periphery of the world capitalist system (Rowe & Schelling 1991) and assume different rhythms of modernity from developed areas (Martins, 2000). As such, Natal presents a hybrid cultural geography of traditional rural culture and conservative sociocultural codes within an urban space of the Northeast. It is also an anthropophagic space in which communities of color push back against the capitalist and white supremacist structures of colonialism. Natal's partial modernity embodies contradictions of modernity in the Northeast and contextualizes the queer anthropophagic spatialities of the city. Its more conservative social environment has resulted in fewer official LGBT + venues than large cosmopolitan cities such as Rio de Janeiro or São Paulo. Many of Natal's LGBT + spaces are queer spaces: marginal, hybrid, and ephemeral in nature. Given the ways in which race, class, gender, and sexuality intersect in Northeast Brazil, the queer spaces I analyze are also nonwhite spaces.

On a smaller scale, the city is formally divided into four zones - North, South, East, and West – shaped by natural features, sociopolitical forces, and historical patterns of development. These zones delineate a specific raced and classed landscape within the city. The oldest neighborhoods are located just south of the *Potengi* river in *Zona Leste*. Also the city center, these neighborhoods were most vibrant during the World War II era when U.S. soldiers and Natal's elite would frequent the area. The upscale neighborhoods of Tirol, Lagoa Nova, Candelaria and Capim Macio are located in the central, south regions. They are easily accessible and close to large commercial centers and Natal's southern tourist districts. The most distant, peripheral areas of Natal are north and east. The city incorporated these zones during Natal's great migratory phase in the 1970s as rural migrants settled in the area (Chianca, 2007b). *Zona Norte* is the most peripheral and marginalized region as it is geographically cut off from the rest of the city by the Pontegi River. The *Igapó* Bridge was the only land route that connected *Zona Norte* to the city until 2007 when the city constructed the Newton Navarro Bridge. GAMI works within *Zona Norte*; it is home to Natal's poor migrant population and subject to many negative stereotypes that mark it as a dangerous and violent space. A space that also drives the economy of the city, most of Natal's urban workforce lives in this sector. Given the socioeconomic, racial, and cultural makeup of *Zona Norte*, it is in many ways a hybrid, queer, subaltern space within the city. The *Arraiá do GAMI*, takes place every year in a rented location in the *Redinha* neighborhood of *Zona Norte*.

The *Arraiá do GAMI*

The Affirmative Group of Independent Women (GAMI) is a nonprofit, community organization of LGBT + women founded in 2003. The group promotes sexual diversity and gender equality in Natal though sport, culture, education, and leisure. GAMI has approximately 1,427 Facebook followers[4] and identifies their target audience as "youth, women, LGBT, and the black population" (GAMI, n.d.a) (Moura, 2008). Located in the peripheral *Zona Norte*, GAMI is connected to many social justice initiatives, such as *Virando o Jogo*, a sports club project for local girls; *Elas nas Exatas*, a professionalization project for women in science; and multiple political events in solidarity with other feminist, black, working-class, and LGBT + groups in the city. The following sections explore some of the ways in which GAMI produces alternate, resistant spaces – queer anthropophagic spaces – that hybridize, absorb, and consume different sociocultural influences to reconfigure the *festas juninas* for queer subjects. Each section focuses on a different type of space including virtual, physical, visual, and auditory, spaces. However, all of these elements intertwine, overlap, and produce each other, and they all come together to configure GAMI's community space.

Social networking and virtual space

Multiple authors have argued that lesbian geographies contest traditional theories of space as territorially congruous and visible areas (Browne & Ferreira, 2015). They have identified social networking (Cattan & Clerval, 2011; Nogueira & Rago, 2005; Rothenberg, 1995; Valentine, 1995) and online social networking (Amari, 2010; Friedman, 2007; Cattan & Clerval, 2011; Saldaña, 2015) as essential mediums through which lesbians establish alternative geographies. In her article on the use of the internet by lesbians, Elizabeth Jay Friedman (2007) argues that online virtual spaces are essential to visibility, community formation, and political action for lesbians in Latin America. For groups that do not historically have their own physical spaces, these de-territorialized, digital spaces offer networks that link individuals across space and time.

GAMI relies on word of mouth and social networking to create and define ephemeral social spaces for LGBT + women. Social networking is the medium through which I came to know about the *Arraiá do GAMI*. After living in Natal for two years, I thought I knew the LGBT + spaces in the city, but I had never heard of the *Espaço Nana Banana,* and I had never been to any lesbian-specific events. Though highly valued in Natal, my white, middle-class, North-American cultural/network capital did not give me easy access to the queer community I sought. All I had to go by was a Facebook cover photo a friend sent me to locate and attend the event. I realized that there are multiple, interlocking, LGBT + communities within virtual spaces connected to Natal that had previously been invisible to me despite the fact that I had spent over two years interacting in Natal's LGBT + community. Unlike events organized at Natal's official gay club, Vogue Natal, GAMI's events are organized primarily for locals and those within GAMI's social network.

Physical, ephemeral space

While the word *arraiá* commonly refers to a party that occurs throughout Brazil in the month of June, an *arraiá* is actually a place. It is a small temporary territory that hosts the events of the *festas juninas*. These festivals, symbolically associated with the Brazilian Northeast, generally maintain heteronormative social values with themes related to reproduction, fertility, and marriage. As previously argued, the space in which GAMI mobilizes is queer and anthropophagic considering the ways in which race and class intersect with sexuality in Natal.

The physical space in which the *Arraiá do GAMI* takes place operates within "strange temporalities" (Halberstam, 2005) to meet the needs of those living in the *Redinha* neighborhood. The *Espaço Nana Banana* is a rented location with a large open-air patio, a stage for performances, a dance floor, and a kitchen area. It is a temporary, multiuse space apparent from the white plastic chairs and tables GAMI arranged under covered areas for guests during the event. It is also an accessible location to those living north of the river. A multipurpose space configured for ephemeral events, it is necessarily fluid, flexible, and adaptable. Similarly, GAMI's event is adaptable as it can move if this location is not available.

The *arraiá* also employs economic practices outside of the capitalist systems of a permanent businesses. In 2014, the group invited a local street vendor to sell typical foods including *pamonha, canjica,* and *bolo de milho* – corn-based products associated with the harvest time of the *festas juninas.* In 2015, GAMI accepted food donations in lieu of an entrance fee and only from those who could afford it. The owner of the *Espaço Nana Banana* is also part of GAMI's community. Unlike the exclusive gay bars and clubs in the southern zones of Natal, GAMI's event did not require a pricy entrance fee.

Finally, the *arraiá* supports "imaginative life schedules," (Halberstam, 2005) welcoming all ages, nontraditional families, and those who manage odd work hours. The event is held on a Sunday afternoon extending late into the night to accommodate day and night workers. In 2014, it drew close to one-hundred-and-fifty people including children, teenagers, middle-aged women, and elders who are often excluded from the bar and club scenes of typical gay life in Natal. Activities included *pescaria* (a fishing game in which players can win small prizes), group dances, a raffle, and a drag *quadrilha* dance presentation by the group *Vice-Versa.* There were several performers including a stage band, a couple of solo singers, and a few dance groups. Most strikingly different from typical LGBT+ spaces in Natal, the event drew a majority of women (cis and trans) who were seated in groups of friends. Situated in a queer time and place, the *Arraiá do GAMI* engages in cultural anthropophagy to create its community space.

Visual and auditory space

GAMI's decorations, music, and visual markers serve an important role in delineating a queer anthropophagic space that is also rural and Northeastern. A group that mobilizes around intersectional issues of race, class, gender, and sexuality, GAMI highlights black and indigenous influences that are often subsumed within the *nordestino* ethnic category. While many of the decorations recreate a traditional setting for the celebration of the *festas juninas* with checkered flags, straw, religious icons, and images of corn or bonfires, others subvert heteronormative themes such as the traditional rural wedding. For example, at the 2015 *arraiá,* GAMI challenged typical representations of marriage at this time of year by centering a statue of an interracial lesbian couple next to the main stage. In the statue, only one of the partners wears a typical white wedding dress and veil while the other's dress features earth tones and floral patterns. Instead of a veil, she wears a white bonnet, not unlike the female version of the *cangaceiro* hat, a symbol of Northeastern banditry culture. Her outfit combines masculine and feminine elements with a black blazer and corsage in her ensemble. The couple merges elements of a traditional Catholic wedding with distinctly Northeastern colors, patterns, and styles while depicting a transgressive marriage. The couple stood next to the main stage, among long strings of triangular, colored flags typical of the *festas juninas* with additional green, yellow, and blue fringe celebrating Brazil.

GAMI also anthropophagizes religious and LGBT + signs to delineate its community space. Instead of rejecting religious symbols which are often associated with homophobia in the Northeast, GAMI incorporates them. In 2014, GAMI hung a hand-drawn religious banner amidst the colorful June festival flags. The banner featured the Virgin Mary holding a dark-skinned baby Jesus. Furthermore, instead of flying a rainbow LGBT + flag, GAMI designed a different symbol for its space. Formed into a square pattern and turned on its side, GAMI's design is reminiscent of the indigenous Bolivian flag[5] that is also square and rainbow colored. Rather than hanging it from a pole, GAMI stitched their design onto a burlap bag – a symbol of agriculture, land, and humble rural communities.

Every year GAMI's members collaboratively document visual elements of the *arraiá* by taking digital photos that they later post to the groups' public Facebook page. In this way, they merge their physical and virtual spaces while giving the ephemeral a more permanent home. Not only does this strategy visibilize GAMI's work for a broader public, but it also allows individuals to participate by liking, tagging, or commenting on photos whether or not they were physically present at the event. In this way, socialization and community formation continue within the virtual space of Facebook well after the event. As Hampton argues in his article on networked sociability (Hampton, 2004), online communities support the formation of larger and more diverse social networks, community organizing, and public participation. These online strategies help form local, regional, and global solidarities.

To define the functionality of their space, GAMI also utilizes different audio strategies including specific music choices. The *arraiá* in 2014 included a *carimbó* dance performance by a group of *senhoras*. *Carimbó* is a dance and a music genre from Northern Brazil with Indigenous origins mixed with African and Iberian elements (Gabbay, 2010). In its original form, it was a sensual dance that often represented social themes such work and class inequality (Gabbay, 2010). It was performed in religious rituals, popular festivals, and social reunions. Unlike most *carimbó* performances, the group at the *Arraiá do GAMI* was made up entirely of elders. Performing the dance as part of a June festival celebration, these women delineated a queer anthropophagic audiovisual space. Uniting musical elements of Northern and Northeastern Brazilian traditions, a couple of the *carimbó* songs emphasized instruments such as the triangle and accordion characteristic of *forró*[6]. An example of cultural anthropophagy, the soundscape of the *arraiá* was heavily influenced by this syncretic musical performance which marked the space of a traditional, popular festival rather than one of a nightclub event. The group of elder women also re-appropriated a sensual dance and re-inserted themselves into LGBT + space. Organized around sexuality and sexual identities, LGBT + spaces often exclude those who are perceived as non-sexual, such as elders. In these ways, the dance performance by senior women was a queer, anthropophagic intervention in audiovisual space. The overall effect of the decorations, music, and visual markers was the merging and melding of cultural influences and traditions - from the nationalistic colors of the Brazilian flag, to Northern/Northeastern styles of music and dress, to the LGBT + rainbow next to religious symbols. GAMI brought all of these elements together within an ephemeral, subversive, and peripheral space to create a place for its community during the *festas juninas*.

Conclusion

Through queer anthropophagic sociospatial practices, GAMI creates space for LGBT + women during the *festas juninas*. Working within a peripheral community in a region scripted by raced, classed, and regionalist narratives, the group utilizes network technology to organize a queer/lesbian event during a time of religious festivals. GAMI mobilizes Brazilian practices of cultural cannibalism to configure a queer community space with multiple dimensions; one that blurs the lines between the internal and external. Consuming foreign, national, and local influences; utilizing different forma-tions of time and space; merging religious symbols with LGBT + practices; GAMI configures a queer and anthropophagic space for its community.

This article has provided a theoretical framework and overview of GAMI's interventions in the *festas*. As such, it did not delve into many of the rich details of the *arraiá* such as an analysis of the drag *quadrilha* dance performance. Furthermore, GAMI's interventions are only one example of how LGBT + communities in the Northeast complicate representations of the region as rural or "anti-modern." While traditional, rural culture of Northeastern Brazil has been coded as conservative, anti-modern and unwel-coming of alternative sexualities and gender expressions, it holds space for LGBT + identities. LGBT + individuals and communities have also made space for themselves within traditional Northeastern culture. This space may look different from that of the Global North or urban South; it might mani-fest itself in different ways, but LGBT + culture in the Northeast continues to exist, adapt, transform, and queer what it means to be traditional.

Notes

1. For work in this vein, see Costa (2013) and Mombaça (2015).
2. See "Anthropophagic dislocations or how we devour Judith Butler" (Colling & Pelúcio, 2015) (translation by author).
3. Referring to the people from the *sertão*: the dry, rural backlands of the Brazilian Northeast.
4. As of August, 2019.

5. The indigenous Bolivian flag, the *Wiphala* is square, multicolored, and made up of squares rather than stripes.
6. A genre of music and a popular dance style of the *festas juninas*.

References

Albuquerque, Jr., D. M. de. (2014). *The invention of the Brazilian Northeast*. Durham: Duke University Press.

Amari, S. (2010). Le cyberespace comme le tiers-espace des lesbiennes de «culture musulmane» dans le monde? *LES Online*, *2*(1), 9.

Andrade, O. D., & Bary, L. (1928). Cannibalist manifesto. *Latin American Literary Review*, *19*(38), 38–47.

Brown, G., Browne, K., Elmhirst, R., & Hutta, S. (2010). Sexualities in/of the Global South. *Geography Compass*, *4*(10), 1567–1579.

Browne, K. (2006). Challenging queer geographies. *Antipode*, *38*(5), 885–893.

Browne, K., & Ferreira, E. (Eds.). (2015). *Lesbian geographies: Gender, Place and Power*. Surrey, UK; Burlington, VT: Ashgate.

Cattan, N., & Clerval, A. (2011). Un droit à la ville ? Réseaux virtuels et centralités éphémères des lesbiennes à Paris [A right to the city? Virtual networks and ephemeral centralities for lesbians in Paris] (C. Hancock, Trans.). *Spatial Justice*, (3), 1–16. Retrieved from http://www.jssj.org/article/un-droit-a-la-ville-reseauxvirtuels-et-centralites-ephemeres-des-lesbiennes-a-paris/

Chianca, L. (2007a). Devoção e diversão: Expressões contemporâneas de festas e santos católicos. *Revista Anthropológicas*, *18*(2), 49–74.

Chianca, L. D. O. (2007). Quando o campo está na cidade: Migração, identidade e festa. *Sociedade e Cultura*, *10*(1), 45–59.

Cohen, C. J. (2005). Punks, bulldaggers, and welfare queens. In E. P. Johnson & M. G. Henderson (Eds.), *Black queer studies: A critical anthology* (pp. 21–51). Durham and London: Duke University Press.

Colling, L., & Pelúcio, L. (2015). Deslocamentos Antropofágicos ou de como devoramos Judith Butler. *Revista Periódicus*, *1*(3), 1–5.

Costa, C. L. (2012). Feminismo e tradução cultural: Sobre a colonialidade do gênero e a descolonização do saber. *Portuguese Cultural Studies*, (4), 41–65.

Costa, G. (2015). *A Presença Feminina na Literatura de Cordel do Rio Grande do Norte*. Natal, RN: Editora 8/Queima Bucha.

Costa, P. (2013, August 14). *Cena Queer: O corpo nu, aqui, é o corpo imigrante [Blog]*. Retrieved September 28, 2018 from http://cenaqueer.blogspot.com/2014/01/o-corpo-nua-qui-e-o-corpo-imigrante.html

England, K. V. L. (1994). Getting Personal: Reflexivity, Positionality, and Feminist Research*. *The Professional Geographer*, *46*(1), 80–89.

Faria, C., & Mollett, S. (2016). Critical feminist reflexivity and the politics of whiteness in the 'field.' Gender. *Place & Culture, 23*(1), 79–93.

Freyre, G. (1933). *Casa-grande e Senzala.* Berkeley, CA: University of California Press.

Friedman, E. J. (2007). Lesbians in (cyber)space: The politics of the internet in Latin American on- and off-line communities. *Media, Culture & Society, 29*(5), 790–811.

Gabbay, M. (2010). Representações Sobre O Carimbó: Tradição X Modernidade. In *Intercom – Sociedade Brasileira de Estudos Interdisciplinares da Comunicação,* 1–15 Rio Branco, Acre.

GAMI. (n.d). *Gami Natal—About.* Retrieved from Facebook Page website: https://www.facebook.com/pg/mariagorettigomes.goretti/about/?ref=page_internal

Green, J. (1999). *Beyond carnival: Male homosexuality in twentieth-century Brazil.* Chicago & London: University of Chicago.

Halberstam, J. (2005). *In a queer time and place: Transgender bodies, subcultural lives.* New York: New York University Press.

Hampton, K. (2004). Networked sociability online, off-line. In M. Castells (Ed.), *The network society: A cross-cultural perspective* (pp. 217–232). Cheltenham, UK; Northampton, MA: Edward Elgar Pub.

Islam, G. (2012). Can the subaltern eat? Anthropophagic culture as a Brazilian lens on post-colonial theory. *Organization, 19*(2), 159–180.

Jáuregui, C. (2012). Anthropophagy. In R. M. Irwin, M. Szurmuk (Eds.), *Dictionary of Latin American Cultural Studies* (pp. 22–28). Gainesville, FL: University Press of Florida.

Johnson, E. P., & Henderson, M. G. (Eds.). (2005). *Black queer studies: A critical anthology.* Durham and London: Duke University Press.

Kobayashi, A. (1994). Coloring the field: Gender, "Race," and the politics of fieldwork. *The Professional Geographer, 46*(1), 73–80.

Kulick, D. (1998). *Travestí: Sex, gender, and culture among Brazilian transgendered prostitutes.* Chicago, IL: University of Chicago Press.

Lugones, M. (2007). Heterosexualism and the Colonial/Modern Gender System. *Hypatia, 22*(1), 186–219.

Martins, J.S. (2000). The hesitations of the modern and the contradictions of modernity in Brazil. In V. Schelling (Ed.), *Through the kaleidoscope: The experience of modernity in Latin America* (pp. 248–274). New York: Verso.

McCann, B. (2004). *Hello, hello Brazil: Popular music in the making of modern Brazil.* Durham: Duke University Press.

Mombaça, J. (2015, January 7). Pode um cu mestiço falar?. Retrieved September 28, 2018, from https://medium.com/@jotamombaca/pode-um-cu-mestico-falare915ed9c61ee

Moura, E. D F. A. (2008). *Organização Política de Lésbicas da Cidade do Natal.* Natal, RN: Top-Gráfica.

Nash, C. J., & Bain, A. (2007). Reclaiming raunch"? Spatializing queer identities at Toronto women's bathhouse events. *Social & Cultural Geography, 8*(1), 47–62.

Neto, J. N. (2015). *Anthropophagic queer: A study on abjected bodies and Brazilian Queer Theory.* New York: Graduate Center, CUNY.

Nicholus, S. (2018). *Queering Tradition: LGBT+Cultural Productions in the Brazilian Northeast* (Dissertation). The University of Texas, Austin.

Nogueira, N., & Rago, M. (2005). *Experiência e Subjetividade. Geografia do Prazer nos espaços de sociabilidade lésbica do Rio de Janeiro dos anos 1950-1960,* 1–7. Londrina: ANPUH: Associação Nacional de História.

Oswin, N. (2008). Critical geographies and the uses of sexuality: Deconstructing queer space. *Progress in Human Geography, 32*(1), 89–103.

Packman, J. (2015). The other other Festa: June Samba and the alternative spaces of Bahia, Brazil's São João Festival and Industries. *Black Music Research Journal, 34*(2), 255–283.

Parker, R. G. (1991). *Bodies, pleasures, and passions: Sexual culture in contemporary Brazil* (2nd ed). Nashville, TN: Vanderbilt University Press.

Puar, J. (2002). A transnational feminist critique of queer tourism. *Antipode, 34*(5), 935–946.

Quijano, A. (2000). Colonialidad del poder, eurocentrismo y América Latina. In E. Lander (Ed.), *La colonialidad del saber: Eurocentrismo y ciencias sociales. Perspectivas latinoamericanas* (pp. 201–246). Buenos Aires: CLASCO.

Rothenberg, T. (1995). And she told two friends': Lesbians creating urban social Space. In *Mapping desire: Geographies of sexualities*. New York: Routledge.

Rowe, W., & Schelling, V. (1991). *Memory and modernity: Popular culture in Latin America*. New York: Verso.

Ruvalcaba, H. D. (2016). *Translating the queer: Body politics and transnational conversations* (1st ed.). London: Zed Books.

Saldaña, P. (2015). The scales and shapes of queer women's geographies: Mapping private, public and cyber spaces in Portland, OR (Master of Urban Studies). Portland State University, Portland, OR.

Slater, C. (1982). *Stories on a string: The Brazilian Literatura de Cordel*. Berkeley, CA: University of California Press.

Valentine, G. (1995). *Out and about: Geographies of lesbian landscapes*. Oxford, UK and Cambridge, MA: Blackwell Publishers.

Valladares, L. (2000). A Gênese da Favela Carioca: A produção anterior às ciências sociais. *Revista Brasileira de Ciências Sociais, 15*(44), 5–34.

WREC. (2010). *Peripheral modernism and third world aesthetics*. Coventry, UK: The University of Warwick. Retrieved March 7, 2017.

Making lesbian space at the edge of Europe: Queer spaces in Istanbul

Ozlem Atalay and Petra L. Doan

ABSTRACT
There is limited research regarding queer spaces in Turkey, and even less on lesbians because women have struggled to have an active public presence in Turkey. Accordingly, lesbian spaces are more embodied and less explicitly visible in public spaces than in the West. This study aims to make the invisible more visible by examining the space-making strategies of the lesbian community during the late 20th and early 21st century when lesbian, gay, bisexual, transgender, and queer (LGBTQ) activism reached a high point in Turkey. In particular, we examined the ways that lesbians challenged narrow conceptions of "territoriality," through their use of spaces such as bars, homes, and restaurants in one neighborhood across time, by reviewing print media archives with LGBTQ coverage and interviewing a sample of activist lesbian women who participated in the lesbian scene in Istanbul during this period. Our findings reveal that lesbians opted to live in Beyoglu due to its multicultural and welcoming character, and formed their businesses as venues to socialize as well as serve LGBTQ clientele. They also expanded the openness of gay bars in the district and opened their houses for home parties within the lesbian community. Furthermore, they used all these arenas as meeting places for lesbian activist support groups.

Introduction

The existing literature on queer spaces tends to use case studies from the Global North, but this article expands that scope, examining the evolution of lesbian spaces in cosmopolitan Istanbul, the meeting place of East and West. This project explores the everyday lives of lesbians and the ways they have constructed public and private community by analyzing the ephemeral networks of lesbian spaces beyond the material landscape (Podmore, 2001). Scholars studying the spatial dimensions of lesbian communities have argued that lesbians are less visible than gay men because women have limited access to capital, are more likely to be primary caretakers of children, and are more vulnerable to male violence (Adler & Brenner, 1992). Lesbian territorial communities are discernible as "concentrations rather than neighborhoods" (Gieseking, 2013, p. 181) in Northhampton, Massachusetts (Forsyth, 1997), the Boulevard St. Laurent area of Montreal (Podmore, 2001; 2006), the Park Slope neighborhood of Brooklyn, New York (Gieseking, 2013), and Toronto (Nash, 2013). Women use space differently than men and are drawn to cosmopolitan spaces where the mobility and chaos of the crowd inhibit the hegemonic relations of power, providing opportunities for haphazard social interaction and a transient sense of communality and desire (Podmore, 2001). Not all lesbian spaces are permanent and rigidly defined, reflecting an evolving meaning of space including temporary, semipublic spaces (Nash, 2001).

Understanding the ways lesbians utilize spaces in their search for community can shed useful light on the complex interactions between lesbian identities and spaces outside the Global North (Olasik, 2015), contesting traditional notions of urban territories as continuous and visible. Our study focuses on the space-making strategies of lesbians in Beyoglu, Istanbul in the 1990s in part because of the first author's lived experiences in that district. In addition, although the existing literature rarely discusses lesbians or lesbian spaces in Turkey, there are several references to Beyoglu in the literature on LGBTQ issues in Istanbul (Erol, 2018; Özbay & Savcı, 2018; Partog, 2012; Selek, 2001; Yenilmez, 2017; Yüzgün, 1993; Zengin, 2014, 2016). Accordingly, Beyoglu was a natural starting place for our snowball sample enabling us to reach lesbian or queer identifying people who lived in the area during the 1990s when the LGBTQ movement in Turkey became substantially more visible with the establishment of LGBTQ organizations such as Lambdaistanbul (Erol, 2011; Görkemli, 2012; Partog, 2012).

Background and context on Turkey

To understand the emergence and shaping of lesbian spaces in Turkey, it is critical to review the background and cultural values of the country. In addition the case study neighborhood of Beyoglu in Istanbul was a critical locus for the evolution of lesbian spaces as well as broader LGBTQ activism starting in 1990s.

Religion and secularism

Both religion and cultural attitudes have an important influence on the attitudes of society towards queer individuals (Çakırlar & Delice, 2012). There has always been a tension between traditional Islam and the secular vision for the modern Turkish nation espoused by Kemal Ataturk. Religion has traditionally imposed expectations on women as wives and mothers (Şahin, 2018) whose place is in the home. Furthermore, any homosexuality or nonheteronomative activity is considered "haram," a kind of sin against God by the majority of Muslims in Turkey (Muedini, 2018).

Discourses of secularism have also shaped women's place in Turkish society (Çınar, 2005; Gökarıksel, 2012; Kandiyoti, 1995), including basic rights such as divorce, inheritance, voting, and eligibility to stand for election (Çınar, 2005). While these efforts were part of "state feminism" in Turkey, they were criticized as insufficient (Gökarıksel, 2012; Gökarıksel & Secor, 2014; Şahin, 2018). For instance, according to Gökarıksel (2012), secularism regulates "not only institutional spaces but also the home and body through transformed norms of dress and conduct and of gender roles and visibilities" (p. 6). Furthermore, Islamic traditional concerns continue to shape the country's institutions and society (Yenilmez, 2017).

Crossroads of East and West; Istanbul, Beyoglu

Prior to the establishment of the Turkish Republic in 1923, Beyoglu had long been the cosmopolitan hub of the Ottoman capital (see Figure 1). In the 18th century, increasing trade between Western Europe and the Ottoman Empire triggered a socioeconomic transformation of the area. During the 19th century globalization, the economic and social environment became vibrant in Beyoglu with increasing numbers of foreign banks, embassies, consulates, office buildings, hotels, department stores, bazaars as well as a variety of leisure spaces such as bars, restaurants, movie theaters, and hammams (Turkish baths).

The multicultural nature of the district declined in the 20th century when the government imposed a strict regulatory regime aimed to "Turkify" the city (Aktar, 2009; Dökmeci & Çıracı, 1999). However, Beyoglu maintained an open door approach, welcoming migrants, including Kurds and African immigrants, who were considered "marginal communities" by the authorities (Adaman & Keyder, 2005; Maessen, 2017). Beyoglu attracted people of all classes due to its affordable housing, available commercial space, and diverse employment opportunities. These features also attracted a variety of political and human rights organizations. Beyoglu and its subdistricts of Tarlabasi and Cihangir played a similar role for the Turkish LGBTQ community to that played by San Francisco and Greenwich Village, New York through their welcome of minorities, artists, as well as gays, lesbians, and the transgender community.

Spatial context of LGBTQ activism

Although anecdotal evidence suggests gay and lesbian people existed in Turkey before and during the Ottoman empire (Delice, 2016; Murray,

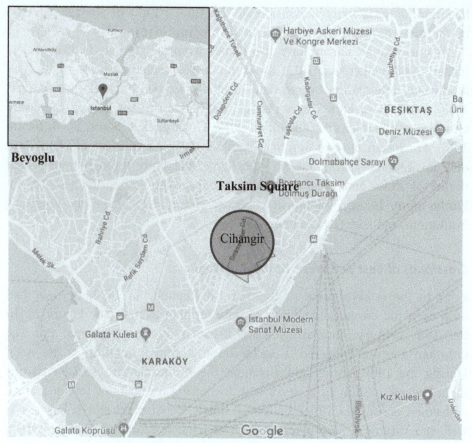

Figure 1. Map of Cihangir, Beyoglu, Istanbul (Google, n.d.) Retrieved April 13, 2019 from https://goo.gl/maps/Yqe9NdAhSTn.

2007), the more public LGBTQ movement can be traced back to the 1970s and the formation of LGBTQ support groups in Ankara and Izmir. However, these organizations were repressed by the harsh policies of the military regime that followed the 1980 coup d'etat (Tapınç, 1992), including oppressive regulations against cross-dressing in bars and clubs.

Similar to the Mattachine Society and Daughters of Bilitis in the 1950s in the United States (d'Emilio, 1983; Jagose, 1996), the LGBTQ movement in Turkey organized quietly after the coup and reemerged in the mid-1980s as part of the Radical Democratic Green Party, composed of anti-militarists, atheists, greens and feminists (Erol, 2011; Partog, 2012). In 1987 this group organized hunger strikes in Beyoglu as well as political demonstrations against police brutality, particularly towards transindividuals, and the silence of the media.

Besides organizing against the oppression of police and bias in the media, the LGBTQ community organized support groups that led to the formation of "Lambdaistanbul" through gatherings at different locations including the gay bars and restaurants that LGBTQ individuals frequented. Furthermore, these activists maintained close contact with feminist groups and human rights organizations such as Insan Haklari Dernegi (Özetle; Lambdaistanbul Ne Yaptı?, n.d.; Yıldız, 2007) and other LGBTQ groups such as "KAOS GL" from Ankara (Erol, 2011; Özetle; Lambdaistanbul Ne Yaptı?, n.d.; Partog, 2012; Yıldız, 2007).

Another lesbian group, the Sisters of Venus, was established by three women in Beyoglu (cad, 1996; Nihal, personal communication, 2018), with ties to feminist organizations such as Kadinin Insan Haklari/Yeni Cozumler Dernegi[1] (Women for Women's Human Rights/New Ways) and Mor Cati[2] (Purple Roof) and provided support and networking (cad, 1996; Nihal, personal communication, 2018).

Emergence of Turkish queer perspectives

Recently literature on LGBTQ communities in Turkey has focused on the social problems of the queer community and its interactions with hetero-sexuals, emphasizing discrimination, exclusion and oppression (Bakacak & Öktem, 2014; Biçmen & Bekiroğulları, 2014; Oksal, 2008; Yenilmez, 2017). Subsequent discussions of queer theory and different sexualities can be seen in works of both scholars and the activists in Turkey (Çakırlar & Delice, 2012; Erol, 2018; Özbay & Savcı, 2018; Savcı, 2016; Zengin, 2014, 2016).

Insightful analyses of police brutality and bias in the media (Yüzgün, 1993), surveillance and harassment of the transgender community in Cihangir (Selek, 2001), as well as the problem of "gender killings" including primarily the cis and transwomen killed by cis men (Zengin, 2014, 2016) add to the understanding of the social and political climate for lesbians as well as others during the study period. A queer lens enables consideration of queer activism and the internet (Görkemli, 2012) and rethinking gay masculinity (Özyeğin, 2012). In addition, queer theorists have challenged heteronormativity and homo/transphobic violence in the Turkish context by re-historicizing that cultural context to highlight a rich history of male dancers (kocek) and diverse representations of gender and sexuality that transcend discussions of religion and secularism (Çakırlar & Delice, 2012).

Other studies used a queer lens to analyze the discourses of LGBTQ-identified protestors (Erol, 2018), activities during Gezi Park Movement (Özbay & Savcı, 2018), and the effects of class on lesbian, gay, bisexual, and transgender (LGBT) (I) political language and political style (Savci, 2016). Finally, Güney and Selçuk (2016) asked how city planning might improve the situation of LGBTQ people in Izmir by using an inclusive city framework.

Adding lesbians to this gap in the literature

This article fills the gap in the literature on lesbians in Istanbul and argues that analyses of lesbians must consider their spatial concentration, in addition to their visibility and community activism. Some lesbians may be concentrated yet invisible due to safety concerns, whereas others may be visible yet scattered around a city due to the affordability of housing. Finally, some lesbians can be both visible and concentrated. In particular, this study examines the ways that lesbians utilize spaces that challenge narrow conceptions of "territoriality," and explores the varying meanings of spaces such as bars, homes, and restaurants.

Materials and methods

Data gathering techniques and sources

Scholars conducting research on queer spaces in the West have used a variety of data sources including voter registration files, mailing lists, locations of gay bars, membership in lesbian and gay associations, and census counts of unmarried partner couples. However, due to the lack of public data in Turkey, this study reviewed a variety of archival records and used personal connections in the field to identify individuals to be interviewed.

Participant observation, direct experience

Direct experience enables the researcher to enter more deeply into the setting under investigation, facilitating a better understanding of the social context of the area. The first author has lived in Istanbul and experienced Beyoglu as a queer person, providing close personal exposure to the lesbian scene in the district. The second author has visited Istanbul and has had numerous experiences in LGBTQ spaces in North America.

In-depth interviews

In keeping with the focus on the lesbian community, we employed "homogeneous sampling" that enables in-depth analysis of a particular subgroup (Patton, 2015, p. 283). This snowball sampling enabled us to reach key informants who lived and worked in Istanbul during the turn of the century, participated in the lesbian scene, and were involved in community activism. In total five individuals were interviewed (three identify as lesbians, one identifies as queer, and one as a straight person). Four of our interviewees spent their twenties and thirties as middle class individuals in Beyoglu, Istanbul.

Our interviewees not only lived in Beyoglu and were actively involved in the lesbian and gay scene during our target time frame, but also owned businesses that served LGBTQ clientele during the 1990s. Prior to their coming out, two of our interviewees had lived in Miami and London for a while, describing their time spent in these cities as helpful to their subsequent coming out processes. After coming back to Turkey, they chose Cihangir to settle down. One interviewee from a small town in the United Kingdom immigrated to Turkey to be with friends so that she could live freely, away from the pressures of family and life in a small British town. Another interviewee lived in Istanbul her whole life and chose to live in Beyoglu. For additional background we also interviewed a straight-identifying woman about the Turkish feminist movement in the 1980s and 1990s to understand the relationships between leftists, feminists, and lesbians.

These interviews were conducted by the first author in Turkish (except for one in English with the British person referred to as Sally) using Skype since both authors live in the United States. Each interview was recorded, lasting over an hour and was translated by the first author. To ensure confidentiality, we do not use the real names of interviewees in our discussion.

Archival records

We analyzed the archives of two LGBTQ organizations in Turkey: Lambdaistanbul and KAOS GL as well as newspaper coverage of LGBTQ activism. We used the websites and digital publications of KAOS GL and Lambdaistanbul, which were established during the 1990s in Ankara and Istanbul. Unfortunately, issues of the magazine *Express* that provided space for LGBTQ voices during the 1990s (Yıldız, 2007; Nihal, personal communication, 2018), were not accessible since they are not available online.

Data analysis-coding process

We coded our data using NVivo software with a deductive coding process based on the conceptualization stage of our study. We took care to avoid imposing our own meanings over those of the participants. Throughout the study, using the "creative process" of "immersion, incubation, insight, and interpretation" (Rossman & Rallis, 2012, p. 274), we developed indigenous categories as they were expressed by the participants themselves. Finally, we developed themes drawing on categories that emerged from our in-depth interviews and analysis of archival records as well as the available literature and our own experience about the topic.

Findings

Our questions revolved around the participants' perceptions of lesbian spaces to see how they socialized and lived. We asked about bars, restaurants, cafés, parks, homes and any places that were important to them during the 1990s. We also asked about the relation between wider LGBTQ activism and the lesbian community, and whether this influenced their ability to navigate the city. In addition, we wanted participants to talk about their coming out processes and life stories.

Journey to home

First, our interviewees mentioned their search for a welcoming place to settle down. It was interesting to see different country choices among our participants. While one of them moved to London, saying that for the first time in her life she was exposed to a lesbian scene, another described her migration from a small town in the United Kingdom to Turkey as emancipation.

> I knew people here in Turkey. The main reason I moved here was to reveal my sexual orientation freely and live accordingly. I was living in a small town in England so there was no way I could live there as a lesbian individual. I wouldn't even be able to explain my feelings. (From interview with Sally)

Kazyak's (2012) analysis of the relationship between place, gender and sexuality reveals that "acceptance of gays and lesbians in small towns is gendered" (p. 826) and shows how meanings of gender presentations change by geographical context. We can read Sally's journey from a British small town to a big Turkish city within this framework. As a feminine lesbian woman, Sally prefers urban life in Turkey to her prior small town life in part because her previous home town undermined the anti-discrimination laws in the United Kingdom that today are inclusive of sexual orientation and gender identity (Browne & Bakshi, 2016), Sally never thought of returning to the United Kingdom because of expected discrimination from her birth family and neighbors.

Turkish family structure is typically traditional, patriarchal and authoritarian where the father of the family is central and masculinity is celebrated (Kandiyoti, 1995). While this structure may vary with the class and ethnicity of families, a lesbian from a traditional family is a daughter and a sister first whose behavior must uphold the honor of the family. Her emancipation from the family home is possible only through marriage to a man. Thus, for a lesbian to leave her family home without a marriage is very difficult unless her family is not conservative. However, increasing participation in education, and the labor market, as well as the effects of globalization, are changing conditions in urban areas to allow more women to leave conservative family homes and create their own more welcoming homes.

Leaving home is not sufficient, since one also needs to find a neighborhood that welcomes single women and same-sex partners. Mills (2007) describes a traditional Turkish neighborhood (mahalle) in Istanbul where everybody knows everyone through the practice of "neighboring" (komsuluk) that reinforces traditional gender roles for women as wives and mothers. In such a neighborhood the intimate bonds among neighbors facilitate high levels of surveillance, making life difficult for lesbians who disrupt expected gender behaviors. Thus, it is no surprise that the traces of lesbian spaces can be found in Beyoglu, Istanbul that provided neighborhood opportunity where lesbians had spaces to breathe.

> "Cihangir, Beyoglu was the place! I did not even think about any other alternatives" (From interview with Nihal).

> Our associations were there. Beyoglu did not belong to anybody, any group or any nation. Nobody, no nation, not even Turks could dominate the area. It had so many immigrants, ethnic groups, a mix of people from different backgrounds. Not having an identity was a way of having identity for Beyoglu. So, it was an area for us where we as LGBTQs, queers, lubunyas,[3] lesbians, gays, trans could breathe relatively comfortably compared to the other places. This is it. (From interview with Ayse)

As stated above by Ayse, the character of this multiethnic and multicultural district attracted many lesbians to the area. One of our informants, Nihal, states that "I don't know, it was not scary for me (referring to the conflicts between transindividuals and polices), I just loved living there." After spending two years in London, Nihal returned to Turkey due to visa issues, describing her experience as a catalyst in her coming out process:

> When I came back from London to Turkey in 1990, with my white t-shirt, torn jeans, DM boots, motor biker black jacket, I was exactly … A lesbian! My short hair … It was the time of Sinéad O'Connor … My hair, style was like hers. Thus, being in London, experiencing it helped me crossing a threshold. (Interview with Nihal)

As a person who sees herself as "a total lesbian," Nihal chose to locate in Cihangir, Beyoglu without considering any other alternatives, because she knew "it was the place." Another informant, Emel, explained her reasons for choosing Cihangir because she met her first long-term girlfriend at a home party there and decided to live with her in that neighborhood surrounded by the safety of many friends. Emel describes this as "a really good decision for us before Cihangir boomed and was discovered by artists, actors, authors and all and became a really hip place. During that time, it was not that expensive."

The limited literature on lesbian geographies has conceptualized the home as a private safe haven, a place where lesbians can escape the heteronormative gaze of society and live their sexual identity (Johnston & Valentine, 1995; Valentine, 1993). For instance, Elwood (2000) found that lesbian homes in Minneapolis, Minnesota were critical as spaces of identity formation, enabling lesbians to contest dominant cultural norms and create their own sanctuaries. However, sometimes even these homes could not protect lesbians from the harassment and hostility of property owners and neighbors. This kind of surveillance over the private spaces of homes is not surprising when home is often considered synonymous with the ideal heterosexual 'family' (Johnston & Valentine, 1995). We saw similar concerns expressed by our interviewees:

> There were so many parties and socializing at homes, we did not have any problems while socializing inside the homes. But, while looking for a home and negotiating with real estate agencies or homeowners, you would not want, for sure, your sexual orientation to be known by them. I would not reveal my sexual orientation to be known by my neighbor, my grocery store ... So, we were not living openly as lesbian individuals. I never kissed on the street, never held the hand of my girlfriend. I was constantly keeping myself under my own surveillance and control. (From interview with Emel)

In spite of the self-surveillance and social control in the neighborhood, Emel explains how moving into a home with her girlfriend contributed to her journey:

> Then, after meeting my girlfriend with whom I would live my first long-term relationship, we moved together to a house in Cihangir, Beyoglu. And, then finally I could be proud of who I am as a lesbian.

Another frequently-mentioned feature was the location of Cihangir near the city center, making it accessible. Beyoglu was the center of nightlife and Cihangir provided affordable and accessible housing stock for transas well as gay and lesbian individuals. Due to its gay and lesbian population, newcomers thought they could feel safe in the district. Basically, Cihangir Beyoglu was the neighborhood for them to make a home and settle down.

These interviews make clear that private homes help stabilize identities. Twenty-first century Western queer theory suggests that gender fluidity can disrupt many things, but in a society where non-normative identities are unwelcome and oppressed, a lesbian may feel the need to declare her sexual orientation as the most rebellious and comforting thing. And homes play an important role in this.

Daily metamorphosis of places

> When I opened the restaurant, it was only a small place at the entry level of a building. At first, it was just for take-out. However, day by day it turned into a restaurant with tables where you could also eat in place. Then, music was added, and then drinks. Then, during nights it turned into a bar-like scene with doors opened to only those who knew it. However, people could bring their friends even though we did not know them personally. So many things have been lived, so many loves, so many parties ... People could come and sit for hours. It was a welcoming place where LGBTQ clientele felt comfortable. (From interview with Emel)

Valentine argues that "lesbians both contest and negotiate heterosexual norms by using time-space strategies" (Valentine, 1993, p. 9). Several of our interviewees started businesses that were open to the public during the day, but at night became venues restricted to lesbians and their friends.

In addition to these lesbian-owned places, during the 1990s several gay bars also welcomed lesbians in Beyoglu. The names of three particular gay-owned bars, Club 14, Club 20 and Prive, repeatedly came up during the interviews.

> In these gay bars, we were welcomed in addition to gay clientele. We could survive in these bars because there were gays and the owner of the bars was also a gay guy. He opened these bars for gay men but we also created our spaces in these places, then there were also bisexuals, transgenders…Then, even straight women who wondered what was going on inside would come and check out the bar. (From interview with Sally)

> We were treated like VIPs after a while. We were treated really well, I cannot really complain about these years and bars…We really had good times…Suddenly, during the night, you were just realizing that there were so many women inside the bar, coming together, including straights who were just curious and lesbians, for sure… (From interview with Nihal)

The metamorphoses of both restaurants and gay bars created safe havens for the LGBTQ community. Lesbian-owned restaurants turned into lesbian bars at night and other gay-owned bars primarily oriented to gay men also welcomed lesbian women to gather. In addition to the physical changes in locations, another kind of personal metamorphosis was also happening:

> After forming my own business, I felt like I did not have to explain my private life to anybody. But, I also did not have anything to hide anymore. While I was hiding it even from myself before…But, then [referring to time after forming her business], if anything happened I was OK. In the end, I did not have to be scared of being kicked out from my job, or anything … (From interview with Nihal)

These quotes also highlight the importance for lesbians of forming their own business to be free from any possible employment discrimination. One of the most crucial problems regarding the discrimination and violation of human rights based on sexual orientation and gender identity is that there is no anti-discrimination legislation in Turkey. An individual who commits murder might plead unjust provocation to reduce their sentence (Yenilmez, 2017). In general, sociopolitical attitudes towards lesbians in Turkey suggest that "[i]f a person is fired because of their sexual orientation, the employers can claim that they are exercising their right to fire their worker because she leads an immoral life" (Yenilmez, 2017, p. 292).

One report indicates that there were 11 hate crime-based deaths, eight incidences of hate-based violence, three violations of housing rights of transgendered individuals, and two (known) acts of workplace discrimination that were carried to the court in 2012 (SPoD, 2013). Several interviewees talked about forming their own businesses as a strategy to eliminate any possibility of facing workplace discrimination because of their sexual orientations. Their lesbian and queer identities shaped their decisions about where to live and how to work. Furthermore, these decisions had profound effects on the lives of other queer people, opening new jobs for LGBTQ individuals and welcoming LGBTQ clientele. Moreover, these business places were also used as safe havens for the meetings of LGBTQ organizations.

> Business owners were really important. You could not imagine a straight owned or managed place, bar or club would organize LGBTQ nights in Istanbul, in Turkey... Still, you cannot imagine it even today. So, for a venue to be gay, it needed an owner who was gay. (From interview with Nihal)

Spaces of activism

In addition to socializing, homes were also a locus for activism. LGBTQ individuals spent a majority of their time in safe homes and bars because of social pressures not only to socialize but also to strengthen their activism (Erol, 2018; Partog, 2012). For instance, the first lesbian organization "The Sisters of Venus" was established in 1995 in one of their members' home. Nihal, one of the co-owners of a restaurant in Cihangir, Beyoglu, explains this as: "we were feeling comfortable at home, we were there to discuss, for brainstorming, but also our homes could provide arenas for us to have intimate moments, such as holding hands." Nihal went on to describe the role of the restaurant as a safe haven for the first meetings of this newly-formed lesbian organization:

> We formed the Sisters of Venus, it is the first in Turkey, the first lesbian organization. There was KAOS GL and Lambdaistanbul but... We were trying to do something through darkness without so much information. We started as three people. Here, also the place mattered a lot for us... How would we communicate, where would we have our meetings? These all mattered... One of these meeting places for us was our restaurant. (From interview with Nihal)

The 1990s were when many feminists joined organizations with various agendas such as developing policies against domestic violence, sexual harassment, and virginity examinations of public employees. Sisters of Venus developed relations and organized activities with other human rights groups such as Women for Women Rights Organization and Purple Roof (cad, 1996; Yıldız, 2007). Nihal explains these connections as:

> Pinar Ilkkaracan, the founder of the Women for Women Rights Organization was a person whom I knew from our high school years. She supported us a lot. She taught

us how to organize. And then, Purple Roof … Everybody was somehow connected to each other at these organizations.

Discussion

This study has documented some of the ways that Beyoglu formed a focal point for the lesbian community to live, work, socialize, and become activists. Although the neighborhood witnessed brutal police repression towards LGBTQ individuals from time to time, it was still a place where lesbians could breathe freely. Although an outsider might not perceive visible concentrations of lesbians, our study illustrates their intense existence in Beyoglu. First, they chose Beyoglu due to its multicultural and welcoming character, then they formed their businesses as venues where they could not only socialize, but also serve LGBTQ clientele and create work opportunities. They not only transformed their own businesses, but also expanded the openness of gay bars in the district. They opened their houses for home parties where they met their partners and developed lasting friendships. Furthermore, they used all these arenas as meeting places for lesbian activism and support groups.

Although the evidence we have gathered does not firmly establish a new form of territoriality, we concur with Gieseking's (2013) findings that "it is not lesbians and queer women who need to change their practices or understandings of their space to 'claim' it, but that definition of neighborhoods must be queered to account for these women's experiences" (p. 195). Our research reveals that within neighborhoods there can be variable meanings and uses of spaces across time for places like bars, homes, and restaurants. Furthermore, we gained insights into the relation between LGBTQ activism and the lesbian community, as well as documented the ways that this connection enhanced lesbians' ability to navigate in the city.

For lesbians, carving out their spaces was not only a means of creating neighborhoods and working environments, but it also enabled them to come to terms with themselves as queer women. Bars or restaurants that welcomed lesbians were not only places to escape the repression of society, but they were sites where intimate relations developed among the clientele and the business owners who recognized the economic and social value of LGBTQ patrons.

For most of this period lesbian visibility was limited; the community avoided pervasive hate crimes and harassment as long as they managed gender performativity and did not reveal their sexual orientation. However, when lesbians organized for the first time as the Sisters of Venus they experienced the difficulties of publicly coming together, even though they had the opportunity to meet either under the roof of feminist organizations such as Purple Roof, or in the organization's members' homes.

Although this article has focused on Beyoglu, Istanbul, this does not mean lesbian spaces do not exist in the other parts of Istanbul or Turkey. However, Beyoglu remains a recognized place among the LGBTQ community across Turkey and continues to exert a gravitational pull on LGBTQ people on far-flung residents (Doan, 2019). Part of the attraction of places like Beyoglu is tied to the careful place making and community building practices of lesbians in Beyoglu in the 1990s.

We recognize that our small sample limits the generalizability of our findings. However, in our study we particularly analyzed the space making strategies of lesbians in 1990s in Beyoglu, Istanbul, although the area was equally important for other LGBTQ persons. In addition, the LGBTQ movement gained much broader visibility and recognition through the 21st century. Today, within the current pro-Islamist, authoritarian and conservative political atmosphere, let alone discussions of rights and anti-discrimination laws, Pride Parades have been banned since 2015 after they reached record attendance numbers in 2013 and 2014 following the Gezi Movement that stands as the largest protest movement in Turkey against the ongoing authoritarian and conservative-neo-liberal practices of the government. Future research should explore later time periods of queer spaces in "New Turkey" through gentrification and urban planning implementations under the governance of the AKP.

Notes

1. Transnational organization that worked to ensure sexual and bodily rights of women.
2. "Mor Cati was established in 1990 by a group of women who organized the campaign against domestic violence in 1987. It was the first autonomous feminist consultation center and shelter that provided services to women survivors of domestic violence" (Marshall, 2013, p. 46)
3. Lubunya means feminine man or trans female in Turkish.

Acknowledgments

We would like to thank the *Journal of Lesbian Studies* anonymous reviewers for their critical suggestions and constructive feedback. We are also grateful to the special issue editor Dr. Emily Kazyak for her patience and encouragement. We also thank our five participants for sharing their stories.

References

Adaman, F., & Keyder, C. (2005). *Poverty and social exclusion in the slum areas of large cities in Turkey*. Report for the European Commission, Employment, Social Affairs and Equal Opportunities.

Adler, S., & Brenner, J. (1992). Gender and space: Lesbians and gay men in the city. *International Journal of Urban and Regional Research*, 1(24), 24–34. Retrieved from https://login.proxy.lib.fsu.edu/login?url=http://search.ebscohost.com/login.aspx?direct=true&db=edsgao&AN=edsgcl.12781939&site=eds-live

Aktar, A. (2009). "Turkification" policies in the early republican era. In C. Duft (Ed.), *Turkish literature and cultural memory* (pp. 29–62). Wiesbaden: Harrassowitz.

Bakacak, A. G., & Öktem, P. (2014). Homosexuality in Turkey: Strategies for managing heterosexism. *Journal of Homosexuality*, 61(6), 817–846.

Biçmen, Z., & Bekiroğulları, Z. (2014). Social problems of LGBT people in Turkey. *Procedia - Social and Behavioral Sciences*, 113, 224–233.

Browne, K., & Bakshi, L. (2016). *Ordinary in Brighton? LGBT, activisms and the city*. Abingdon, UK: Routledge.

cad. (1996). Turkey: Feminists, lesbians organize. *Off Our Backs*, 2(26), 7.

Çakırlar, C., & Delice, S. (Eds.). (2012). *Cinsellik muamması: Türkiye'de queer kültür ve muhalefet* [The sexuality conundrum: Queer culture and dissidence in Turkey]. Istanbul: Metis Yayinlari.

Çınar, A. (2005). *Modernity, Islam, and secularism in Turkey: Bodies, places, and time* (Vol. 14). Minneapolis, MN: University of Minnesota Press.

Delice, S. (2016). The Janissaries and their bedfellows: Masculinity and male friendship in eighteenth-century Ottoman Istanbul. In G. Özyeğin (Ed.), *Gender and sexuality in Muslim cultures* (pp. 131–152). Farnham, Surrey: Routledge

d'Emilio, J. (1983). *Sexual politics, sexual communities: The Making of a homosexual minority in the United States*. Chicago: University of Chicago Press.

Doan, P. L. (2019). Cultural archipelagos or planetary systems. *City and Community*, 18(1), 30–36. doi: 10.1111/cico.12380

Dökmeci, V., & Çıracı, H. (1999). From westernization to globalization: An old district of Istanbul. *Planning History*, 21(3), 13–22.

Elwood, S. (2000). Lesbian living spaces. *Journal of Lesbian Studies*, 4(1), 11–27.

Erol, A. (2011). Eşcinsel kurtuluş hareketinin Türkiye seyri [The course of LGBT movement in Turkey]. In S. Ozturk (Ed.), *Cinsel yonelimler ve queer kuram* [Sexual orientations and queer theory] (pp. 65–66). Cogito: Yapı Kredi Yayınları.

Erol, A. E. (2018). Queer contestation of neoliberal and heteronormative moral geographies during# occupygezi. *Sexualities*, 21(3), 428–445.

Forsyth, A. (1997). Out' in the Valley. *International Journal of Urban and Regional Research, 21*(1), 38–62.

Gieseking, J. J. (2013). Queering the meaning of 'neighborhood': Reinterpreting the lesbian-queer experience of Park Slope, Brooklyn, 1983–2008. In Y. Taylor, & M. Addison (Eds.), *Queer presences and absences* (pp. 178–200). Basingstoke, UK: Palgrave MacMillan.

Gökarıksel, B. (2012). The intimate politics of secularism and the headscarf: The mall, the neighborhood, and the public square in Istanbul. *Gender, Place & Culture, 19*(1), 1–20.

Gökarıksel, B., & Secor, A. (2014). The veil, desire, and the gaze: Turning the inside out. *Signs: Journal of Women in Culture and Society, 40*(1), 177–200.

Görkemli, S. (2012). Coming out of the internet" lesbian and gay activism and the internet as a "digital closet" in Turkey. *Journal of Middle East Women's Studies, 8*(3), 63–88.

Güney, M. E., & Selçuk, I. A. (2016). LGBTTs of Turkey between the east and the west–the city and the world through their eyes in the case of Izmir. *Gender, Place & Culture, 23*(10), 1392–1403.

Jagose, A. (1996). *Queer theory: An introduction.* New York: New York University Press.

Johnston, L., & Valentine, G. (1995). Wherever I lay my girlfriend, that's my home: The performance and surveillance of lesbian identities in domestic environments. In Bell, D. & Valentine, G. (Eds.), *Mapping desire: Geographies of sexuality* (pp 88–103). London: Routledge.

Kandiyoti, D. (1995). Ataerkil oruntuler: Turk toplumunda erkek egemenliginin cozumlen-mesine yonelik notlar [Patriarchal patterns: Notes about the solution of man hegemony in Turkish society]. In Tekeli, S. (Ed.) *1980'ler Turkiyesi'nde kadin bakis acisindan kadin-lar* [Women from the perspective of women in 1980s' Turkey] (pp. 367–382). Istanbul: Iletisim Publishing.

Kazyak, E. (2012). Midwest or lesbian? Gender, rurality, and sexuality. *Gender & Society, 26*(6), 825–848.

Maessen, E. (2017). Reading landscape in Beyoglu and Tarlabasi: Engineering a 'brand new' cosmopolitan space, 1980-2013. *International Journal for History, Culture and Modernity, 5*(1), 47.

Marshall, G. A. (2013). *Shaping gender policy in Turkey: Grassroots women activists, the European Union, and the Turkish State.* Albany, NY: Suny Press.

Mills, A. (2007). Gender and mahalle (neighborhood) space in Istanbul. *Gender, Place and Culture, 14*(3), 335–354.

Muedini, F. (2018). *LGBTI rights in Turkey: Sexuality and the state in the Middle East.* Cambridge, UK: Cambridge University Press.

Murray, S. O. (2007). Homosexuality in the Ottoman Empire. *Historical Reflections, 33*(1), 101–116.

Nash, C. J. (2001). Siting lesbians: Sexuality, space and social organization. In Goldie, T. (Ed.), *In a queer country: Gay and lesbian studies in the Canadian context* (pp. 235–256). Vancouver: Arsenal Press.

Nash, C. J. (2013). Queering neighbourhoods: Politics and practice in Toronto. *Acme: International E-Journal for Critical Geographies, 12*(2), 193–213.

Oksal, A. (2008). Turkish family members' attitudes toward lesbians and gay men. *Sex Roles, 58*(7-8), 514–525.

Olasik, M. (2015). Location, location: Lesbian performativities that matter, or not. In K. Browne & E. Ferreira (Eds.), *Lesbian geographies: Gender, place and power* (pp. 201–217). Farnham, Surrey: Ashgate Publishing Limited.

Özbay, C., & Savcı, E. (2018). Queering commons in Turkey. *GLQ: A Journal of Lesbian and Gay Studies, 24*(4), 516–521.

Özetle; Lambdaistanbul Ne Yaptı?. (n.d.). Retrieved March 13, 2019, from http://www.lambdaistanbul.org/s/hakkinda/ozetle-lambdaistanbul-ne-yapti/

Özyeğin, G. (2012). Reading the closet through connectivity. *Social Identities, 18*(2), 201–222.

Partog, E. (2012). Queer teorisi bağlamında Türkiye LGBTT mücadelesinin siyasi çizgisi. [The politics of Turkey's LGBTT struggle in the context of queer theory]. In C. Çakırlar, S. Delice (Eds.), *Cinsellik muamması: Türkiye'de queer kültür ve muhalefet* [The sexuality conundrum: Queer culture and dissidence in Turkey] (pp. 162–184). Istanbul: Metis Yayinlari.

Patton, M. Q. (2015). *Qualitative research & evaluation methods: Integrating theory and practice.* Thousand Oaks, California: SAGE Publications, Inc. Retrieved from https://login.proxy.lib.fsu.edu/login?url=http://search.ebscohost.com/login.aspx?direct=true&db=cat05720a&AN=fsu.033001810&site=eds-live

Podmore, J. (2001). Lesbians in the crowd: Gender, sexuality, and visibility along Montreal's Boulevard St. -Laurent. *Gender, Place, and Culture, 24*, 191–217.

Podmore, J. (2006). Gone "underground"? Lesbian visibility and the consolidation of queer space in Montreal. *Social & Cultural Geography, 7*(4), 595–625.

Rossman, G. B., & Rallis, S. F. (2012). *Learning in the field: An introduction to qualitative research* (3rd ed.). Thousand Oaks, CA: Sage.

Şahin, O. (2018). From home to city: Gender segregation, homosociality and publicness in Istanbul. *Gender, Place & Culture, 25*(5), 743–757.

Savcı, E. (2016). Who speaks the language of queer politics? Western knowledge, politico-cultural capital and belonging among urban queers in Turkey. *Sexualities, 19*(3), 369–387.

Selek, P. (2001). *Maskeler süvariler gacılar: Ülker Sokak: Bir alt kültürün dışlanma mekanı.* Ankara, Turkey: Ayizi Kitap.

Social Policies, Gender Identity, and Sexual Orientation Studies Association (SPoD). (2013). 2012 Cinsel yönelim ve cinsiyet kimliği temelli insan hakları ihlalleri izleme raporu. Istanbul. Retrieved from http://www.spod.org.tr/SourceFiles/pdf-2018112216376.pdf.

Tapınç, H. (1992). Masculinity, femininity, and Turkish male homosexuality. In K. Plummer (Ed.), *Modern homosexualities: Fragments of lesbian and gay experiences* (pp.39–49). London: Routledge.

Valentine, G. (1993). (Hetero)sexing space: lesbian perceptions and experiences of everyday spaces. *Environment and Planning D: Society and Space, 11*(4), 395–413.

Yenilmez, M. I. (2017). Socio-political attitude towards lesbians in Turkey. *Sexuality & Culture, 21*(1), 287–299.

Yıldız, D. (2007). Turkiye tarihinde escinselliğin izinde escinsellik hareketinin tarihinden satir baslari-2:90'lar. *Kaos Gl, 93*, 46–49. Retrieved from http://kaosgldergi.com/dosya-sayfa.php?id=2208

Yüzgün, A. (1993). Homosexuality and police terror in Turkey. *Journal of Homosexuality, 24*(3–4), 159–170.

Zengin, A. (2014). Trans-Beyoğlu: Kentsel dönüşüm, sehir hakkı ve trans kadınlar. [Trans-Beyoglu: Urban transformation, right to the city and trans women]. In A.B. Candan, and C. Özbay (Eds.), *Yeni Istanbul calismalari: Sınırlar, mücadeleler, acilimlar.* Istanbul: Metis Yayinlari.

Zengin, A. (2016). Mortal life of trans/feminism: Notes on "gender killings" in Turkey. *Tsq: Transgender Studies Quarterly, 3*(1–2), 266–271.

Balancing safety and visibility: Lesbian community building strategies in South Korea

Chelle Jones (iD)

ABSTRACT

Heteronormative and gender hierarchical organization of economic, legal, and family life intersect to marginalize the lesbian community in South Korea. Lesbian, gay, bisexual, transgender, and queer (LGBTQ) and women's rights movements achieved some gains after democratic transition in the 1990s, but anti-LGBTQ activists target lesbians with harassment and violence. How do lesbians build networks and safe space under these conditions? How do they balance competing needs for visibility and safety? Drawing on 16 months of participant observation and ethnographic interviews, I analyze the relationship between lesbian community growth and safety practices. My intersectional approach examines the heterosexist context in which lesbian social spaces are maintained, and relations of power among LGBTQ, feminist, and anti-LGBTQ groups. Under threat of intersectional violence, lesbian social entrepreneurs withhold information, screen members and rely on spatial tactics to hide in plain sight, prioritizing safety over visibility. Finally, I discuss how some community members marginalized by these safety practices gain access to lesbian spaces.

Introduction

As a lesbian rights movement formed in South Korea in the early 1990s, it lacked alliances with either women's or gay men's rights organizations. I discuss how the lesbian movement negotiated homophobic and misogynist violence as they built women-only safe spaces. I analyze spatial tactics and strategies local lesbian social entrepreneurs deploy as they balance competing needs for safety and visibility and discuss the exclusions such strategies produce.

Women's and LGBTQ rights movements emerged after a widespread democracy movement ended military dictatorship in the late 1980s. But heteronormative legal, economic, and family dynamics constituting local gender relations continued to marginalize lesbians and obstruct alliances.

Rising anti-LGBTQ evangelical Christian activism (Kim, 2016; Yi, Jung, & Phillips, 2017) targets lesbians with harassment, involuntary "outing" and physical violence. Despite these challenges, local organizers have established an impressive array of venues and social networks that continue to expand. How do lesbians build networks and establish safe space under these conditions?

This article engages literature on LGBTQ community-building and safety strategies by considering how a new lesbian community in the 1990s established despite a patriarchal, gender segregated, and heteronormative social context. I use an intersectional approach to argue that the heterosexist context and relations of power among LGBTQ, feminist, and anti-LGBTQ groups influence lesbian social entrepreneurs' strategic prioritization of safety over visibility. I draw on participant observation and ethnographic interview data to explain strategies, such as: withholding information, hiding venues in plain sight, screening patrons by gender marker, and maintaining safe spaces. I discuss the consequences of these safety strategies, which may make the community challenging to access.

Review of literature

"Coming out" is a complex decision with different levels of risk for LGBTQ people who face discrimination compounded by intersecting gender-, class- or race-based oppressions (Collins & Bilge, 2016; Meyer, 2015; Valentine, 2007). Recent research suggests that because high visibility LGBTQ spaces can become targets for violence, they may deter participants who prefer lower profile venues (Croff, Hubach, Currin, & Frederick, 2017; Hanhardt, 2013; Hartal, 2016). Yet, visibility has become central to Western LGBTQ politics (Fraser, 1999; Ghaziani, Taylor, & Stone, 2016).

Visibility politics and "coming out" discourse shape global LGBTQ politics by normalizing high visibility strategies, and often designate the East as backwards (Manalansan, 1995). Important contributions push back against this narrative by demonstrating how local LGBTQ communities in India, Singapore, and Myanmar successfully build community without emphasizing visibility politics (Chua, 2016; Dave, 2010; Tang, 2012). Unfortunately, lesbian studies may overlook successful community building alternatives to visibility politics precisely because their outcomes are carefully guarded insider knowledge.

The external pressure of homophobic and misogynist violence can compel lesbian communities to design low visibility safety strategies that produce complex, and perhaps unintended, marginalization and from lesbian spaces. The existing literature on anti-LGBTQ violence has not paid enough attention to how safety strategies can themselves produce exclusions within the community. An intersectional analysis of lesbian community safety practices can reveal how, in the pursuit of safety, specific identities can be normalized for membership in LGBTQ space, reflecting local race, gender, and class dynamics.

Background: Gender and LGBTQ rights in Korea

Korean lesbian organizers established their community while navigating the democratic transition from decades of military dictatorship. As Korean democratization gave rise to social movements, lesbian community leaders struggled against their marginalization by potential allies, in addition to facing familist social pressure, political homophobia, and social discrimination.

Korean society has long emphasized heteronormative marriage, while not recognizing same-sex unions. Although homosexuality and transgender identities are not criminalized in Korea, LGBTQ rights protections are lacking. There are no protections from employment, housing, educational, or healthcare discrimination. Marriage strategically mobilizes families in the pursuit of national economic growth (Kendall, 1996; Nelson, 2000). LGBTQ Koreans face intense social, legal, economic, and cultural pressure to marry heterosexually and reproduce their family line (Cho, 2009; Kim & Hahn, 2006; Kimmel & Yi, 2004; Moon, 2008). For many LGBTQ Koreans, severing family bonds is a pressing fear (Cho, 2009; Kim & Hahn, 2006).

Local homophobia is based primarily on one's responsibility to reproduce this family-nation system, rather than on religious or biological arguments (Na, Han, & Koo, 2014). However, anti-LGBTQ Christian activists organized a strong local movement, and joined transnational campaigns against LGBTQ rights (Yi et al., 2017). Anti-LGBTQ activists occupy the space surrounding LGBTQ rights organizations to violently disrupt their activities (Korean Society of Law and Policy on Sexual Orientation and Gender Identity (KSLPSOGI), 2017) and target individuals with violence, harassment, and involuntary "outing" (Kim, 2016; Yi et al., 2017). Consequently, the need for safety shapes LGBTQ community strategies.

A lack of allies affected early lesbian community building strategies. The local women's rights movement emerged in the 1980s, fighting against gender roles that limit women's autonomy and economic security (Chang & Song, 2010; Kim & Kim, 2014). Campaigns against sexual harassment, sex crimes, and domestic violence emerged (Moon, 2002). Activists achieved reform of the Korean family registration system in 2008, making it possible for a woman to be designated as head of the family (Yang, 2013). Although these campaigns were also important to lesbians, major women's rights movement organizations refused to work with lesbian activists until the mid-2000s (Park-Kim, Lee-Kim, & Kwon-Lee, 2007).

Furthermore, divisive gender relations emerged within the LGBTQ community and a once unified organization splintered by the end of 1993. Lesbian activists formed a separate organization in 1994, citing gay male activists' emphasis on "coming out" publicly, disagreement over the allocation of funds, and gay male activists' disregard of gendered sexual violence against lesbians (Lee, 1999). Although lesbian and gay organizations collaboratively hosted the first pride parade in 1999 (Han, 2018), lesbian activists worked alone for much of the 1990s and 2000s. At first, lesbians had very few physical spaces where gatherings were possible, especially outside Seoul and outside college campuses (Kwon Kim & Cho, 2011). A national economic crisis in 1997 made it harder to establish lesbian-only spaces, but a few bars and a nightclub formed by the end of the decade. The number of lesbian venues slowly grew, then spread rapidly after prominent early lesbian business owners retired in 2015.

Data and methods

I combine ethnography with 86 semi-structured interviews of lesbian and LGBTQ community members in Korea. I am a white U.S. citizen, identify as a member of the LGBTQ community, speak Korean at the advanced intermediate conversational level, lived in Korea for 8 years, and my home institution is in the United States, so respondents seemed confident that I would keep their identities anonymous. I was able to access outsiders to the local lesbian community, such as foreign residents. Key gatekeepers in Korea's LGBTQ communities interacted with me before I began researching the community and later vouched for me as I frequented LGBTQ venues over 16 months from mid-2017 through 2018. I resided in Seoul and took monthly trips to visit Busan, Daegu, Daejeon, Gwangju and Jeju. I observed public events and informal social gatherings; volunteered at festivals; visited organization headquarters; and regularly patronized several LGBTQ bars, cafés, and nightclubs. I organized group tours of lesbian venues that helped me learn about vetting and safety policies. For ethical reasons, I participated in vetting strategies and maintained the integrity of safety practices by leaving out some details. I have changed the names of all interviewees, venues, and organizations.

Empirical analysis

In the sections that follow, I discuss lesbian exclusion from LGBTQ spaces and identify lesbian venue safety strategies. Lesbian entrepreneurs emphasized that screening patrons and limiting visibility is important to protecting lesbian spaces from anti-LGBTQ activists. They cited incidents of bars infiltrated by anti-LGBTQ women activists who took photos and harassed patrons. Patrons also experienced harassment and violence from men. Thus, lesbian social entrepreneurs adapted by sacrificing visibility for safer community space. Finally, I discuss how such strategies produce intentional or inadvertent exclusions that marginalize some who seek lesbian spaces.

Gender segregated LGBTQ spaces

LGBTQ neighborhoods in Korea are generally sex segregated. Korea's oldest sexual minority neighborhood in the Jongno District of Seoul serves cisgender gay men (Seo, 2001). A second gayborhood in the Yongsan District hosts numerous cisgender gay-only venues, at least five all-gender inclusive bars, two lesbian-only bars, and several venues operated by trans Korean citizens. Finally, the Mapo District has a lesbian neighborhood. Busan and Daegu follow a similar pattern with sex-segregated LGBTQ venues and neighborhoods.

Gay venues in Jongno often ban or limit the entry of women, foreign residents, and transgender people. Several interviewees reported being denied entry unless accompanied by Korean cisgender gay men. Blair (35, F, European) visited a bar in this area with two cisgender gay male tourists and was told that "foreigners and women usually can't enter," but since the bar was empty, they could have a drink if they left after Korean patrons arrived.

In contrast, Yongsan is a multicultural area of the city near a US military base and tends to receive foreign patrons. However, I observed several venues that posted signs in Korean and English excluding potential patrons based on nationality, sex, or race. Signs read "no foreigners" while others specified "No Southeast Asians," or "no army." Some venues deter women and transgender patrons by charging them double or triple the admission fee, while others deny their entry outright or maintain a quota limiting their numbers. I also witnessed harassment and sexual violence targeting women inside gay venues.

Gayborhood gatekeeping

In Yongsan there are two lesbian bars, Bar Unni and Bar Diamond. The rise and fall of a third lesbian venue, Club Push, points to the gendered challenges the lesbian community continues to face today. Club Push opened for just a few weeks before closing in 2018. Club Push staff collaborated with nearby lesbian entrepreneurs to cross-promote their businesses by temporarily serving as bartenders at both lesbian bars. The manager of Bar Diamond introduced me to Club Push staff a few weeks ahead of their launch, as they trained for opening night. Local lesbian bar owners hoped a nightclub would boost traffic to their businesses. Club Push was successful for about 4 weeks, crowded from 11 pm to 2 am every weekend, as were both bars. This briefly transformed the narrow back alley of a street full of gay bars as women queued to enter, smoked and flirted outside, and visited all-gender inclusive and lesbian bars nearby. The strong preference for gender segregation, particularly among cisgender gay men, produced conflicts hastening Club Push's demise. Partnering lesbian bar staff later reported that Club Push staff received many complaints and criticisms from within the LGBTQ community; it was closed within a month and never re-opened.

I observed and heard from interviewees about cisgender gay men vocalizing frustration at the influx of women onto "their" street. Some merely muttered rude comments such as, "it reeks of pussy (*boji naemsae*)" as they passed the club on the way to nearby gay men's venues. According to Kyungmin (27, F, Korean), five cisgender gay men surrounded and verbally confronted her on the street, yelling "There are too many vaginas on the hill, get out of here!" I met her immediately after this conflict and accompanied her as she attempted to join a group of friends at a gay bar. We were refused entry by the owner and bartender, who angrily informed us that it was a bar for gay men, and that there were already too many women inside. They threatened to call the police, insisting that we leave. After some protest from gay friends, we were able to join them at the bar, but the bartender continued to verbally harass us throughout our short stay.

Lesbian venue safety strategies

Due to the marginalization lesbians had long experienced in gayborhoods, they opened lesbian-only businesses in separate areas of Seoul, Busan and Daegu. In the early 1990s Korea's sole lesbian organization *Kkirikkiri* expanded its membership and several lesbian venues opened in Seoul (Seo, 2001). By my count, from 2016 to 2018 in the Mapo District of Seoul there were six lesbian nightclubs, over a dozen lesbian bars, at least ten lesbian-owned businesses, and a health co-operative for lesbians lacking the care resources typically provided by family. In Busan, there were at least six lesbian bars, a nightclub, and three businesses. In Daegu there were two lesbian bars.

Limiting public access to information

Operating in a legal environment that inadequately protects LGBTQ people from discrimination, lesbian venues in Korea carefully curate the information they release to the public. Lesbian venues withhold both online and offline information about operating hours and location. Although a few lesbian bars are featured in English-language guidebooks for LGBTQ travelers, these listings contain outdated information and many venues have closed or relocated. Even on Korean-language websites, public information is quite limited. Some lesbian bars can only be found by calling for directions. Photography is not allowed inside most venues. Community members tend to share details about venues only with people they trust.

Hiding in plain sight

LGBTQ communities that deemphasize visibility should not be simply regarded as passively responding to social repression. Lesbian business owners actively build cultural respite from heterosexist society by deploying safety strategies in the design of their venues. Most bars use simple nondescript signboards. In contrast to neighboring (heterosexual) bars, they typically lack neon fixtures, tend not to be colorful or embellished with eye-catching decoration, and are located out of sight near the top of a building. A typical signboard is simple, with a distinctive local color pattern and code words legible only to those who have local cultural resources to decipher its meaning. Lesbian bar signboards are often rendered in English or use English names, not to target an English-speaking audience, but to avoid garnering attention from the Korean public. Lesbian bars are rarely located on the first floor, typically occupying the basement or top floor, and in alleys away from major foot traffic and obscured from street view. In contrast, cisgender gay men's bars are often located on the first floor, in neighborhoods with higher concentrations of LGBTQ venues. Korean bars and clubs that cater to lesbian clientele utilize a variety of barrier structures at their entrances and typically have tinted glass, or lack exterior windows.

Some lesbian bars more elaborately mask their presence, cleverly remaining hidden in plain sight. Bar Very Nice offers an excellent example: despite my existing knowledge of masking mechanisms, it took three visits before I could find its entrance. According to a Korean informant and her U.S. citizen fiancé, Bar Very Nice was near a local lesbian club, in a four-story building that hosted arcade game cafes. The building had a single cramped elevator lobby with a dark, dingy stairwell full of cardboard boxes, with walls lined with advertisements for popular games. Signs listed the names of second and third floor arcades, operating hours, and contact information. On my first visit, I could not find any information about Bar Very Nice and left. I visited again a few days later; this time I noticed a single small sign for *Arcade* Very Nice. I entered the elevator, along with several teenagers, but there was no placard listing *Arcade* Very Nice. Slightly embarrassed, I remained in the elevator as it opened, teens spilling out into the second and third floor arcades. On my third attempt, several weeks later, I carefully examined the *Arcade* Very Nice sign. It did not indicate that Very Nice was a bar. Instead, the sign advertised an arcade, including pictures of games and snacks. The only information listed on this sign was a phone number for group reservations, and in smaller font that it was located on the fourth floor and rooftop. However, once in the elevator, I confirmed once again that there was no placard listing for *Arcade Very Nice*. Next to the buttons were labels for the first through third floors. Two additional buttons seemed unused and lacked a business name placard or floor number. I pushed the unlabeled button and was pleasantly surprised when the elevator opened to a cramped lobby full of chain-smoking women. There was not a single arcade game in the venue. In a neighborhood dominated by neon signs, this lesbian pub relied on subtlety to build a loyal following.

Patron screening

Lesbian clubs often post professional security guards at their exterior entrance. Most venues ban minors and those without identification from entering, and screen patrons based on gender markers. Some lesbian bars subtly exclude unwanted patrons by labeling their venues "alumni pubs." Here, the term "alumni" is code for lesbian. The owner of Bar Diamond told me that if men find their way up the external stairwell to her third story bar, she prevents conflict and exposure by simply pointing to the "alumni pub" signs and explaining that she is hosting a reservation-only alumni event. Those newcomers who figure out the local codes gain access to lesbian community spaces if they can provide the appropriate identification. However, screening may exclude queer newcomers and foreign residents who are unfamiliar with its use in lesbian networks.

This tactic is also deployed to discourage heterosexual women. I experienced a revealing instance in which the owner of a lesbian bar explained the unwritten rule that their bar was not for straight women. One wintry evening, I met Kay (27, biracial Korean American) so we could check out a new bar together. As we entered Bar Vertigo, the owner (37, Korean) approached us to ask in English, "Do you know where you are?" I responded, "Yes, Bar Vertigo." The owner subsequently mentioned that it was an "alumni" pub. We assured her, "We are alumni." Just in case her question had been too vague, or possibly because she wasn't certain we understood, she asked directly, "Are you lesbian?" Once we affirmed our LGBTQ community membership and explained how we knew about her relatively new bar tucked away in an otherwise empty alley, the owner apologized for the awkward screening. Like several other owners, she cited safety concerns and a history of anti-LGBTQ and misogynist violence. She invited us in for a drink and chatted with us throughout the night. Either she could not read us as LGBTQ, or because we were clearly foreign residents and could have wandered into the bar accidentally, the owner slipped out of coded language and resorted to asking directly if we belonged. This interaction revealed the importance social entrepreneurs place on screening and sharing information about the privacy governing lesbian spaces in Korean cities.

Early morning safe spaces

Women fear for their safety, particularly as sexual harassment and sex crimes rise in areas of Seoul where women socialize, study, and work (Lee et al., 2017). My interviewees reported feeling vulnerable when walking or taxiing home after a night out. Interestingly, some lesbian bars coordinate their schedules to remain open until public transportation resumes in the morning. These venues coordinate with nearby lesbian clubs so that women have safe spaces nearby to stay after nightclubs close at around 4am.

Safety strategies and exclusion

Heterosexual men and women

Heterosexual men are not welcome in Korea's lesbian bars. While most use the strategies previously outlined, two lesbian gastropubs in Seoul post exterior signs indicating that they are for women only. However, Korean lesbian venues also generally discourage heterosexual women from entering, citing the importance of safe spaces and cultural respite from heteronormative society.

Gay cisgender men

Gay men are also generally barred from entry unless it is a rare "LGBTQ night" or they are accompanied by women who secured permission in advance from the owner.

Foreign residents

Unlike some of the cisgender gay men's bars in Jongno and Yongsan that exclude patrons based on national origin, the lesbian bars in Mapo District welcome foreign residents. As a Korean-speaking, white U.S. citizen frequenting lesbian spaces, I never experienced or witnessed exclusion based on national origin or ethnicity. As explained in the preceding section, Kay and I were not excluded from Bar Vertigo for being foreigners, but the owner did want us to understand the sexual identity boundaries that govern admission to her bar. I interviewed 86 LGBTQ foreign residents in Korea and never heard of any ban from a lesbian bar based on national origin, regardless of their ethnoracial identities, or their Korean proficiency.

However, the use of local cultural codes to protect the community does make it difficult for those who struggle to find such venues, including foreign residents. Foreign residents were sometimes questioned about their sexuality. For example, bar staff occasionally asked if I was a member of the lesbian community, if I knew I was in a lesbian bar, or how I had heard about the bar. Given the lack of outright exclusions, it seems that lesbian social entrepreneurs are concerned with avoiding involuntary "outing" or misogynistic threats to community safety, not with excluding patrons based on their national origin. This contrasts the exclusionary practices at some cisgender gay bars, which did not cite safety as motivating entry policy, instead emphasizing that their clients do not want women or foreigners present.

Trans marginalization

It is legally possible, but challenging, to change one's gender marker in Korea. During my fieldwork, Korean law required parental consent before adult transgender citizens could change their legal gender identity. While this policy was ruled unconstitutional by the courts in August 2019 (Korean Society of Law and Policy on Sexual Orientation and Gender Identity (KSLPSOGI), 2019), current law continues to mandate that transgender adults changing their legal gender identity be unmarried and have no minor children (Na et al., 2014). Citizens of other countries must typically return to their birthplace in order to petition for a change to the gender marker on their passport, and then return to Korea to have their ID reissued. In this context, screening patrons by gender markers can produce exclusion for those who are unable or unwilling to submit to the bureaucratic procedures necessary to change their ID.

However, when I invited some transwomen to lesbian venues as part of a large group of lesbians and queer women, they gained entry despite lacking identification that matches their gender identity. At four different lesbian venues in Seoul, I observed (and occasionally facilitated) transgender patrons securing entry when a mutual contact vouched for them. These trans patrons relied on their companions to secure initial access to these venues, but as they became familiar with staff, they were able to gain entry independently. These exceptions to formal policies screening based on gender suggest that lesbian venues do not necessarily aim to exclude transgender patrons. Rather, they respond to a history of homophobic and patriarchal violence by anti-LGBTQ activists when they establish procedures that screen based on sex.

Conclusion

Korean lesbians struggle against the external forces of homophobia and misogyny, common in many countries. In addition to being targets for homophobic and misogynist physical, sexual, and verbal violence, the fear of involuntary "outing" is especially strong in the lesbian community in Korea. They must face not only relational but also socioeconomic consequences of such "outing" due to the Korean government's family-centered laws and lack of LGBTQ nondiscrimination policies. Marginalization of lesbians from both the women's and gay men's rights movements challenged early lesbian community building and drove the establishment of lesbian-only spaces. Nevertheless, lesbian communities in Korea have shown impressive growth since the 1990s, due to strategies that prioritize safety over visibility, but also produce complex patterns of inclusion and exclusion.

Korean lesbian social entrepreneurs draw on their available resources to establish carefully protected and sometimes hidden safe spaces to cope with homophobia, misogyny, and marginalization. They try to minimize the risk of harassment and violence through strategies common to other gayborhoods documented in the literature, such as employing security staff and checking patron IDs. Bar staff promote safety by staying open until public transportation resumes and by redirecting men who wander in by labeling themselves "alumni" pubs. The spatial tactics, community vetting, and interactional strategies that local lesbian social entrepreneurs deploy as they strive to balance competing needs for safety and visibility resulted in impressively variegated lesbian social spaces in several cities. Visibility should not be regarded as the default strategy for community building; it is a strategic choice that suits particular conditions.

Taking an intersectional analytical approach focused on relations of power and marginalization helps to highlight how these strategic responses to violence produce complex patterns of inclusion and exclusion from lesbian space. It is difficult for lesbians who lack knowledge of local cues or preexisting ties to find and navigate lesbian space. I have documented several instances of cisgender gay venues explicitly excluding patrons, deploying quotas or charging high admissions fees based on gender and national origin to maintain social spaces for cisgender gay locals. In contrast, lesbian community admissions screening practices differ in purpose; they emphasize safety rather than applying a gender discriminatory fee for access to LGTBQ space. The practice nevertheless reifies binary gender markers and excludes on the basis of sex, though some accrue the social capital to secure an exception to the policy.

By centering already highly visible LGBTQ communities in the West, the existing literature oversimplifies not only our understanding of how contextual constraints and resources shape lesbian community building but also how intersectional violence, operating variedly in different contexts, shapes safety strategies and alliances. Gender segregation, homophobic violence and socioeconomic discrimination against LGBTQ people in Korea mean that visibility politics can expose an already marginalized group to increased risk of intersectional violence and discrimination. The Korean case supports queer theorists' claim that invisibility can provide protected and productive spaces to imagine and build queer selves and communities (Seidman, 1998) rather than simply being a passive reaction to homophobia. By minimizing visibility and establishing an array of creative safety mechanisms to protect patrons and staff from harassment and violence, lesbian social entrepreneurs in Korea successfully established many long-running safe spaces. Within just twenty years, the once small and marginalized lesbian social scene rapidly grew into dozens of lesbian-only safe spaces.

Acknowledgments

The Korean LGBTQIA + community made this project possible. Thanks to Jaeeun Kim's invaluable support, Emily Kazyak, anonymous reviewers, Todd Henry, Hae Yeon Choo, Barbara Anderson, Carla Pfeffer, Jeff Lockhart and Bryan Parsons for helpful feedback.

Funding

A Fulbright Grant and funding from the University of Michigan Nam Center's Core University Program through the Republic of Korea Ministry of Education and Academy of Korean Studies Korean Studies Promotion Service (AKS-2016-OLU-2240001), CEW+, IRWG, Rackham, and Department of Sociology supported this research.

ORCID

Chelle Jones 🆔 http://orcid.org/0000-0002-2402-8548

References

Chang, K. S., & Song, M. Y. (2010). The stranded individualizer under compressed modernity: Korean women in individualization without individualism. *British Journal of Sociology*, 61(3), 539–564.

Cho, S. P. (2009). The wedding banquet revisited: "Contract marriages" between Korean gays and lesbians. *Anthropological Quarterly*, 82(2), 401–422.

Chua, L. J. (2016). Negotiating social norms and relations in the micromobilization of human rights: The case of Burmese lesbian activism. *Law & Social Inquiry*, 41(3), 643–669.

Collins, P. H., & Bilge, S. (2016). *Intersectionality*. Hoboken, NJ: John Wiley & Sons.

Croff, J. M., Hubach, R. D., Currin, J. M., & Frederick, A. F. (2017). Hidden rainbows: Gay bars as safe havens in a socially conservative area since the pulse nightclub massacre. *Sexuality Research and Social Policy*, 14(2), 233–240.

Dave, N. N. (2010). To render real the imagined: An ethnographic history of lesbian community in India. *Signs: Journal of Women in Culture and Society*, 35(3), 595–619.

Fraser, M. (1999). Classing queer: Politics in competition. *Theory, Culture & Society*, 16(2), 107–131.

Ghaziani, A., Taylor, V., & Stone, A. (2016). Cycles of sameness and difference in LGBT social movements. *Annual Review of Sociology*, 42(1), 165–183.

Han, W. (2018). Proud of myself as LGBTQ: The Seoul pride parade, homonationalism, and queer developmental citizenship. *Korea Journal*, 58(2), 27–57.

Hanhardt, C. B. (2013). *Safe space: Gay neighborhood history and the politics of violence*. Durham, NC: Duke University Press.

Hartal, G. (2016). The politics of holding: Home and LGBT visibility in contested Jerusalem. *Gender, Place & Culture*, 23(8), 1193–1206.

Kendall, L. (1996). *Getting married in Korea: Of gender, morality, and modernity*. Berkeley, CA: University of California Press.

Kim, N. (2016). *The gendered politics of the Korean protestant right*, 81–114. Cham: Palgrave Macmillan.

Kim, S. K., & Kim, K. (2014). *The Korean women's movement and the state: Bargaining for change*. London, UK: Routledge.

Kim, Y., & Hahn, S. (2006). Homosexuality in ancient and modern Korea. *Culture, Health & Sexuality*, 8(1), 59–65.

Kimmel, D. C., & Yi, H. (2004). Characteristics of gay, lesbian, and bisexual Asians, Asian Americans, and immigrants from Asia to the USA. *Journal of Homosexuality*, 47(2), 143–172.

Korean Society of Law and Policy on Sexual Orientation and Gender Identity (KSLPSOGI). (2017). Human rights situation of LGBTI in South Korea. Retrieved from http://annual.sogilaw.org/review/intro_en

Korean Society of Law and Policy on Sexual Orientation and Gender Identity (KSLPSOGI). (2019). Daebeob-won teulaenseujendeo seongbyeoljeongjeong bumodong-uiseo yogu pyeji hwan-yeonghanda [Supreme Court abolishes parental consent requirement for trans gender change]. Retrieved from https://sogilaw.org/m/76?fbclid=IwAR1JkoIZLe-l7vBnR9RhZwLj8XlVX965WqSbuA_WFoNABx-IEKXuEJy_n_Y

Kwon Kim, H. Y., & Cho, S. P. (2011). The Korean gay and lesbian movement 1993–2008: From "identity" and "community" to "human rights. In *South Korean social movements*, edited by G. Shin and P. Chang, 220–237. Routledge.

Lee, H. S. (1999). Hanguk Lesbian Inkwonoondong-ui Yeoksa [History of the Lesbian Rights Movement in South Korea]. In *Hanguk Yeoseong Inkwonoondongsa* edited by H. Shin, K. Min, H. Lee, C. Chung, H. Lee, H. Jung, H. Lee and E. Kim, 359–403. Seoul: Hanwool.

Lee, Y. N., Park, J. H., Kim, B., Kim, D. J., Han, J. W., Han, K. T., & Kim, S. J. (2017). Violent crimes in a community and quality of life for its inhabitants: Results of a multi-level study in South Korea. *Psychiatry Research*, 257, 450–455.

Manalansan, M. F. IV. (1995). In the shadows of Stonewall: Examining gay transnational politics and the diasporic dilemma. *GLQ: A Journal of Lesbian and Gay Studies*, 2(4), 425–438.

Meyer, D. (2015). *Violence against queer people: Race, class, gender, and the persistence of anti-LGBT discrimination*. New Brunswick, NJ: Rutgers University Press.

Moon, H. (2008). Shin-jayujueui shidae nodonggwa kajokeui jaeguchohwa [Restructuring of labor and family in the era of neoliberalism]. *Yeo/seong Eeron*, gyeolho.

Moon, S. (2002). Carving out space: Civil society and the women's movement in South Korea. *The Journal of Asian Studies*, 61(2), 473–500.

Na, T. Y. J., Han, J. H. J., & Koo, S. W. (2014). The Korean gender system: LGBTI in the contexts of family, legal identity, and the military. *Journal of Korean Studies*, 19(2), 357–377.

Nelson, L. C. (2000). *Measured excess: Status, gender, and consumer nationalism in Korea*. New York, NY: Columbia University Press.

Park-Kim, S. J., Lee-Kim, S. Y., & Kwon-Lee, E. J. (2007). The lesbian rights movement and feminism in Korea. *Journal of Lesbian Studies*, 10(3-4), 161–190.

Seidman, S. (1998). Are we all in the closet? Notes towards a sociological and cultural turn in queer theory. *European Journal of Cultural Studies*, 1(2), 177–192.

Seo, D. (2001). Mapping the vicissitudes of homosexual identities in South Korea. *Journal of Homosexuality*, 40(3-4), 65–79.

Tang, S. (2012). Transnational lesbian identities: Lessons from Singapore? *Queer Singapore: Illiberal citizenship and mediated cultures*, edited by A. Yue and J. Zubillaga-Pow, 83–96. Pokfulam, Hong Kong: Hong Kong University Press.

Valentine, G. (2007). Theorizing and researching intersectionality: A challenge for feminist geography. *The Professional Geographer*, 59(1), 10–21.

Yang, H. (2013). *Colonialism and patriarchy: Where the Korean family-head (hoju) system had been located, Law and society in Korea*. Northampton, MA: Edward Elgar Publishing.

Yi, J., Jung, G., & Phillips, J. (2017). Evangelical Christian discourse in Korea on the LGBT: The politics of cross-border learning. *Society*, 54(1), 29–33.

"You out-gayed the gays": Gay aesthetic power and lesbian, bisexual, and queer women in LGBTQ spaces

Amy L. Stone

ABSTRACT

In lesbian, gay, bisexual, transgender, and queer (LGBTQ) spaces, gay male practices, sexualities, and priorities often dominate. I argue that in mixed-gender LGBTQ festival spaces in the South, gay aesthetics are normative, which often minimizes the contributions of lesbian, bisexual, and queer (LBQ) women. I compare two festival events run by the LGBTQ community—Cornyation, a mock debutante pageant that is part of Fiesta in San Antonio, Texas, and Osiris Ball, a formal Carnival ball during Mardi Gras in Mobile, Alabama. This research is based on participant observation data collected at both events over several years and 38 interviews conducted with event participants. I argue that at these events, gay aesthetic power is exerted through the expectation that LBQ women should master these aesthetics, a dynamic that often relies on gay men as arbiters of successful mastery. These processes were more dramatic in organizations and spaces where men were a numerical majority. This marginalization fits within a pattern of androcentric bias in both the arts and the workplace.

In a re-boot of *Queer Eye for the Straight Guy*, the Fab five are at it again, swooping in to mostly heterosexual men's homes and lives to instruct them on the finer aspects of house decorating, hair sculpting, and clothing fashion, along with emotional conversations about masculinity, vulnerability, and relationships. There is a long history of gay men being associated with the arts and design. For example, being referred to as a culturally sophisticated man was a coded way of talking about homosexuality in the 1950s (Stone, 2016). Scholars analyze the way gay culture contributes to musical theater (Clum, 1999) and historical preservation (Fellows, 2005). In artistic fields like fashion design, gay men's contributions are valorized and rewarded above women and other men's accomplishments (Stokes, 2015). Gay men's fashion advice dominates on the original version of *Queer Eye for the Straight Guy*, giving the gay consultants "aesthetic power"

(Hart, 2004; Papacharissi & Fernback, 2008), a narrowly focused form of power organized by ability to design, judge, and consult on aesthetics. This research extends this concept of aesthetic power to analyze the way gay aesthetics dominate LGBTQ spaces.

I argue that in mixed-gender LGBTQ festival spaces in the U.S. South, gay aesthetics—particularly designing campy or outrageous centerpieces, costumes, and skits—become the normative aesthetic for other participants to master, which obscure the contributions of lesbian, bisexual, and queer (LBQ) women. In this article, I compare two large festival events run by the LGBTQ community—*Cornyation*, a mock debutante pageant and political satire performed during the Fiesta festival in San Antonio, Texas, and the *Osiris Ball*, a formal Carnival ball put on by the Order of Osiris as part of Mardi Gras in Mobile, Alabama. I argue that gay men exert aesthetic power through judging LBQ women's ability to master gay aesthetics, and expectations of mastery of gay aesthetics contributes to a history of androcentrism in LGBTQ spaces.

Some of this marginalization is linked to the dominance of gay culture. Scholars like David Halperin (2012) study the various elements of U.S. gay culture, including camp, the appropriation of non-gay items, attention to aesthetics, being "over the top," and "laughing at situations that *to others* are horrifying or tragic" (p. 140). Although gay culture can be performed by anyone, there is a long history of gay men being protective or territorial over gay culture and cultural elements like camp or drag (Newton, 1996). In her classic work "Dick(less) Tracy and the Homecoming Queen" Newton (1996) analyzes the cultural marginalization of lesbian women in the gay resort town of Cherry Grove, New York, in which campy theatrical rituals that were at the center of community life were considered to be the exclusive territory of gay men. When a butch lesbian wins a coveted drag contest, gay men contest this victory, and the lesbian victor has to constantly navigate the protectiveness of gay men over camp and drag.

Aesthetic power demonstrates the power dynamics between gay men and LBQ women in mixed LGBTQ spaces, in which the labor of creating the space is divided between both men and women but the normative aesthetics of the space is gay culture. Several scholars document uneven resources and gendered labor within LGBTQ spaces and organizations (Bailey, 2013; Ward, 2008). Papacharissi and Fernback (2008) explain that the aesthetic power of the Fab 5 in *Queer Eye for the Straight Guy* is a weak power, limited in duration and contained in the apolitical realm of consumption and aesthetics. I contend that this aesthetic power is used to dominate and organize mixed-gender spaces and the labor of design within them. This aesthetic power operates through expectations about aesthetics, which are at times reinforced with gay male judgement or social exclusion of LBQ women. The operation of aesthetic power was most dramatic in organizations that were majority male, where these networks of social exclusion were the most powerful.

Methods and background

This project is part of a larger study of LGBTQ visibility and cultural citizenship in four urban festivals in the U.S. South and Southwest. In this article, I focus on two of the largest LGBTQ multigendered festival organizations in these four cities: the Osiris Ball during Mardi Gras in Mobile, Alabama, and Cornyation during Fiesta in San Antonio, Texas.

Mardi Gras is celebrated all over the Gulf South, from Galveston, Texas, to Pensacola, Florida during several weeks that span the winter Carnival season. The Carnival season includes private, formal, adult events as well as family-friendly street parades. Mobile, Alabama, is often described as the birthplace of the U.S. Mardi Gras tradition, dating its celebration back to the 1700 s (Roberts, 2015). The city hosts over 25 parades and 65 formal balls organized by over 70 organizations, impressive for a city of less than 200,000 people (Roberts, 2015).

Order of Osiris is a *krewe* or mystic society, a festival organization that sponsors a masque ball and/or parade during Carnival season. *Masque balls* are elaborate, costumed affairs attended by guests who are typically invited through the krewe members' social networks. Most krewes crown their own royalty— "kings" or "queens" or emblems of the group—at the ball, recognizing longtime group members. All of these balls include refreshments, decorations, music, and a *tableau* of acting, dancing, or visual displays. Order of Osiris is the largest of four krewes that are openly inclusive of LGBTQ people in Mobile and is the oldest gay and lesbian organization in the city (Roberts, 2015). Osiris is primarily composed of white gay men and lesbians, and the Osiris Ball is attended by almost 2,000 people every year. The group began as a majority male group in the 1980s but gradually integrated throughout the 1990s and now is a majority women group.

Fiestas are festivals common throughout Texas, New Mexico, and Southern California. These fiestas tend to include multiple parades, fairs, theatrical events, and the crowning of festival royalty over the course of several weeks. Fiesta San Antonio consists of hundreds of events across the city, such as the Battle of the Flowers Parade, the second largest parade in the United States. Many Southwestern festivals rely on historical pageantry about the Western frontier, romanticized Spanish history, and stories of racialized conquest. San Antonio Fiesta began as a celebration of the Battle of San Jacinto (the Alamo), but the festival has become gradually disconnected from this historical pageantry (Hernández-Ehrisman, 2008).

In 1951, Cornyation began as a satire of the major Fiesta San Antonio event, The Coronation of the Queen of the Order of the Alamo, a serious coronation of Anglo upper-class debutantes that dates back to the turn of the 20th century (Haynes, 1998). In the 1950s and 1960s, Cornyation was a mock debutante pageant run by artistic Anglo gay men for a public, family audience. The show quickly became a political satire of national and local politics, using camp aesthetics to critique class and political relations in the growing city of San Antonio (Stone, 2016; 2017). After a hiatus of about fifteen years, Cornyation was revived in the early 1980s at a gay bar and became a popular Fiesta event attended by approximately 5,000 people a year and fundraising over two million dollars for humanimmunodeficiency-virus (HIV)/AIDS service organizations. The show has its own royalty ("King Anchovy") who is attended by about ten queens and their entourage (their "house"), each spending about four minutes on stage satirizing a different element of contemporary politics and culture. A typical "house" has one queen, six or seven additional performers, and one or more designers who fashion the costumes, music, and aesthetics of the piece. Cornyation drag comes out of a strong Anglo and Latino drag community in San Antonio that has roots back into the 1970s bar culture (Stone, 2017). Most of the Cornyation participants are men, and identify as Latino, Latina, or Latinx.

The data for this paper come from participant observation at Cornyation and Osiris Ball between 2012 and 2016, including attending each event at least twice and associated activities like lunches, parties, fundraisers, and dress rehearsals for the affiliated organizations. For Cornyation, I worked as a stage hand for two years and a performer ("duchess") for two years, experiences that came about as a result of conducting my research.

I interviewed members of each event, including the major organizers, totaling 38 interviews all together. In Cornyation I interviewed 23 people: 16 cisgender men, seven cisgender women. Ten interviewees identify as Latino, Latina, or Hispanic, and thirteen interviewees identify as White or Anglo and not Hispanic. In Osiris I interviewed 15 people: nine cisgender men, six cisgender women. All interviewees were White except for one Black woman. Most interviewees were in their thirties, forties, and fifties and modestly middle class in education and income. For the Osiris interviews and one Cornyation interview, an undergraduate research assistant attended the interview as well and asked probing questions. In addition to formal interviews, I informally interviewed dozens of men and women involved in each organizations and spent over fifty hours in each space as a participant observer.

Each interview was transcribed and I analyzed all interview transcripts and fieldnotes using the qualitative software program NVivo for consistent analytical themes. Included in this article is all analysis of themes about the involvement and contributions of LBQ women in these two organizations. No information is included about the role of transgender women because there were few transwomen involved in either organization during the time of research.

Findings

Women are involved in both events as artistic designers and performers. In Osiris, women and men are equally involved in the group, including in royalty and leadership. Women often serve as ball captains, the lead organizer who selects the theme of the ball and coordinates the event. Krewe members in Osiris all decorate tables for their guests in accordance with the theme of the annual ball. More senior members of the organization also "costume," in which they create costumes, a small float, and a sketch or dance that corresponds to the theme of the ball. Many Osiris members design their own costumes and floats by hand; others pay artists to craft the items for them.

In Cornyation, the over 100 performers in the group are divided between ten or twelve "houses," each of which with their own artistic designers and one "duchess" (or "queen" or "empress"), who must be a transgender or cisgender woman per the Cornyation guidelines. In many houses, the duchess is one of the few women in the group, and the remainder of the group is men. The designers in each house conceptualize the theme of the year, design costumes, arrange music, and/or choreograph routines or pay people to do so on their behalf. There is a long history of gay men designing for Cornyation dating back to the 1950s and 1960s (Stone, 2016). A few women design for the show currently. In 2017, three of the twelve Cornyation houses were led by female designers. Not all designers and performers are LGBTQ. Increasingly, heterosexual designers work on the show, and some "houses" are known for being more straight than others. The organization is mostly led by Latino and Anglo gay men with some Anglo heterosexual women and men in support positions. The stage crew has been led by a lesbian woman for several decades, often jokingly referred to as the "head dominatrix," and the board includes at least two LBQ women. The aesthetics of both shows feature campy and outrageous gay aesthetics. The Osiris Ball operates by the ethos "Never Too Big, Never Too Much," emphasizing the use of outrageous design work with creative flamboyance. Large costumes, hair, floats, centerpieces, and personality were central to this aesthetic. Indeed, the group gave a yearly award for the design work that best represented this ethos. Cornyation often presented gay aesthetics that were corny, campy, and low culture. Materials made out of old costumes, discarded items, gallons of glitter, and amateur artistry have been part of the show since its inception as a mockery of the high class expensive pageantry of debutante coronations in the 1950s. As a "duchess" in the show, my costumes included cheap Hallowe'en costumes, a glitter-spray-painted Snuggee, a pink bathrobe with feathers formerly worn by a drag queen, the ugliest dress I have ever bought from a thrift store, a rhinestone graduation gown, and combat boots. The performances of drag queens are emphasized, often highlighted in the promotion of Cornyation in flyers and website images, although in both events women also perform dressed as drag kings or as male characters.

LBQ women's contributions were often measured against this gay aesthetics in both organizations. This normative use of gay aesthetics was most extreme in the majority male group Cornyation, where gay social networks of exclusion operated most strongly.

Outgaying the gays at the Osiris Ball

I thought about the complexity of this aesthetic power while walking around the convention center during ball preparations for the Osiris Ball. It was late morning, and I thought wistfully about my lunch plans as I helped put together various table decorations throughout the room. Later that evening, almost 2000 people would come into the venue to participate in the annual ball. Guests typically enter the event in mandatory formal wear, help themselves to refreshments and liquor, sit at assigned tables decorated by their host, and enjoy the multihour tableau of costuming put on by the krewe members followed by an evening of dancing and revelry. This morning, krewe members are busy setting up elaborate tables for their guests that correspond with the theme of the ball, "Magical Mythical Places." Tables include thematic centerpieces about magical, alternate worlds like the dystopian world from *The Hunger Games*, the board game Candyland, *Rocky Horror Picture Show*, and the world of Harry Potter. Compared to other Mobile Mardi Gras balls, the LGBTQ events have more elaborate, inventive table designs (Roberts, 2015). Each set of tables has gift bags or presents for guests.

I notice something as I circulate around the convention center. I investigate a table with a Harry Potter theme designed by a white, older lesbian couple. They show me the creatively designed props on their table—the various recyclable bottles they saved over the year to turn into potions containers, the pictures they printed off the internet. They comment that they just do not have as much money as the gay men in the group and have to be more creative. Their table is charming to me, a longtime Harry Potter fan. Across the convention center, one of the most visible tables is decorated with huge, glittery centerpieces that rise above all the others. Someone admits to me that the white gay man who did those decorations paid someone to design his outfit, float, and table decorations. Several other designs by white men are elaborate, large, and fabulous. An older white gay couple shows me how their tables are decorated sparsely, that they used an old, painted Spam can to make the foundation of their centerpieces; they enjoy traveling and do not want to spend their limited income on table decorations. Throughout my fieldnotes, I notice that even in this space that includes slightly more woman participants, gay aesthetics are often more visible in the ball space. At times, gay designs and creations literally take up more space and tower above those created by LBQ women. However, not all gay designs are so prominent, as economics restrict artistic production.

I am hosted by a butch-femme lesbian couple who have spent the last several months constructing elaborate centerpieces to create an Alice in Wonderland themed area; they made these centerpieces on the weekends with a group of lesbian friends, their chosen family with whom they also regularly vacation together. My table is the Mad Hatter's table, which comes with a gift bag full of related paraphernalia, including my own teacup, Mardi Gras beads, and drinking glasses. My seat is labeled with a little card with my name on it. One of the established members of the group, an older white woman, comes over to inspect the elaborate tables; she shakes her head and exclaims to the butch lesbian woman who designed the tables, "you out-gayed the gays this time."

At the Osiris Ball, the size and scale of the event is a point of pride, signifying the effort and attention the krewe members give to their annual ball. Being grandiose and fabulous is valued. Sometimes this aesthetics reflect class and economic differences between LBQ women and gay men in the group, although not all gay men are economically well off. The time and money resources to produce grandiose aesthetics were not available to all participants.

The table, costume, and float designs that are produced by LBQ women participants are judged in relation to gay aesthetics. I am struck by the way the lesbian-decorated tables are described as "out-gaying the gays," describing tables decorated by a group of lesbians as both a gay aesthetic accomplishment and besting gay aesthetics. For example, a femme Osiris woman in Mobile described herself as having "a little gay man inside me" due to her artistic ability. These LBQ women are indeed recognized by their group members as contributing to the design work of the event. There was much appreciation for other types of LBQ labor in the organizing of the Osiris Ball, for example. However, this recognition is always framed in relation to gay aesthetics, even when produced by LBQ women. In this group, LBQ women were just as likely to judge or arbitrate these gay aesthetics as gay men.

Although less common in Osiris, this mastery of gay aesthetics included some protectiveness about this aesthetic. This same femme woman, who did elaborate table and costume designs yearly for the event, tells me in her interview that the gay men in the club were resistant to voting her into the group, because she was visibly femme and artistic. Her partner insinuates that the men did not want a femme group member who could master gay aesthetics better than them, that they did not want a femme woman "besting" them.

It's still to some extent a man's territory in Cornyation

In Cornyation, the aesthetic contributions of LBQ women are rendered almost entirely invisible. Indeed, while writing a history of the show, a longtime Latino male designer in the group returns a draft of the manuscript to me with all the references to "lesbians" crossed out. "There's no lesbians in the show," he tells me, ignoring the fact that he is speaking to one. All the major senior designers are Anglo and Latino men, and their milestones are featured prominently in the show and are eulogized after their death with commemorative skits. Newspaper accounts of the show disproportionately feature the works of male designers.

LBQ women who designed for the show often described it as an old boys club in which women had to "prove themselves" in their ability to master gay aesthetics and fit in. LBQ women suggested that it took them a long time to gain the respect of gay designers, who often ignored them until they did an "epic" costume or performance. Penny, a gay woman who designed for the show in the 1980s and 1990s and now helps organize the show, described it as "still to some extent a man's territory." She said that the gay men in the show almost completely ignored her until she did a grandiose design in her second or third year of the show and was recognized by some of her fellow designers.

> With the boys I knew I was finally *in*. I was the first girl that was really in. In fact, I was the only female designer for a long time. I knew I was in when [a male designer] came up to me and said "Penny, you peed" and I thought "I don't know that that it is but it's gotta be good." And then they would talk to me. It really was the breaking in of the old boys' club.

Penny and other designers were excluded from recognition and respect for their aesthetic accomplishments of designing costumes and themes for the show; they often had to work harder or longer to get similar kinds of respect for their designing accomplishments.

I met Valeria backstage when I worked as a stage crew member. Valeria is one of the youngest designers at Cornyation, a Latina bisexual woman who was the artistic genius behind the four-minute sketch that her group performed to parody cultural and political events. I ran on stage to hold up glittery cardboard props of the Alamo and other San Antonio landmarks while she and her crew of Latino men danced in crudely-made fat suits dressed as children to parody concerns about the rising rate of childhood "obesity" in San Antonio. Valeria arrived as the "queen" of the sketch, the only role in each sketch required to be filled by a woman, to rescue the day dressed as a huge pizza. Later, we sit at the outside tables of a well-known local gay brunch place talking about her experience in the show with her partner, Julian, a young Latino man who often designed and performed in the show as well. During that interview I learn that she became involved in the show as an older teenager, working with her gay theater mentor from a local children's afterschool program, and when her mentor passed away she stepped into his shoes. I did not know until then just how long Valeria had been designing for the event, over a decade. When I ask her about her experience fitting into the show, she shrugs "I've felt a little outcast for the most part, but I guess maybe finally just letting it go." When I question this further she notes that "I've been in Cornyation for so long and even now I feel like 90% of the people in the show don't know who I am, but I know who they are. I've always felt like they don't view me as part of the show or something, I'm not part of the clique or something, you know." She mentions that she's one of the few female designers, that others have come and gone over the years, but she is still not considered a senior designer. She is not certain if it is because she is a woman, Latina, perceived as straight, or a combination of these factors. People do not seem to notice that her crew is entirely Latino gay men except for her, her partner, and one Latina woman who performs with them. She arches her eyebrow and questions "is our gay ratio not high enough in our group," insinuating that a group needed to have a certain number of gay members to be considered legitimate. Valeria was excluded from gay male designer networks of support and recognition, including being ignored, not being recognized as a senior designer, or being considered illegitimate.

Discussion

In both organizations LBQ women participate as designers who contribute to the creation of these LGBTQ festival events and spaces, but their work is constantly measured against the expectations of their mastery of gay aesthetics. This research compares two spaces: one in which men and women are evenly represented and one in which men outnumber women dramatically. In both types of spaces, LBQ women's design contributions were measured against gay aesthetics, although this marginalization was more extreme in Cornyation, where male designers outnumbered women.

There are some limitations to these findings. Both organizations included few Black LGBTQ people. Both spaces are shaped by middle-class economics, although not all designers, gay or otherwise, are middle class. Both events began as events that were dominated by Anglo gay men. Future research may investigate whether these same dynamics of aesthetic power operate in organizations that began as multigendered organizations, racially diverse, or as women-only organizations. Additionally, the spaces created by these events were both temporary and recurring. Aesthetic power may operate differently in permanent spaces.

This aesthetic power centers on gay aesthetics as normative. When Penny describes Cornyation as "still to some extent a man's territory," she is describing the way gay-created designs shape and define the way aesthetics are supposed to operate in the space of the show. Gay aesthetics become normative by shaping what other designers are supposed to aspire to, exerting androcentric ideals into LGBTQ spaces. Upholding these LBQ aesthetic contributions may operate through networks of social exclusion or judgement, particularly in the majority male group Cornyation. A few LBQ women in Cornyation mentioned methods of social closure (Parkin, 1974), such as gay designers not talking to LBQ women designers. This closure echoes earlier research done by Newton (1996) on the protective and territorial relationship that gay men have to cultural forms like camp and drag. This protective control of aesthetic adds to the systematic marginalization of LBQ women in LGBTQ spaces and organizations (Casey, 2004; Doan, 2007; Orne, 2017; Podmore, 2006; Pritchard et. al., 2002; Stone & Shapiro, 2017; Taylor, 2007). These methods of social closure mirror gendered patterns of discrimination and acceptance in the workplace, fitting a pattern of women's labor being judged or accepted based on norms established by men. For example, gender-fluid LBQ women in the tech industry are more easily integrated into male-dominated workplaces when they are able to demonstrate mastery of geek culture (Alfrey & Twine, 2017).

The consequences of aesthetic power is mostly a social one, but the privileging of gay aesthetics fits into a history of women's labor being judged against a standard set by men, including the construction of the ideal worker as a man (Kelly, Ammons, Chermack, & Moen, 2010). The privileging of cultural forms from gay culture echoes other ways that masculine ideals and men's cultural forms have been privileged in field like language (Bodine, 1975; Kristeva, 1980), music (Koskoff, 1989) and visual arts (Broude, 2018). For example, the possibility of LBQ women having their own aesthetic never came up in my fieldwork. Despite a rich history of LBQ women's artistry in fields like music and visual arts (see Murray, 2007 for examples), lesbian aesthetics especially operate as a punchline, a reliable anti-aesthetic. A tweet in July of 2019 by scholar Michelle Nolan joked about "Queer Eye but with a team of butch lesbians who buy you six pairs of the same jeans because they're comfortable and point out that the reason you have no time for self care is capitalism." The tweet got over 75,000 likes and 12,000 retweets. When I presented this paper at a conference, I made a slide titled "Devaluing of Lesbian Aesthetics" that included a screenshot from the online game "Lesbian or Redneck?", a Birkenstock, *Xena*, and a Subaru ad with a white, middle-aged lesbian in it. This slide resonated uncomfortably with many conference attendees. When I posted the slide on Facebook, a friend joked that "Aren't lesbian aesthetics anti-aesthetics?!?" This paper does not have space to answer the question of how LBQ women contribute their own unique aesthetics to these events but raises the question of what other aesthetics operate alongside normative gay aesthetics in LGBTQ spaces.

Acknowledgments

This research was collected with the grant support of the American Sociological Association Fund for the Advancement of the Discipline, the National Geographic Society, the Mellon Foundation initiative for undergraduate summer research, and the Society for the Psychological Study of Social Issues. I was assisted by indispensable undergraduate research assistants: Caitlin Gallagher, Jady Domingue, Analicia Garcia, Elizabeth Gilbert, Rosa Perales, Danielle Hoard, Beatrice Roman, Georgina Continas, and Maria Olalde.

Disclosure statement

No financial interest or benefit has arisen from the application of this research.

References

Alfrey, L., & Twine, F. W. (2017). Gender-fluid geek girls: Negotiating inequality regimes in the tech industry. *Gender & Society, 31*(1), 28–50.
Bailey, M. M. (2013). *Butch queens up in pumps: Gender, performance, and ballroom culture in Detroit*. Ann Arbor, MI: University of Michigan Press.
Bodine, A. (1975). Androcentrism in prescriptive grammar: Singular 'they', sex-indefinite 'he', and 'he or she'1. *Language in Society, 4*(2), 129–146.
Broude, N. (2018). *Feminism and art history: Questioning the litany*. Abingdon: Routledge.
Casey, M. (2004). De-dyking queer space (s): Heterosexual female visibility in gay and lesbian spaces. *Sexualities, 7*(4), 446–461.

Clum, J. M. (1999). *Something for the Boys: Musical Theater and Gay Culture*. New York, NY: St. Martin's Press.

Doan, P. L. (2007). Queers in the American city: Transgendered perceptions of urban space. *Gender, Place and Culture, 14*(1), 57–74.

Fellows, W. (2005). *A passion to preserve: Gay men as keepers of culture*. Madison, WI: Univ of Wisconsin Press.

Halperin, D. M. (2012). *How to be gay*. Cambridge, MA: Harvard University Press

Hart, K. P. R. (2004). We're here, we're queer—and we're better than you: The representational superiority of gay men to heterosexuals on Queer Eye for the Straight Guy. *The Journal of Men's Studies, 12*(3), 241–253.

Haynes, M. T. (1998). *Dressing up debutantes: pageantry and glitz in Texas*, Oxford: Berg.

Hernández-Ehrisman, L. (2008). *Inventing the Fiesta City: Heritage and Carnival in San Antonio*. Albuquerque, NM: UNM Press.

Kelly, E. L., Ammons, S. K., Chermack, K., & Moen, P. (2010). Gendered challenge, gendered response: Confronting the ideal worker norm in a white-collar organization. *Gender & Society, 24*(3), 281–303.

Koskoff, E. (Ed.). (1989). *Women and music in cross-cultural perspective* (Vol. 79). Champaign, IL: University of Illinois Press.

Kristeva, J. (1980). *Desire in language: A semiotic approach to literature and art*. New York, NY: Columbia University Press.

Murray, H. (2007). Free for all lesbians: Lesbian cultural production and consumption in the United States during the 1970s. *Journal of the History of Sexuality, 16*(2), 251–275.

Newton, E. (1996). Dick (less) Tracy and the homecoming queen: Lesbian power and representation in gay male Cherry Grove. In Ellen Lewin (ed.), Inventing Lesbian Cultures, (pp. 161–193). Boston, MA: Beacon Press

Orne, J. (2017). *Boystown: Sex and community in Chicago*. Chicago, IL: University of Chicago Press.

Papacharissi, Z., & Fernback, J. (2008). The aesthetic power of the Fab 5: Discursive themes of homonormativity in queer eye for the straight guy. *Journal of Communication Inquiry, 32*(4), 348–367.

Parkin, F. (1974). Strategies of social closure in class formation. In Frank Parkin (ed.), *The social analysis of class structure* (pp. 1–18). London: Routledge

Podmore, J. A. (2006). Gone 'underground'? Lesbian visibility and the consolidation of queer space in Montréal. *Social & Cultural Geography, 7*(4), 595–625.

Pritchard, A., Morgan, N., & Sedgley, D. (2002). In search of lesbian space? The experience of Manchester's gay village. *Leisure Studies, 21*(2), 105–123.

Roberts, L. C. (2015). *Mardi Gras in Mobile*. Charleston, SC: The History Press.

Stokes, A. (2015). The glass runway: How gender and sexuality shape the spotlight in fashion design. *Gender & Society, 29*(2), 219–243.

Stone, A. L. (2016). Crowning King Anchovy: Cold War Gay Visibility in San Antonio's urban festival. *Journal of the History of Sexuality, 25*(2), 297–322.

Stone, A. L. (2017). *Cornyation: San Antonio's Outrageous Fiesta Tradition*. San Antonio, TX: Maverick Book/Trinity University Press.

Stone, A. L., & Shapiro, E. (2017). You're really just a gay man in a woman's body!" The possibilities and Perils of Queer Sexuality. *Men and Masculinities, 20*(2), 254–272.

Taylor, Y. (2007). If Your Face Doesn't Fit…': The misrecognition of working-class lesbians in scene space. *Leisure Studies, 26*(2), 161–178.

Ward, J. (2008). *Respectably queer: Diversity culture in LGBT activist organizations*. Nashville, TN: Vanderbilt University Press.

"That crosscountry 1969 vw squareback and holiday inn affair": lesbian mobility

Liz Millward

ABSTRACT

This article argues that lesbian mobility contributed to the development of lesbian identity in North America in the 1960s and 1970s. Drawing primarily on published accounts, it explores the ways in which women achieved and sustained their lesbian identity in part through their access to what cultural geographers term a transportation assemblage or constellation of mobility. This was constituted through the symbolic meaning of mobility for predominantly white women, the existence of new highway networks and Volkswagen vehicles, which were popularized through countercultural branding, and lesbians' embodied experiences of fear and desire.

In 1973 Jill Johnston's *Lesbian Nation* was published. It was a collection of essays taken from *The Village Voice*, a countercultural newspaper, and described the process by which Johnston developed her feminist and lesbian politics. Crucial to this process was her mobility: it was through her journeys and experiences and encounters along the routes that she began to develop a sense of herself as a politicized lesbian, not just an individual woman who happened to be in love (yet again) with another woman. In 1969 she undertook a trip across the USA in a Volkswagen Type 3 squareback sedan. She wrote that in "january & february 1969 I was traveling in a VW squareback south and West and back east again 12000 miles in seven weeks with a lover and partways with a friend of hers from canada and finland who weighed over 200 and protected us through the badlands of the south. In el paso we sent him flying on. We were in love and he was a jealous party. We stayed in every holiday inn along the way" (Johnston, 1973, p. 75). This is a key account, in which the trip was a chance for the two lovers to partially escape the external forces of homophobia and the long reach of family control. They were also running towards something that felt new: for Johnston in particular that was a shift from occupying a highly individualized (and suffering) subject position towards seeing herself as a lesbian, a political identity that lay outside of patriarchy and was a threat to it.

What made Johnston's mobility possible and significant was not just the two women's lust and desire "to live happily ever after with yer [sic] one true beloved or perish in the effort" (Johnston, 1973, p. 76). It was instead facilitated by a "transportation assemblage" (Stewart, 2014) or "constellation of mobility" (Cresswell, 2011), a combination of several components that together make a particular form of mobility both possible and meaningful. In the late 1960s and early 1970s this assemblage was constituted by the symbolic meaning of mobility for white women, the existence of new highway networks and their associated facilities, freshly established women's lands, and Volkswagen vehicles, which were themselves a combination of material object and clever countercultural branding. This article looks at three examples of lesbians negotiating this specific assemblage: Johnston's account of her 12,000-mile road trip and of her travels in a Volkswagen camper van; the Womanshare Collective's use of vehicles; and the experiences of the Van Dykes. These negotiations contributed to the experience and development of a specific, primarily white, version of North American lesbian identity that combined a sense of personal agency with a commitment to sexual freedom. This mobility was not available to all lesbians. Even when women shared the political goals of lesbian feminism they could not necessarily go on the road in pursuit of them if they were limited by working-class or racialized travel horizons, including the expectation of staying close to home or supporting family.

Analyses of lesbian geographies tend to study particular types of spaces that women inhabit in their attempts to consolidate lesbian community, of which lesbian lands provide perhaps the best-known example (Jennings, 2018; Sandilands, 2002). In the urban setting lesbians have struggled to be visible (Podmore, 2006), but from at least the end of the Second World War and certainly by the 1960s and 1970s they were working hard to maintain spaces where lesbian culture and politics could thrive (Chenier, 2004; Millward, 2015). These lesbian geographies were not static. Lesbian groups came and went as members burned out, were kicked out, or made out and left of their own accord, and both groups and individual women frequently relocated. Between 1973 and 1976, for example, Montreal Gay Women changed its meeting space eight times (Millward, 2015, p. 119). Indeed, Nash and Gorman-Murray (2015) suggest that looking at why lesbian place-making is so mobile "has the potential to rewrite the historical geographies of lesbians' urban landscapes from one of 'failure' or 'lack of potential' to create or maintain urban territories [compared to gay men] to one that understands gendered and sexual differences as truly mediating distinctive sociospatial relations, urban experiences and place making" (p. 177).

Expanding the lens to look beyond urban sites adds to this approach. The increasing numbers of lesbian-organized events such as conferences and music festivals in the 1970s provided one significant motivation for certain lesbians to travel, while Gorman-Murray (2007) suggests another: "a need queer people often feel to find *somewhere* – some *place* – to explore alternative ways of being, *at the same time* recognizing that this search is *ongoing*, generating *movement between places*" (p. 113, emphasis in original). These desires led lesbians abroad as they engaged in transnational circuits of mobility at the global scale (Jennings & Millward, 2016). All of this work attends to movement but does not necessarily consider the journey itself or what can be learned from the "constellation of mobility" (Cresswell, 2011, p. 165) that made something like "that crosscountry 1969 vw squareback and holiday inn affair" possible (Johnston, 1973, p. 86).

Mobility is political. As Cresswell (2011) explains, it is "implicated in the production of power and relations of domination" (p. 166). The questions of who can move where and by what mode of transportation, what this means, and what it feels like, together constitute pervasive "constellations of mobility" in particular time periods (Cresswell, 2011, p. 165). In the USA in the 1960s, for example, all African Americans battled to overcome forced immobility (the legacy of slavery with its brutal regime to control movement) and the violent repression of racial politics, while across North America indigenous people fought to assert their ancient practices of free movement around the continent in the face of government pass systems that tried to restrict them to reserves. The freedom of movement of women from these and other groups was constrained by a stifling patriarchy, in part for economic reasons but also through cultural meanings and the threat of violence if they stepped out of line. In this context, automobility in general provided a symbolic sense of power and control.

What automobility meant

Automobility has a long history of deep symbolism beyond its functional aspect as a mode of transportation. In his aptly named *Republic of Drivers*, Seiler (2008) argues that in U.S. culture "the belief in self-directed motion as an agent of liberation, cleansing, edification, and nationalization is powerful and venerable" (p. 16). The particular form of motion is significant. He argues that it is "the *act of driving*, rather than the utilitarian and status-conferring automotive object," which matters since it provides "the crucial compensation for apparent losses to the autonomy, privacy, and agency registered by workers under the transition to corporate capitalism, and therefore [is] an important ideological tool for the preservation of hegemony" (Seiler, 2008, p. 13). He goes on to argue that "the subjects produced by the apparatus of automobility pronounce and feel themselves free with an intensity that asserts motion to be the epitome, and not simply one possible dimension, of freedom" (Seiler, 2008, p. 149). Particular groups worked collectively to try and ensure that they had access to this freedom. Seiler draws attention, for example, to innovations such as the *Travelguide* and *The Negro Motorist Green Book* that "simultaneously protested the discrimination that confronted black motorists on American roads and proffered the hegemonic image of American freedom through driving" (Seiler, 2008, p. 115).

Driving as freedom has a particular valence for women, although being on the road quickly exposed the limits and constraints of that liberty (Ganser, 2006). Parkins (2009) demonstrated that the idea of women achieving autonomy through mobility predated the rise of automobility itself, making its way into cultural representations in novels and serials from the 1850s onwards, but it is Scharff (1991) who made the link that it was explicitly driving that fostered U.S. women's feelings of freedom and autonomy. This idea has since been developed by Clarke (2007) and Clarsen (2008) who trace the widespread representation of automobility as a powerful signifier of independence for women in Australia, Britain, and the USA during the early decades of motoring. Women drivers who were seeking a way to establish themselves as independent beings might feel liberated through their displays of technological competence: filling a tank at a gas station, performing routine maintenance tasks like oil changes, or undertaking roadside repairs such as changing a tire. They expanded their travel horizons by navigating using maps and finding their way in unfamiliar landscapes. Farr (1995) shows that U.S. feminist novelists refreshed the link between driving and women's political and emotional freedom in books written in the 1970s and 1980s. Ganser (2006), however, cautions against a simplified reading of that link, at least in terms of cultural representations that include hitch-hiking as well as driving and being a passenger. She argues that "most road literature by women […] is wary of celebrating the illusory freedom of travel, but emphasizes instead the importance of making women visible in public space, in this case entailing the road itself as well as the roadside, with its truck stops, diners and motels" (Ganser, 2006, p. 164).

Although Ganser (2006) suggests caution around the mobility-as-freedom narrative, it seems that during the 1960s and 1970s many people wholeheartedly embraced it. Mobility was a major component of the zeitgeist. The lesbian author Lee Lynch (1988) remarks that "frequent moving had become a generational phenomenon by 1971, at least for the middle-class kids I knew" (p. 162). In Canada, hitchhiking by young people in the late 1960s had become such a popular form of what Cohen (1973) called "drifter-tourism" that the Liberal Government under Prime Minister Pierre Trudeau felt pressured into a formal response: a *Transient Youth Enquiry*. It recommended youth hostels as a way to manage the potential disruption represented by white, middle-class mostly young men hitchhiking across Canada in large numbers (Mahood, 2014). Each summer an estimated 50,000 to 100,000 hitchhikers went through Winnipeg, which is generally considered to be the geographic center of North America (Mahood, 2014). Such self-directed mobility, in contrast to forced relocation or the postwar migrations of displaced persons, had become "the new God," as Rivers (1972) put it in *The Restless Generation*. While environmentalists began to fret over the ways in which the combined vested interests of governments, oil and transportation companies and tourism operators managed to bull-doze their way through any critique of unbridled mobility, women (like the men, mostly but not exclusively white, middle-class and young) took up the opportunities that were created. Thousands hitchhiked, but others drove relatively cheap cars on subsidized roads using relatively cheap pet-rol, flew overseas on the new jet airliners, or ventured afield on flat-rate Greyhound coach tickets.

Highways and Volkswagen vehicles

This "new God" (Rivers, 1972) of mobility was dependent on "moorings," or infrastructure components such as highways, Holiday Inns, hostels and camping grounds, filling stations, and – for lesbians specifically – lesbian land, each with their own history and significance, without which long-dis-tance driving could not become commonplace. In terms of highways, Stewart (2014) argues that the "road is not finished matter or representa-tion but an assembling, registering machinery of impacts and potentialities" (p. 553). Certainly, infrastructure development increased the possibilities for independent travel. In 1950 work began on the Trans-Canada Highway, which had first been floated as an idea before World War I and for which funding was allocated under the Canada Highways Act of 1919 and again in the 1949 Trans-Canada Highway Act (Saywell, 1975). The highway offi-cially opened in 1962, even though it was not actually finished until 1970. Its construction was justified as part of a prominent ideology of unification through transportation. A 1978 Canadian government report listed key transportation infrastructure projects whose role was to support the Canadian "common market" and to provide, as the report's title suggested, a "unifying link" (MacNeil, 1978). These roads changed the relationships between communities, as railways had done before them, and "would enable the strung-out Canadians to get to know each other a little better, and know their country a little better too" (Saywell, 1975, p. 163).

Similarly, while the famous Route 66 (from Chicago to Santa Monica) had been completely paved during the 1930s, the US Interstate highway system was not begun until 1956. It was finally declared complete in 1992 and was portrayed as "the fulfillment of middle-class Americans' desires for automotive safety, national security, economic prosperity, and expanded mobility. It was the largest public works project in human history: from 1956 to 1975, over 42,500 miles of the continental U.S. would be paved; and a federal trust fund would raise and distribute an estimated $41 billion (in actuality, over $100 billion) in construction costs" (Seiler, 2008, p. 71). Like the Trans-Canada Highway, its impact was complicated. Its progress was used to justify the bulldozing and displacement of poorer urban communities dominated by Black and Latino people while simultaneously consolidating the power of urban centers at the expense of what became dismissed as "fly-over country." For African American drivers in particular it had a contradictory effect because by opening up the continent it increased the potential for racist encounters, but the homogenization of roadside services simultaneously reduced the frequency of these moments. As Seiler (2008) puts it, "it was precisely in the act of driving through unfamiliar territory that the inescapability of race became [...] so apparent" (p. 114), although the development of the limited-access highways with their "increasingly national 'McDonaldized' amenity businesses at the interchanges" ameliorated this experience to some extent (p. 128). And although the network as a whole might contribute to a sense of sameness everywhere the highways went, some routes carried more specific meanings. Herring (2010) singles out the I-80 east-to-west coast highway as one that generated a profound queer imaginary, linking, at least symbolically, Christopher Street in New York City with the Castro District in San Francisco. Lynch (1988) meanwhile refers to I-5, the Canada-to-Mexico freeway, as a main trunk of the "Amazon Trail." This claim was supported by the Womanshare Collective, based in Oregon, who were interested in connecting to lesbian feminists living outside their land. They noted that "this community lives all along Interstate Highway 5 from San Francisco to Seattle. Some members of the community are our very close friends and lovers, others we don't know yet" (Womanshare Collective, 1976, p. 172). The existence of the highway would make it possible to meet and get to know them.

The mode of transportation used on those highways also mattered. David Gartman (1994) among others details the role that particular makes of vehicle play in creating and sustaining a driver's sense of self, as they buy into advertising messages promoting "expressive individualism," or the ability to achieve individual fulfillment and exercise personal choice through car ownership (Seiler, 2008, pp. 33-35). Nelson remarked in 1970 that the Volkswagen company "knows that the VW is not just a mode of transportation (which was the only purpose for which Porsche designed it); it knows that the car amuses and delights, as well as transports, its owners" (Nelson, 1970, p. 248). Or, as Bernhard Rieger (2013) puts it, "beyond its undisputed mechanical qualities and its economy, the Beetle possessed an intangible charm," and the VW Beetle was a noticeable favorite with women drivers from the 1950s onwards (pp. 196-202).

Literally capitalizing on the odd charm of the Volkswagen stable of vehicles, the famous advertising campaign for them started in 1959 by the DDB agency effectively created the idea that Volkswagen drivers were countercultural. Frank (1997) asserts that these advertisements launched "a form of anti-advertising that worked by distancing a product from consumerism" (p. 68) and that persuaded consumers that they should "buy this to escape consumerism" (p. 69). One woman who "drove a VW bus then still remembers" a specific advertisement that listed the qualities of the "wife" who would embrace the VW Transporter, also known as a Station Wagon or a Bus in the USA and as a Microbus or Camper in the UK. She would be able to bake her own bread and let her daughter have a pet snake, among many other qualities. The woman explained that that advertisement "made me feel cute as a button and interesting as hell" (Rowsome, 1970, p. 100). Lesbians involved in the counterculture were equally influenced by this form of driver/owner subjectivity and VWs became the vehicle of choice for many of them. To give just three examples: Lynch's (1988) dream car in 1970 was a "brand new Bug" that she named Lana Cantrell after the singer. When this was stolen she replaced it with a red VW Beetle that she called Blue. In 1971 Dian, who went on to found the Womanshare Collective, "wanted to buy a vw van and do some traveling, because my life felt as if it had dead-ended" (Womanshare Collective, 1976, p. 65), while Reva, her daughter, and their guinea pig were squeezed into a "loaded down Volkswagen" at the beginning of a cross-Canada trip to start their lives afresh in 1975 (Reva, 1975, 2).

From their earliest incarnations automobiles have been a "means to privacy and seclusion, and an enclosed space for unsanctioned sexual contact" (Seiler, 2008, p. 57). They can also represent a "mobile living room" or personal zone of safety for women venturing into the explicitly hostile public realm (Clarsen, 2008). The VW van in particular seemed to create both of these conditions for those white lesbians with access to one. In an essay from 1973 Johnston (1998) remarked that "we all have these camper phases even if you don't actually get one" (p. 218). She used hers for one "three month junket to the coast and back" during which time she "parked it for a week on an island off maine overlooking some reefs and seaweed and holed up inside to write very comfortably as though I'd discovered the all-purpose self reflecting box with a window on the ocean of the world" (Johnston, 1998, p. 217). She noted that "when you have a car that you *can't* sleep in nobody wants you to stay in their regular plumbing and elec-trified houses and when you *do* have one they're quite eager for some rea-son to put you up, so the true benefits deriving from a camper are those of increased and unlimited visitation rights" but added that "i had a very important sexual experience in my camper, so I guess it was worth it" (Johnston, 1998, pp. 220-221).

Dykes on the road

Johnston remained fairly individualist in her Volkswagen van excursions, but the "Van Dykes," a loose group of predominantly white and middle-class Canadian and U.S. lesbians, committed to a collective experience of adventure in their several Volkswagen vans. In 1976 Heather, one of the original Van Dykes who eventually changed her name to Lamar (most of the Van Dykes changed their names at some point), met Ange Spalding, "who was glowing and tan after almost a year of living out of her van in warm places. Ange talked about the anonymity and freedom of life on the road" (Levy, 2009, p. 31). In spite of the fact that Heather was then in a relationship with Chris Fox and sharing a life on a farm with her and two other lesbians at Cavan in Ontario, Canada, she left with Ange and they spent 1977 on the road. Returning to Canada in 1978 Heather met a new lover, Judith:

> But what Heather really wanted was to be on the road – not so much with a partner as with a pack. The dramatic potential of a van gang appealed to Judith, and she enlisted her friend Nancy, a woman who was just getting out of a bad marriage. Nancy wanted to share the spoils of her divorce with other women and experiment with a new way of life. She quickly transformed from Nancy, a heterosexual with children, into Sky Van Dyke, a lesbian separatist with a van. (Levy, 2009, p. 34).

Sky paid Chris Fox (who changed her name to Thorn Van Dyke) to renovate her van, and together with Ange and another woman who joined Sky, the six of them, in separate combinations, made their various ways by VW van to a rendezvous in San Antonio, Texas and eventually on to Mexico. Heather remarked that "you could actually go all around the coun-try from Women's Land to Women's Land and you met all these other women who were doing the same thing" (Levy, 2009, p. 35). However, the whole ethos of living in vans and constant mobility could be challenging. As Fox, who was working class, explained, "Some people had vans; other people didn't have vans. I didn't have a van. So, if I didn't always have to sleep with somebody in a van, then I needed a place to live, too" (Fox, 2012). By the early 1980s, most of the Van Dykes had put down roots and given up life on the road.

The Van Dykes explicitly committed to mobility as a means to create and experience their lesbian subjectivity. Other lesbians were also exploring and developing their personal lesbian identity in part through their relationship to automobility. In 1972 Dian from the U.S. lived with Carol (whom she had met ten years earlier at college) and Billie in a collective in Nova Scotia, Canada, and the three of them subsequently opened a not-for-profit women's craft store called The Flaming Apron in Montréal. They became dissatisfied with their lives in that city and in the summer of 1973 Dian persuaded the other two (by then a couple) to drive West with her where she hoped to find "a safe space to live, to work, to help create the women's culture she dreamed of" (Womanshare Collective, 1976, pp. 62-63). Having traveled for a while they finally purchased some land in southern Oregon in April 1974 and set up home there, along with a number of other women who came and went, and founded the Womanshare Collective. By 1976 the Womanshare Collective owned three vehicles: a Toyota pickup truck and two VW Beetles named "Tootie" and "Gussie." In addition to teaching themselves how to look after the vehicles they had to negotiate over who could use them for which trips, not just with each other but also with their lesbian neighbors, Sally, Shannon and Tori. In a "Sample Car Rap" they demonstrate this process:

> Carol: OK, let's talk about the trips we want to go on in the next month.
>
> Dian: Nelly and I are going to the city on January 9th. We want to take a car.
>
> Sue: I'm going to Seattle on the 9th also and I want to take Gussie.
>
> Billie: Tori and I are going to go snowshoeing, but we're taking Tori's van.
>
> Carol: I'm staying here. Susann's coming.
>
> Sue: Well, Tootie and Gussie both need a tune-up and to get lubed at the gas station. I'll do the tune-up.
>
> Carol: (To Sue) You and I can take Gussie in when we go to get the car insurance.
>
> Sue: OK. So I guess Dian and Nelly can take Tootie.
>
> Dian: I'll take Tootie to get her lubed. (Womanshare Collective, 1976, pp. 114-115)

This car rap indicates two factors. First, women such as these who founded and maintained the lesbian lands across North America were not immobile: they took frequent trips and their mobility was part of their identity. Second, in choosing what to highlight in their account of collective living they picked this rap, which on the one hand is a straightforward negotiation around resources and on the other is a document of their technological competence and sense of agency. More than merely a meta-phor for learning how to inhabit lesbian nation, these skills helped women develop confidence in themselves and in the possibility and existence of an alternative worldview.

Embodied lesbian mobility

The third component of Cresswell's (2011) "constellation of mobility" is embodiment, or what it feels like. In their accounts of their mobility these white lesbians reveal how fraught it could be. For any lesbians traveling across the North American continent, the highways and Holiday Inns often seemed at a minimum to be heteronormative spaces and at worst fre-quently dangerous, either physically or, in Johnston's case, to her and her lover Polly's tenuous sense of lesbian selfhood. She wrote that "more than two days in any one place was a luxury we couldn't seem to afford [...] Either there really was a menace out there or it was all in my paranoid les-bian mind. I think it was both. But basically I thought the world was after us and we had to keep moving. And basically I was right. We were an illegal couple" (Johnston, 1973, p. 77). The couple was beset by threats to their relationship at every turn, from their own internalized doubt about its validity to the encounters with men they met along the way who demon-strated everything from active aggression to damaging disrespect. Johnston refers to the trip as a series of escapes. Some of these were minor: "we escaped every bad baboon and his wife in the holiday or other inns by just paying and leaving and not looking crosseyed" (Johnston, 1973, p. 94). Others were more disturbing: from "a bunch of refugee hippies in taos in a muddy shack serving up health shit leering lust and luftwaffe after me and polly but especially polly" to "these creative alcoholic cigar smoking woman fucking husbands and artists whose attitude toward me and polly was no better than all the others I mentioned and so typically we fled to a holiday inn in detroit before driving on to Pittsburgh" (Johnston, 1973, p. 94). In their case the VW Squareback was the zone of safety and the only space where their illicit sexuality seemed able to exist, at least until they pulled into a gas station or Holiday Inn and had to encounter the oppressive weight of homophobic patriarchy at the end of each day.

For other lesbians the space inside the vehicle was equally intense and freighted with significance. Endlessly driving and living out of motel rooms, in tents, and in VW vans was physically and emotionally draining. Chris Fox (2012) pointed out that remaining on the road without a van of her own was unsustainable, and the emotional toll of the sexual jealousies and political disagreements became exhausting. For Dian, Billie and Carol, the trip out West in search of lesbian community was a challenge on many levels. "Leaving was hard," they wrote, "leaving the familiar, leaving old friends. Traveling was also hard." The three women struggled to negotiate their interpersonal dynamics. "They all felt pain, anger, and jealousy; and struggle as they did, they were unable to be a happy threesome. It was hard being in the car together so much, such a small space. And there were just the three of them. There were no other women to help change their emotional dynamics." Having left Montreal, they "struggled across the U.S., through Mexico, and up and down the West Coast." When those "emotional dynamics" reached breaking point, they set down roots in Oregon (Womanshare Collective, 1976, p. 64).

Whereas the first two components of the "constellation of mobility" (Cresswell, 2011), the means and the meanings, indicate that some white lesbians could subvert the hegemonic goals of nationalist, capitalist and resolutely patriarchal mobility and adapt them to their own ends, their experience of that subverted mobility was more sobering. Their accounts of embodied experiences of fear, threat, exhaustion and jealousy can be read as the exposure of the illusory nature of the dream of mobility as freedom. Alternatively, however, they can be read as evidence of these women's determination to keep moving, to maintain both their circuits of mobility and their VW vans and meet up with new women in new places for new sexual and political encounters in spite of the emotional toll that mobility took.

Conclusion

Johnston's tale points to the significance of automobility for white and mostly middle-class lesbians during the 1970s. French geographer Marianne Blidon (2015) suggests that scholarship on lesbian geographies should extend beyond its typical focus on urban and rural-separatist communities to explore the scale of the nation and globe, while also considering the transnational mobility of cultural products and social networks. This paper takes up that suggestion in order to explore the factors that contributed to lesbian mobility at the scale of the North American continent at a time when a political identity was becoming both possible and sustainable. In particular their side-opening Volkswagen vans provided the mobile homes in which they could spend years driving around the burgeoning lesbian community: from Womyn's Land to music festivals or to make side trips to see (and have sex with) other lesbians they had heard about. Although not accessible to many lesbians through the particular politics of race and class, in the 1960s and 1970s the new highways and lodging places, the significance of the Volkswagen brand, and the cultural meanings of both contributed to a politics of mobility that supported lesbian community formation and a different sense of self.

Disclosure statement

No potential conflict of interest was reported by the author.

References

Blidon, M. (2015). Putting lesbians geographies on the geographical map – A commentary. In K. Browne & E. Ferreira (Eds.), *Lesbian Geographies: Gender, Place and Power* (pp. 243–247). Farnham: Ashgate.

Chenier, E. (2004). Rethinking class in lesbian bar culture: Living "The Gay Life" in Toronto, 1955-1965. *Left History, 9*(2), 85–118.

Clarke, D. (2007). *Driving women: Fiction and automobile culture in twentieth-century America*. Baltimore: Johns Hopkins University Press.

Clarsen, G. (2008). *Eat my dust: Early women motorists*. Baltimore: Johns Hopkins University Press.

Cohen, E. (1973). Nomads from affluence: Notes on the phenomenon of drifter-tourism. *International Journal of Comparative Sociology XIV, 14*(1–2), 89–103.

Cresswell, T. (2011). Towards a politics of mobility. In M. Hvattum, B. Brenna, B. Elvebakk, & J. Kampevold Larsen (Eds.), *Routes, Roads and Landscapes* (pp. 162–177). Farnham: Ashgate.

Farr, M. T. (1995). Freedom and control: Automobiles in American women's fiction of the 70s and 80s. *The Journal of Popular Culture, 29*(2), 157–169.

Fox, C. (2012). Personal interview. May 27

Frank, T. (1997). *The conquest of cool: Business culture, counterculture, and the rise of hip consumerism*. Chicago: University of Chicago Press.

Ganser, A. (2006). On the asphalt frontier: American women's road narratives, spatiality, and transgression. *Journal of International Women's Studies, 7*(4), 153–167.

Gartman, D. (1994). *Auto opium: A social history of American automobile design*. New York: Routledge.

Gorman-Murray, A. (2007). Rethinking queer migration through the body. *Social & Cultural Geography, 8*(1), 105–121.

Herring, S. (2010). *Another country: Queer anti-urbanism*. New York: New York University Press.

Jennings, R. (2018). Creating feminist culture: Australian lesbian-separatist communities in the 1970s and 1980s. *Journal of Women's History, 30*(2), 88–111.

Jennings, R., & Millward, L. (2016). A fully formed blast from abroad"? Australasian lesbian circuits of mobility and the transnational exchange of ideas in the 1960s and 1970s. *Journal of the History of Sexuality, 25*(3), 463–488.

Johnston, J. (1973). *Lesbian nation.* New York: Simon & Schuster.

Johnston, J. (1998). *Admission accomplished: The lesbian nation years (1970-75).* London: Serpent's Tail Press.

Levy, A. (2009, March 2). Lesbian Nation: When Gay Women Took to the Road. *The New Yorker,* 30–37.

Lynch, L. (1988). *The Amazon trail.* Tallahassee: Naiad Press.

MacNeil, P. H. (1978). *Transportation: a unifying link.* Ottawa: Government of Canada.

Mahood, L. (2014). Hitchin' a Ride in the 1970s: Canadian youth culture and the romance with mobility. *Histoire Sociale/Social History, XLVII*(93), 219–220.

Millward, L. (2015). *Making a Scene: Lesbians and community across Canada, 1964-1984.* Vancouver: UBC Press.

Nash, C., & Gorman-Murray, A. (2015). Lesbians in the city: Mobilities and relational geographies. *Journal of Lesbian Studies, 19*(2), 173–191.

Nelson, W. H. (1970). *Small wonder: The amazing story of the Volkswagen.* Rev. ed. Toronto: Little, Brown and Co.

Parkins, W. (2009). *Mobility and modernity in women's novels, 1850s-1930s: Women moving dangerously.* Basingstoke: Palgrave Macmillan.

Podmore, J. (2006). Gone "underground"? Lesbian visibility and the consolidation of queer space in Montréal. *Social & Cultural Geography, 7*(4), 595–625.

Reva. (1975, October). When a dyke goes west. *Long Time Coming,* 2–3.

Rieger, B. (2013). *People's car: A global history of the Volkswagen beetle.* Cumberland: Harvard University Press.

Rivers, P. (1972). *The restless generation: A crisis in mobility.* London: Davis-Poynter.

Rowsome, F. (1970). *Think small: The story of those Volkswagen ads.* Brattleboro, Vermont: Stephen Green Press.

Sandilands, C. (2002). Lesbian separatist communities and the experience of nature: Toward a queer ecology. *Organization & Environment, 15*(2), 131–163.

Saywell, J. T. (1975). *Across mountain and muskeg: Building the Canadian transportation system.* Discussion paper (Economic Council of Canada); no. 22. Ottawa: Economic Council of Canada, pp. 141–163

Scharff, V. (1991). *Taking the wheel: Women and the coming of the motor age.* New York: Free Press.

Seiler, C. (2008). *Republic of drivers: A cultural history of automobility in America.* Chicago: University of Chicago Press.

Stewart, K. (2014). Road registers. *Cultural Geographies, 21*(4), 549–563.

Womanshare Collective. (1976). *Country lesbians: The story of the Womanshare collective.* Grants Pass, Oregon: WomanShare Books.

From situated space to social space: Dyke bar commemoration as reparative action

Japonica Brown-Saracino

ABSTRACT

Drawing on an ethnography of dyke bar commemoration in four U.S. cities, this article applies Sedgwick's concept of "reparative reading" to commemorative practices, tracing how commemorators leverage this reading to guide a *logic of reparative action*. They commemorate material spaces rooted in place, but cultivate mobile and inclusive space. That is, commemorators, most of whom have had limited exposure to the spaces that they mourn, carefully situate the lost dyke bar, highlighting geographic, esthetic, demographic, and temporal attributes. The images they construct of the *situated bar* contrast with their commemorative events, which emphasize social over alternate attributes. Commemorators repair and critique the situated bar – not to restore it, but to harness it for their forward-facing efforts – by using memory to advocate for a move from specificity to generality; from situated to mobile and inclusive *social spaces*. I elucidate how this turn toward social space and bar commemoration itself emerges not merely from institutional and territorial loss, but from commitments to diversity, inclusivity, and queer identities and politics.

Introduction

The 1969 Stonewall riot served as a defining origin story for the gay and lesbian movement (Armstrong & Crage, 2006; D'Emilio, 2002). This story positioned the bar and the riot that took place there as a meeting place for racially and economically heterogeneous lesbian,gay,bisexual,transgender,and-queer (LGBTQ) individuals, including, among others, butch lesbians, drag queens, cisgender gay men, and transgender individuals (Bravmann, 1997). This account underlines LGBTQ individuals' shared marginality, and downplays divisions and exclusions (Seidman, 2013); it locates sexual and gender minorities, together, in the same bar, battling the police. This narrative partially facilitated 20th-century gay and lesbian politics that presented sexual difference as providing inimitable common ground (Bernstein, 1997).

This article spotlights a different origin story, centering a different bar. Drawing on an ethnography of dyke bar commemoration, it asks why activists leverage memories of a much less demographically diverse bar to achieve similar aims of cultivating community and identity. Commemorators offer a notably detailed portrait of the bar, positioning it in a specific time, locale, and esthetic genre, and emphasizing working-class, cisgender female clientele. In other words, they offer narratives of the *situated* bar: an (exclusive) institution presented in narrow temporal, spatial, esthetic and demographic terms.[1]

Their situated narratives are part of what Eve Sedgwick terms "reparative reading" (Sedgwick, 2003). While diagnosing the inequalities and exclusions of the dyke bar (in a mode characteristic of Sedgwick's "paranoid reading"), commemorators also admire and rescue elements of the bar for the future, particularly its capacity for generating a sense of "we" and related community. By combing dyke bar histories for successes and failures, they leverage new strategies for fostering identities and communities. In this sense, they adopt a critical yet hopeful – or reparative – reading of extant dyke bars.

If Stonewall narratives gesture to shared fate and identity among disparate individuals, commemorators present the situated dyke bar in nearly opposite terms: as a place where everyone knows your name because everyone is *like* you. They present it as an institution inaccessible to many, particularly nonwhite, cisgender "dykes," but that cultivated identities and communities. Going forward, commemorators are committed to a *logic of reparative action* or a set of strategies culled from their reparative reading of the situated bar; from their recognition that "the future may be different from the present" (Sedgwick, 2003, p. 146; see Love, 2007) and their desire to jumpstart that future both via commemoration and future events they hope to inspire. Specifically, they seek to organize gatherings that are *not* oriented around specific identities, and *not* rooted in time or place. They imagine a future in which heterogeneous queer (writ-large) individuals intermingle at a variety of times and places; this is at the heart of the *social space* they work to constitute: mobile, temporary, inclusive, and socially heterogeneous interactional contexts that foster identity and community.

Crucially, desire for social space does not merely emerge from institutional loss. Commemorators read the bar against the backdrop of the diversification of sexual and gender identities, which renders "lesbian" identities they associate with dyke bars passé and problematic (Podmore, 2006, Stein, 2010). Indeed, most commemorator-informants are under 35, identify as queer; a handful are genderqueer or transgender. Most possess a BA (many from elite institutions), are from middle-class households, mindful of intersectionality (Crenshaw, 1991), and steeped in "diversity discourse" (Berrey, 2005). Thus, personal and political commitments to diversity, inclusivity, and radical queer and intersectional politics are central to their vision for future social space (Muñoz, 2009). They present themselves as privileged custodians of dyke bar histories, and regard the cultivation of social space as a responsibility that extends from their privilege. They implicitly reject visions of a "postgay" world (Brown, 2006; Ghaziani, 2011) in which alliances emerge from non-sexual traits. They seek to bring disparate queer individuals together, despite reduced sexual-marginality. Indeed, contra existing literature, more than institutional and identity changes, ideological commitments drive their work.

Below, I locate the article in existing literatures, introduce methods, and trace representations of the situated dyke bar. Ultimately, I reveal how histories, read reparatively, shape a logic of action aimed at cultivating mobile and inclusive social space (Ward, 2008).

Literature review
Changing identities and institutions

Dyke bar commemoration emerged with broad changes in LGBTQIA institutions; those that served LBQ individuals, from bars to bookstores, have taken new shape or withered with cultural, political, and social changes (Nash, 2011; Stone, 2013). Among these are the proliferation and diversification of sexual and gender identities (Faderman, 1991; Gamson, 1995; Stein, 1993); transgender, queer, and genderqueer individuals' increasing visibility; sexual minorities' expanding legal and cultural gains; their related integration into traditionally heterosexual spaces and vice versa (Hartless, 2018; Orne, 2017); broad claims of a move toward "postgay" identities (Brown, 2006; Forstie, 2018); and advancing gentrification (Gieseking, 2016). Scholars and others trace how institutions have faltered as they grapple with changing base, and face pushback for exclusions and biases (Browne, 2011; Hogan, 2016), and how surviving institutions serve as anchors (Greene, 2014). By commemorating dyke bars, commemorators engage and navigate this evolving terrain.

Literature on nostalgia predicts that activists would leverage commemoration to preserve identities associated with bars (Milligan, 2003). Instead, they reject the "meta-narrative of gay identity formation that glosses over difference, anomaly, and specificity" (Bravmann, 1997, p. 44) – one they associate with bars. In contrast, they embrace inclusivity and center "queer" or nonnormative orientations (Warner, 2000). Thus, commemoration is only partially a response to institutional and territorial loss (cf. Ghaziani & Stillwagon, 2018). Instead, commemoration emerges with commitments to diversity, inclusivity, and queer politics.

Public memories and reparative action

To construct social space, commemorators rely on the formation of "public memories" (Dunn, 2016) of the situated bar. Their presentation of the situated bar calls out a sense of community from nostalgia, recognition of the *absence* of a common bar-past, and commitment to inclusivity.

Commemorators are not alone in turning to memory to organize a public. Their bar-mythology constitutes a "queer [fiction] of the past" (Bravmann, 1997, p. x), which aids the formulation of "queer fictions of the present" (ibid) and future. Like others, they place memories of queer pasts on display so that "like-minded members can constitute, de-constitute, and reconstitute identities" (Dunn, 2016, p. 8).

Thus, this article underlines how memory can be future-oriented (Pickering & Keightley, 2006). This builds on scholarship on how memories are rooted in "conceptions and needs of the present" (Olick & Robbins, 1998; Schwartz, 1982). Scholars call for consideration of how even nostalgia is forward-facing, recognizing "aspects of the past as the basis for renewal and satisfaction in the future" (Pickering & Keightley, 2006, p. 921).

Extending from this, I explore the bar's "queer after life" (Dunn, 2016). To understand that after-life, I begin with the remembered bar. Yet, it is important not to lose sight of the "the constitutive role that the future imaginary plays in" commemoration (Mische, 2014; see also Puar, 2007, Tavory & Eliasoph, 2013). That is, like other markers of difficult pasts (Wagner-Pacifici & Schwartz, 1991), bar-commemorations are not entirely or even largely affirmative; there is a future imaginary in nuanced representations (McDermott, 2002).

Commemorators' hopes for the present and future take the form of what Sedgwick terms a "reparative reading" (Sedgwick, 2003) of the bar. Sedgwick writes:

> Hope…. is among the energies by which the reparatively positioned reader tries to organize the fragments and part-objects she encounters…. Because the reader has room to realize that the future may be different from the present, it is also possible for her to entertain such profoundly painful, profoundly revealing, ethically cruel possibilities as that the past, in turn, could have happened differently (Sedgwick, 2003, p. 146).

For commemorators, reparative reading – their eye for elements of the past that can be "rescued" and put together differently – guides a logic of *reparative action* or a set of future-facing strategies, an unexplored facet of reparative reading.[2] The pages that follow reveal efforts to rescue elements of the situated bar, namely its association with community and collective identity, as commemorators formulate mobile and inclusive social space.

Methods

I draw on my ethnography of dyke bar commemoration in New York, New Orleans, Chicago, and San Francisco. At the center of the study is the work of four collaborative commemorative organizations that constituted, to the best of my knowledge, collaborative dyke bar commemoration in the U.S. during the study period (2016 – 2019).[3] These include: the New Orleans theater troupe, *Last Call*, which used oral history interviews to create a dyke bar musical and podcast series; *New York Dyke Bar Takeover*, which used oral history research to create a Lost Dyke Bar Walking Tour in Greenwich Village and hosts bar takeovers; San Francisco's *Lexington Archival Project*, which created a short documentary on the Lexington Club (circa 1997 – 2015); and Chicago's *Lost & Found*, a series of events – from DJed yoga to panels – organized around an exhibit on lost dyke spaces. Table 1 summarizes additional data sources.

I collected field notes at events related to the above organizations, films, and exhibits (see Table 2). On occasion, commemorators directed me to additional scenes, such as a bar and exhibit, and I collected notes there. The range of data points facilitates examination of scripted narratives, such as those in tours and performances, as well as of informal interactions.

Table 1. Films, exhibits, and plaque.

Films	Exhibits & Plaque
Documentary footage from Macon Reed's *Eulogy for the Dyke Bar* (Brooklyn, 2015)	*To Know Herself* (San Francisco Wattis Gallery, 2019)
J.D. Samson's *Last Lesbian Bars* (Vice 2015)	Partial reproduction of *Eulogy for the Dyke Bar* (Wattis Gallery, 2019)
Sapphic Laser's music video *Dyke Bars Never Last* (2018)	Plaque commemorating San Francisco's Lexington Bar
Lexington Archival Project's short film, *Never a Cover* (2017)	
Documentary on lost lesbian spaces, *All We've Got* (2019)	

Table 2. Fieldnotes and Interviews.

City	Fieldnotes	Interviews
New Orleans	Performances of Last Call's *Alleged Lesbian Activities;* workshop; dinner for oral history informants; public reading; and lecture	Core organizers and cast members of Last Call
New York	New York Lost Dyke Bar Walking Tours (2017 & 2019); and Dyke Bar Takeover events in Manhattan. Observation of a public lecture pertaining to *All We've Got* (2019)	Core organizers of Dyke Bar Takeover, as well as with organizers of *All We've Got* and *Eulogy for the Dyke Bar.*
Chicago	Chicago's *Lost & Found* Exhibit	Core organizers
San Francisco	*To Know Herself* exhibit, Wattis Gallery (2019); and at scenes recommended by informants	Interviews with core organizer of exhibit, and organizers of Lexington Archival Project and Lexington Plaque.

I also interviewed twenty-four individuals, including primary commemorators and several others engaged in related work. Three interviews were conducted at commemorators' recommendation. They urged me to speak with a memoirist, podcast organizer, and an "elder" informant. With the exception of the elder, all responded to questions about educational, occupational, family, and residential backgrounds; and how they became engaged in commemoration, organizational structure and goals, nightlife, and demographics. In addition to interview and observational data, I coded videos in the same manner in which I coded ethnographic data (beginning with open coding, and moving to purposive).[4]

With the exception of San Francisco informants who tend to be in their forties, nearly all are in their early thirties. New Orleans commemorators are diverse in terms of race and gender; core organizers include several African American and genderqueer or transgender members. With four exceptions, beyond New Orleans informants are White cisgender queer women; this article pursues the origins of organizers' commitments to inclusivity and diversity given their relative gender and racial homogeneity. Throughout I refer to informants by pronouns they use to describe themselves.[5] Finally, with only two exceptions, commemorators hold degrees from highly-selective colleges and universities.

The remembered dyke bar: Portraits of situated institutions

Dyke bar commemorative projects offer fine-grained portraits of bars, situating them in time and space, and sketching patrons' demographic characteristics and bar esthetics. Emphasizing bars' specificity, which commemorators present as generative of community and identity *and* of exclusions and biases, facilitates public engagement with reparative reading (Sedgwick, 2003). Below, I describe commemorators' portrait of the situated bar, before exploring how they rescue and dispense with elements of that bar for social space.

Activists commemorate bars located in what they describe as dyke-dense neighborhoods that were, at the time, ungentrified or at an early stage of gentrification. At a *Lost Dyke Bar Tour*, a speaker listed a plethora of shuttered bars. She said, "These were *lesbian* bars." She linked bar-density to affordability: "There was the 6th Avenue elevated train. It made Greenwich Village, because it made property cheap. NYU wasn't there – fortunately. There were lesbian bars instead!" Later, she said, "All of these things are gone, because of ...." and then paused, rubbing her thumb and index finger together, until someone yelled, "Rent!" Likewise, facing eviction because of back-due taxes, the bartender in Last Call's musical laments how "all of the old places are gone."

Though commemorators point to different times periods that were the "hay gays" of lesbian bars (1970s and 1980s for most, but 1990s - early 2000s for the Lexington), the narratives share a reading that the dyke-density, pregentrification era of lesbian bars allowed for a specific dyke esthetics and politics: radical, working-class, butch-femme, predicated on racial exclusion. Commemorators rely on the "dyke" to evoke working-class histories and locations, but also to gesture to distaste for sexual and gender integration; they imply, in admiring and critical terms, that bars served a specific population.[6]

Crucially, for most, the dyke is working class. A commemorator said dykes no longer share territory "because of gentrification and financialization.... Young dykes can't afford to live in San Francisco." She specified that "'Queerness" comes "out of academia instead of from working class cultures – from lesbian cultures." The dyke and bar this commemorator evokes are not academic or professional; commemorators remember cisgender, working class, female-identified dykes. *Lost & Found* included a visual image of this individual: "[There was] a dyke paper doll that you could cut out and it has different sun glasses and like a leather jacket, and also like a fancy dress just in case, and armpit hair." This commemorator describes the dyke in admiring terms, but she also conveyed distance between this doll and her own identity and self-presentation as a White, femme, cisgender queer professional. Indeed, an article on the exhibit depicts the organizers posed in makeup and dresses – a far cry from the paper-doll. This distance, like her temporal and spatial distance from dyke-dense 1970s neighborhoods, aids and abets her reparative reading.

While there is near uniformity about the above attributes, commemorators vary in terms of how (or whether) they explicitly ascribe the dyke racial characteristics. New Orleans organizers acknowledge that bars often served discrete racial groups, underlining racism and exclusions. This awareness led them to think of the bar they evoke as serving African Americans. As a result, many New Orleans organizers explicitly reference the African American dyke, whereas commemorators in other cities are more circumspect, relying on either racially heterogeneous images of dykes (Chicago) or depicting predominately White individuals (San Francisco). In three cities, as part of their reparative work, commemorative events include discussion of racism; a *Lost Dyke Bar Tour* guide said, "Black lesbians were not always welcome. Audre Lorde would describe being always carded." A Lost & Found commemorator also spoke to the bar exclusions: " ... Racism in the community; people of color having to bring several IDs to get into bars that white women only had to bring one." They instruct audiences to mourn bars, while remaining mindful of their problems.

Commemorators also present bars in gendered terms. Across the cities they remember dyke bars as spaces in which butch/femme identities flourished. Commemorators model a combination of wistfulness for and criticism of this history. An *Alleged Lesbian Activities* song, "Butch/ Femme," celebrates such identities, while also making light of rigid gender roles. Cast members change their gender appearance as they sing, concluding, "There's no regular woman.... If you decide to change your mind that's okay. Or reject the whole dichotomy." Building on this, they highlight transphobia that they associate with bars. A *Lost & Found* commemorator said: "[It was] a very .... flawed thing that was probably not all bad all the time ... [T]here were debates about our transwomen."

Commemorators' narrative of the situated bar, which arises from and facilitates reparative reading, serves as a touchstone for cultivating social space. After all, most yearn for the sense of community they associate with the bar; a genderqueer African American New Orleans commemorator said, "I don't have a space that I really go to.... [I]t doesn't feel like [there is] a space." As the pages that follow demonstrate, commemorative events become spaces that they *can* go to; they craft events with the situated bar as touchpoint.

"What space do we *want*?": mapping social space

Bar commemorators leverage public memories to gather people together now, and to gesture to an as-yet-hazily-defined future. One said, "We don't want to go back to something.... we're *creating* something." They aim for their reparative reading to guide *reparative action*.

What is it that they are creating and how do they aim to "repair"? The notion that they do *not* want to replicate the bar guides their vision. One said, "[journalists] are always reaching out.... asking, 'Why aren't there lesbian spaces?' ... [W]e might need to.... ask a different question, which might be: What spaces do we want? What is our future?" Another said, "now that we have a little more mobility, I think the question is: what kind of space does our community actually need?"

Commemorators partially answer this negatively, holding up bar failures: "We can't just look to bars to be our sanctuaries," and: "I don't think [bars are] a solution." They are unflinching in naming bars' problems: "[W]e also heard a lot of stories about violence. And addiction. One of things we talk about in the piece is racism...." Commemoration, then, is less about celebrating the past than about convening a public to contemplate errors and identify successes: "It doesn't feel like we're glorifying the bars because we don't shy away from talking about the problems.... [W]e wanted to tell a complicated story." This "complicated story" is front and center; in all cities commemoration underlines violence, alcoholism, transphobia, and racism.

Organizers leverage criticisms of bars to shore up commitment to inclusivity. To move away from exclusions and biases of the situated bar, they seek to organize gatherings that are mobile and heterogeneous, particularly along the lines of race, gender, and age. Their belief that lost bars were age diverse, but fell short on racial and transgender inclusion, influences their events and vision for social space.

In both preparing for commemoration and in the events themselves, organizers stress the need to be inclusive and work to reach varied participation in terms of age, race, and gender. A Chicago commemorator emphasized the life stage, racial and geographic heterogeneity of *Lost & Found* audiences: "age and ethnicity and race and background was all over the map .... we had lesbians that drove in from like the suburbs that were like 60 and 70, and then we had .... Twenty-one year-olds ... So many people told me, 'I've never been in a space with like that many queer women.'" Echoing this, a New York organizer said: "A couple of [panelists] were transmasculine. I almost .... have a checklist. Being like, 'How many white people are speaking vs. not white people?'" Last Call's inclusivity-efforts include those they interviewed and commemorate, cast-membership, and organization of rehearsals. One explained, "we would just cancel rehearsal if there was only one person of color who could attend." This policy emerged from recognition of how diverse – and segregated – bars were: "[T]hey were really segregated .... We shouldn't create this thing that is centered around dyke bars in New Orleans when there's like hardly any Black people involved in the process of making it."

Likewise, Last Call sought to capture transgender experiences: "[Jay's] story was also in the last piece, and he's trans. And he talked a lot about feeling excluded from those spaces once he transitioned." To address age inclusivity, Last Call, for instance, strategically offers matinees: "The elders .... they'd mostly come to the daytime shows. Let's be real, because nighttime driving is a thing .... Every time we run we like to have at least one matinee .... Because, again, accessibility." Another commemorator noted that she "wanted to do everything I could to make it as accessible and open as possible." She asked panelists: "'What do you need from me in order to feel safe from this space? What are you concerned might come up? .... How can I show up for you? .... Any time I had a person of color who was involved in the project that would be like, 'What do you need?'" She intervened when someone used the term "tranny," explaining why her language was hurtful. Thus, they articulate commitment to inclusion – specifically along the lines of age, race and gender – that extends from planning to commemorative events.

Ultimately, bringing heterogeneous individuals together to commemorate – and even navigating contentious terrain – served what, in retrospect, she identifies as an implicit purpose: "part of it was about dyke bars .... The sneaky part .... is that *it was also really about having an excuse to bring people from different sides of that conversation into a room and not talk about it directly, but just share stories about things*" (emphasis added).

She offered a concrete example of the exchange she values:

> There was one person who is in her 70s .... She had been homeless and lived near Stonewall .... during the riots. And had been put in jail so many times because she wasn't wearing gender appropriate clothing.... [S]he just talked about how important it was, how healing it was, for her to stand in a room full of queer people and [have them] hear her story, and the young people were crying.

Inadvertently she reveals her implicit aims: the creation of conversation across areas of difference. Another said that organizing panels for *Lost and Found* opened her eyes to political possibilities that in-person intergenerational exchanges generate. She said:

> We had a panel of [women] who ran lesbian centers and spaces .... We got on some challenging topics especially when talking about trans exclusionary radical feminism.... some folks in the audience [said] 'we just want like lesbian space. It's not that we don't support trans women or trans men, but we just want to have this space.' That would have been a conversation that would have got really nasty on the internet, but in person it was so deep and nuanced.... [I]t's okay that it is challenging.

She imagines a future in which (challenging) engagement is more frequent. A Last Call organizer also underlines the political potential of intergenerational events:

> [S]ome of [the elders] have felt really pushed by our work and it made them have to think about.... the spaces that they ran and were they actually integrated or... segregated.... I think that we needed to lean into complications.

Thus, they consciously create spaces that "might push some people".

Even as commemorators focus on bars, they also conclude that they do not need bars or gatherings in a fixed, material locale. Yet, they yearn for *space* and the community and identity it might facilitate. One gestured to a space that would serve myriad purposes, and include some whom one might not find in a bar, "I would love .... a queer art center .... for everybody to do their hustles and sewing machines and laundry." For its part, Last Call's focus has moved from nightlife to collecting "Stories of Queer Resistance." Paralleling this, a filmmaker avoids commemorating bars, because she wishes to underline the risks of losing spaces that, in her view, better cultivate political action. She said, "Queer bars really don't function as social spaces for all people .... I'm interested in politics and how people form that. So bars aren't my thing ...." Going forward, she wishes to cultivate local, inclusive spaces that foster dialogue.

Commemorators also point to how commemorative events, and the space they provide, foster communion. One said that crowds that linger after

"Alleged Lesbian Activities" performances, is "a testament.... of how much the show, this performance, worked to fill this void.... or this lack of spaces in the city for queer women." For them, commemoration constitutes inclusive, mobile gatherings. However, they express excitement about cultivating future spaces that are not organized around remembering bars. Dyke Bar Takeover formed the Queer Visibility Collective: "a parent organization underneath like an umbrella of organizations that provide spaces. I mean we're all dykes so we know dyke spaces and what dykes need.... and so maybe somebody who is transgender will know how to create transgender events.... and that could be like another little branch.... So the idea [is] extremely inclusive space for everybody." This, of course, hints at organizers' sense of the limitations of their reparative action, and perhaps even recognition of how their social spaces replicate their own normative practices and exclusions (Orne, 2017). In this sense, they read their own reparative action reparatively – with an eye for elements to preserve, discard, and rearrange. Having, in their view, fallen short of full-inclusivity, they explore alternate directions, and, ironically, gesture to the possibility of distinct spaces for distinct groups – despite their criticism of bars' exclusivity and homophily.

Ultimately, commemorators want to generate warm and witty exchanges between strangers that they fantasize once unfolded on bar stools. However, having read – reparatively – dyke bar histories, they conclude that those exchanges, more often than not, took place among individuals with shared traits, in specific institutions. This homophily misaligns with their commitment to inclusivity, and weak attachment to situated space. Thus, that barstool – and the yearning for associated community and identity that they recognize – serves primarily as a symbol to harness for inclusive, mobile social space; while partially aware of the shortcomings of their own events, they hope that by embracing flexibility and fluidity they will be less apt to replicate bar exclusions and biases.

Conclusion

In recent years, residents of four cities have gathered in a recreated dyke bar, toured storefronts that once housed bars, observed a plaque marking a lost bar, and browsed material artifacts of dyke spaces. Despite the concrete encounters with history commemorators facilitate, and their habit of situating the lost dyke bar in time and place, they resist creating brick and mortar bars. Their commemorative events are mobile and sporadic. While they celebrate the Lexington for having always been open on Christmas – providing a place one could always go – commemorators turn away from future situated spaces. Instead, they desire mobile "social space" characterized by the inclusion of queer individuals of diverse racial, gender and age backgrounds. And, increasingly, they seek to set the stage for a future in which disparate individuals come together without the bar as anchor.

Despite their criticisms of bars' homophily and exclusivity, they nonetheless desire space – in the present and future – and refer to a "we" that will utilize it. Who is the "we" that they evoke, and what kind of space do they yearn for? Perhaps by design or because their work is ongoing, their "we" is underspecified. However, it remains a *local* we; not a "we" that inhabits a neighborhood bar, but, instead, one culled from their metro-area. This "we" shares sufficient familiarity with extant bars to join in commemoration, and is primed for public reparative reading of bars.

Why do commemorators underspecify the "we"? A definitive answer is beyond my scope because commemorators still grapple with this. However, there are plausible sources. First, under-specification likely emerges from queer and transgender-turns. It may also arise from encounters with conversations about intersectionality and queer theory among academics and broader professional and artistic publics.

Why do they reject situated space in favor of mobile social space? Again, the answer must remain speculative, but commitment to inclusivity is key; they believe that situated space produces exclusivity, and mobility and flexibility enhance inclusivity. Beyond this, their embrace of mobile, inclusive space may emerge from technological developments that facilitate communication beyond personal networks, and that permit events to occur intermittently (Ghaziani & Stillwagon, 2018). Their embrace of social space is also a response to the perceived dispersion of LBQT individuals out of hyper-gentrified bar neighborhoods. Indeed, *Alleged Lesbian Activities* includes the line, "We don't have anywhere anymore." In this sense, I read their embrace of social space as partially adaptive (to external conditions) and partially affirmative (of commitment to inclusivity and identity fluidity).

In sum, commemorators read their remembered object reparatively (Sedgwick, 2003) – with a critical eye, as well as with a hope of rescuing and rearranging elements of the past for the spaces and "we" they construct. Their commemoration does not emerge, as one might suspect, from anxiety about the reduced salience of "lesbian" identity or even about institutional loss (Mattson, 2019), but, rather, from desire to call out a new future.

One might expect commemorators to echo filmmaker Barbara Hammer, who reflected: "'we don't want to forget the lesbian, and we don't want her to be lost. She might not even be known in twenty years, as a population or as a language. A mode of being, a vocabulary, a particular way we cut our hair'" (Gessen, 2019). Instead, commemorators are of two minds about the dyke and her bar. On the one hand, they ask, in the words of *Alleged Lesbian Activities*, "How can we know where we are going if we don't know where we came from?" The "we" that they evoke here, though, is not the same "we" or "she" Hammer conjures. As the musical closes, the bar's owner, Franki, facing property tax debt, leaves the keys to the bar. After she departs, a butch African American woman and an African American transgender woman, Janice, remain. Ultimately, Janice takes Franki's keys and the butch woman says, "So maybe I'll see you tomorrow night?" and Janice, surveying the bar with a smile, says, "Maybe." As they exit, the cast sings "maybe we can rebuild this family." This "family" does not have a specific haircut, bar, or neighborhood, but commemorators hope it has a future – one that builds off of but also repairs elements of the past.

Notes

1. Situated and social space are not truly separable (Latour, 2000). Commemorators do not regard situated space as divorced from demographics; they insist on the import of the location and form of the lost bar, and social traits of commemorative events.
2. See Love 2007 on reparative reading's radical potential.
3. I relied on media analysis, observations, and interviews to identify organizations.
4. On coding see Emerson et al, 2011.
5. Of course, patrons included, among others, transgender individuals (Doan, 2007; Mac & Kayiatos, 2019).
6. On working-class lesbian politics see Kennedy & Davis (1993). Commemorators blur histories of gay bars and lesbian-feminist separatism.

Acknowledgments

For helpful feedback, the author thanks Robin Bartram, Debbie Becher, Leslie Hinkson, Emily Kazyak, Sara Shostak, and students and faculty at Oberlin College – especially Greggor Mattson and Jaleh Jalili. The author also thanks the reviewers and editors for their recommendations, and the Boston University Center of the Humanities and BU Sociology Morris Fund for research support.

Disclosure statement

No potential conflict of interest was reported by the author.

References

Armstrong, E., & Crage, S. (2006). Movements and memory: The making of the Stonewall myth. *American Sociological Review, 71*(5), 724–751.

Bernstein, M. (1997). Celebration and suppression: The strategic uses of identity by the lesbian and gay movement. *American Journal of Sociology, 103*(3), 531–565.

Berrey, E. (2005). Divided over diversity: Political discourse in a Chicago neighborhood. *City and Community, 4*(2), 143–170.

Bravmann, S. (1997). *Queer fictions of the past: History, culture, and difference.* Cambridge, UK: Cambridge University Press.

Brown, G. (2006). Cosmopolitan camouflage:(post-) gay space in spitalfields. In *Cosmopolitan urbanism* (pp. 142–157). New York, NY: Routledge.

Browne, K. (2011). Beyond rural idylls: Imperfect lesbian utopias at Michigan Womyn's music festival. *Journal of Rural Studies, 27*(1), 13–23.

Crenshaw, K. (1991). Mapping the margins: Intersectionality, identity politics, and violence against women of color. *Stanford Law Review, 43*(6), 1241.

D'Emilio, J. (2002). *The world turned: Essays on gay history, politics, and culture.* Durham, NC: Duke University Press.

Doan, P. (2007). Queers in the American city: Transgendered perceptions of urban space. *Gender, Place and Culture, 14*(1), 57–74.

Dunn, T. (2016). *Queerly remembered: Rhetorics for representing the GLBTQ past.* Columbia, SC: University of South Carolina Press.

Emerson, R., Fretz, R., & Shaw, L. (2011). *Writing ethnographic fieldnotes.* Chicago, IL: University of Chicago Press.

Faderman, L. (1991). *Odd girls and twilight lovers: A history of lesbian life in twentieth-century America.* New York, NY: Columbia University Press.

Forstie, C. (2018). Ambivalently post-lesbian: LBQ friendships in the rural Midwest. *Journal of Lesbian Studies, 22*(1), 54–66.

Gamson, J. (1995). Must identity movements self-destruct? A queer dilemma. *Social Problems, 42*(3), 390–407.

Gessen, M. (2019). Barbara Hammer's Exit Interview. New Yorker, March 26.

Ghaziani, A. (2011). Post-gay collective identity construction. *Social Problems, 58*(1), 99–125.

Ghaziani, A., & Stillwagon, R. (2018). Queer Pop-ups. *Contexts, 17*(1), 78–80.

Gieseking, J. J. (2016). Crossing over into neighbourhoods of the body: urban territories, borders and lesbian-queer bodies in New York City. *Area, 48*(3), 262–270.

Greene, T. (2014). Gay neighborhoods and the rights of the vicarious citizen. *City & Community, 13,* 99–118.

Hartless, J. (2018). Questionably queer: Understanding straight presence in the post-gay bar. *Journal of Homosexuality, 66,* 1035–1057.

Hogan, K. (2016). *The feminist bookstore movement: Lesbian antiracism and feminist accountability.* Durham, NC: Duke University Press.

Kennedy, E. L., & Davis, M. D. (1993). *Boots of leather, slippers of gold: The history of a lesbian community.* New York, NY: Routledge.

Latour, B. (2000). When Things Strike Back: A Possible Contribution of 'Science Studies' to the Social Sciences. *British Journal of Sociology, 51*(1), 107–123.

Love, H. (2007). Compulsory happiness and queer existence. *New Formations, 63,* 52.

Mac, A., & Kayiatos, R. (2019). *Original Plumbing: The Best of Ten Years of Trans Male Culture.* New York, NY: Feminist Press.

Mattson, G. (2019). Are gay bars closing?. Trends in United States gay bar listings, 1977–2017.

McDermott, S. (2002). Memory, Nostalgia, and gender in a thousand acres. *Signs: Journal of Women in Culture and Society, 28*(1), 389–407.

Milligan, M. (2003). Displacement and identity discontinuity: The role of nostalgia in establishing new identity categories. *Symbolic Interaction, 26*(3), 381–403.

Mische, A. (2014). Measuring futures in action: Projective grammars in the Rio+ 20 debates. *Theory and Society, 43*(3-4), 437–464.

Muñoz, J. E. (2009). *Cruising utopia: The then and there of queer futurity*. New York: NYU Press.

Nash, C. J. (2011). Trans experiences in lesbian and queer space. *The Canadian Geographer / Le Géographe Canadien, 55*(2), 192–207.

Olick, J., & Robbins, J. (1998). Social memory studies: From "collective memory" to the historical sociology of mnemonic practices. *Annual Review of Sociology, 24*(1), 105–140.

Orne, J. (2017). *Boystown: Sex and community in Chicago*. Chicago, IL: University of Chicago Press.

Pickering, M., & Keightley, E. (2006). The modalities of nostalgia. *Current Sociology, 54*(6), 919–941.

Podmore, J. (2006). Gone 'underground'? Lesbian visibility and the consolidation of queer space in Montréal. *Social & Cultural Geography, 7*(4), 595–625.

Puar, J. (2007). Introduction: Homonationalism and biopolitics. In Terrorist Assemblages: Homonationalism in Queer Times, 1–36. Durham, NC: Duke University Press

Schwartz, B. (1982). The social context of commemoration: A study in collective memory. *Social Forces, 61*(2), 374–402.

Sedgwick, E. K. (2003). *Touching feeling: Affect, pedagogy, performativity*. Durham, NC: Duke University Press.

Seidman, S. (2013). *Beyond the closet: The transformation of gay and lesbian life*. New York, NY: Routledge.

Stein, A. (2010). The incredible shrinking lesbian world and other queer conundra. *Sexualities, 13*(1), 21–32.

Stein, A. (1993). Sisters and queers: The decentering of lesbian feminism. *Radical Society, 22*(1): 33

Stone, A. (2013). Flexible queers, serious bodies: Transgender inclusion in queer spaces. *Journal of Homosexuality, 60*(12), 1647–1665.

Tavory, I., & Eliasoph, N. (2013). Coordinating futures: Toward a theory of anticipation. *American Journal of Sociology, 118*(4), 908–942.

Ward, J. (2008). *Respectably queer: Diversity culture in LGBT activist organizations*. Nashville, TN: Vanderbilt Press.

Wagner-Pacifici, R., & Schwartz, B. (1991). The Vietnam Veterans Memorial: commemorating a difficult past. *American Journal of Sociology, 97*(2), 376–420.

Warner, M. (2000). *The trouble with normal: Sex, politics, and the ethics of queer life*. Cambridge, MA: Harvard University Press.

Index